# Audio Recorders to
# Zucchini Seeds

# AUDIO RECORDERS TO ZUCCHINI SEEDS

## Building a Library of Things

Mark Robison and Lindley Shedd, Editors

**LIBRARIES UNLIMITED**™

An Imprint of ABC-CLIO, LLC

Santa Barbara, California • Denver, Colorado

**Library of Congress Cataloging-in-Publication Data**

Names: Robison, Mark (Mark D.), editor. | Shedd, Lindley, editor.
Title: Audio recorders to zucchini seeds : building a library of things / Mark Robison and Lindley Shedd, editors.
Description: Santa Barbara, California : Libraries Unlimited, an Imprint of ABC-CLIO, LLC, [2017] | Includes index.
Identifiers: LCCN 2016056960| ISBN 9781440850196 (hardcopy : acid-free paper) | ISBN 9781440850202 (ebook)
Subjects: LCSH: Libraries—Special collections—Nonbook materials. | Special libraries—Collection development. | Libraries—United States—Case studies.
Classification: LCC Z688.N6 A93 2017 | DDC 025.2/1—dc23
LC record available at https://lccn.loc.gov/2016056960

ISBN: 978-1-4408-5019-6
EISBN: 978-1-4408-5020-2

21 20 19 18 17   1 2 3 4 5

This book is also available as an eBook.

Libraries Unlimited
An Imprint of ABC-CLIO, LLC

ABC-CLIO, LLC
130 Cremona Drive, P.O. Box 1911
Santa Barbara, California 93116-1911
www.abc-clio.com

This book is printed on acid-free paper ∞

Manufactured in the United States of America

# Contents

# Acknowledgments

The editors would like to thank all our contributors: Michelle Coleman Alvarado, Justin Azevedo, Adam Broner, Brian Burns, Amy Calhoun, Patrick "Tod" Colegrove, Betsy Goodman, Jennifer Harvey, James Hill, Eric D. M. Johnson, Ed Kazzimir, Sue Kirschner, Rochelle Hunt Krueger, Shelly McCoy, Erin DeWitt Miller, Sue Parks, Tara Radniecki, Diane Robson, Celia Rozen, Mitchell Shuldman, René Tanner, Helen Woods, and Jill Youngs. These authors are nobly experimenting with great ideas in their libraries.

We would also like to thank Sharon Coatney and Lise Dyckman at ABC-CLIO for seeing this project through, from the generation of concept until the moment the book hit the presses.

We owe a special "thank you" to Patricia Ratkovich for her skill in interpreting cataloging jargon to noncatalogers.

We also want to thank the University of Alabama Libraries and the Christopher Center Library Services at Valparaiso University for their support of this project.

Finally, Mark Robison would like to thank his friends and family—especially his husband, Matt—for their insights about things collections and for their willingness to have yet another conversation about the cool things that libraries are doing. He wishes his grandmother, Marjorie Robison, who first taught him to love libraries, were here to see this book in print. He also owes a debt of gratitude to Ann Bourne, who graciously provided her sun porch as a makeshift office.

Lindley Shedd would like to thank family, friends, and colleagues for their encouragement and support, especially her partner, Paul Francoeur, for his never-ending encouragement and much-needed reminders to stop, eat, and rest as this project moved toward its completion. She would also like to thank her grandmother and aunt, Dorothy Taylor and Maude Carruth. Both women have been Lindley's lifelong supporters, making this project just another thing (but a big thing), which makes all the checking in and "you can do it's" all that much more important.

# Introduction

Attentive observers of today's library landscape will agree that a new movement is under way. Across the United States, libraries of all types are experimenting with building collections of items that defy tradition and expectation. The "things collection" movement is here. From the public library lending guitars and cake pans to the academic library offering umbrellas and green screens, libraries are reimagining and reinventing their roles by making "things" available for circulation to their users.

In contrast to the printed and audiovisual media so long associated with libraries, these "things" are not sought for their informational value. Instead, they typically serve a practical purpose as tool, equipment, or good. Consider, for example, the burgeoning seed library movement, exemplified by libraries such as the Pima County Public Library (Arizona), the La Crosse Public Library (Wisconsin), or Arizona State University. Seed collections put actual, sowable seeds into the hands of their patrons. Seeds might include those for growing edible fruits and vegetables, local flowers, and even grasses and varieties of wheat. In exchange, patrons are expected to save and to return a portion of the seeds from the plants they grow, to replenish the seed collection. In the process, patrons learn about gardening, seed saving, food sustainability, and other aspects of horticulture by way of workshops sponsored by the library. They also help to cultivate plants that are adapted to the local environment and promote genetic diversity among plants. The seeds in these collections are not some clever ploy invented by librarians to trick patrons into checking out gardening books— although many seed libraries do make such materials available. Rather, the circulation of seeds is the end goal itself. Though not a printed or electronic publication medium, seeds serve important practical and educational purposes to a library's community of users.

Another example of this movement is the growing number of academic libraries that collect and circulate video game consoles. Examples include the University of North Texas Media Library, DePaul University Library, and College Library at the University of Wisconsin-Madison. Although innumerable libraries offer

*[handwritten marginalia: Functional needs / Not information needs / seems to be compatible/in conjunction w/ the makerspace movement / — also community building! / — resource sharing / — in conjunction w/ programs]*

1

video games, most fail to take the next step of lending the actual equipment that would allow patrons to play the games in the comfort of their own homes (or dorm rooms). This trend is attributable to many factors, including the growing academic emphasis on gamification and new literacies, such as technology literacy and media literacy (Alexander, 2009; Apperley & Beavis, 2013; Sanford & Madill, 2007). But it also speaks to librarians' valiant creativity and willingness to experiment with new services. As libraries have done for generations, these institutions identified a need among their patrons and satisfied it by acquiring, describing, and circulating a collection of items. Only these items are video games and consoles, instead of books.

From bicycles to sewing machines, from violins and ukuleles to prom dresses, libraries are recognizing the value of building new types of collections for their patrons. This introduction starts by defining what "things collections" are and explaining why they deserve to be distinguished from other library collections. It then situates the movement in the larger cultural and library landscape. We argue that this movement is closely tied to the rise of the digital sharing economy and its focus on sustainability and local community. Things collections are also influenced by the do-it-yourself (DIY) mentality and by DIY's revival through the makerspace. We believe the cultivation of things collections is one way that libraries are demonstrating their value to stakeholders. More than 20 years into the information age, having shed many of their traditional roles, libraries are working to define their new objectives and to reassert their importance to their communities in new and creative ways. Lending "things" is one such way that libraries can leverage their strengths to provide innovative and truly beneficial service to their users. This introduction closes with an overview of the contributed chapters that follow.

## DEFINING A MOVEMENT

The differences between things collections and other types of library collections are difficult to define, but the biggest distinction is that of utility. Unlike books or movies or journals, seeds and video game consoles (not to mention hammers, telescopes, bicycles, video cameras, and musical instruments) have a practical purpose. Rather than supporting an *information* need, they satisfy a practical, *material* need in accomplishing a task. Here we must be very careful. Information resources—whether for research, education, or for leisure—are also practical. Information is needed to solve problems, conduct a home repair, or create a video project. However, unlike the formats that have long dominated libraries' attentions and budgets, things collections are not information media. Instead, they consist of the tools, equipment, and goods whose use is *informed* by the knowledge contained in print and electronic media.

A second necessary distinction will feel slightly closer to home for readers: things collections circulate. Libraries have long been in the business of amassing collections of strange and intriguing objects. Special collections and archives can boast holdings ranging from the historical—such as the ivory anatomical manikins and 400-year-old surgical saw in Duke University History of Medicine Collections[1]—to the contemporary, such as the UCLA Library Special

Collections' Heavy Metal Archive, with its hundreds of posters promoting heavy metal rock concerts.[2] In fact, special collections are one way that libraries stake a claim to uniqueness in the face of otherwise considerable overlap in print and electronic holdings. (However, as Carter [2012] argues, even special collections are feeling intensified pressure to demonstrate their value in quantifiable terms of scholarship and learning.) Circulation is the key difference between the ephemera of special collections and the contents of things collections. Whereas special collections implement rigorous policies to prevent theft and to preserve their holdings, seed and tool libraries want patrons to leave the building with their items and put them to use.

Other characteristics distinguishing things collections could be noted. These collections often have a focus on improving conditions for the socioeconomically disadvantaged (or the collegiate impoverished) by providing patrons with items they need but cannot afford. They also have a "wow" factor meant to attract patrons who might not be regular library users. Lastly, they at once complement and defy libraries' typical processes for selecting, intaking, circulating, storing, and marketing their collections. However, although these characteristics are useful in understanding things collections, none of them is exclusive to the things movement. Libraries have long pursued the mission of making expensive items available to all through collective ownership. Also, as noted previously, the "wow" factor is not unique to things collections, but is sought by special collections, archives, and even in the design of library buildings or the planning of programs. Libraries frequently attempt to prove their value by impressing their patrons and delivering the unexpected. And although the development of a things collection usually necessitates creative approaches to cataloging and storage, one need only look to the shelves of oversized books or to the drawers crammed with maps to see that every format was once new and posed challenges to the institutions tasked with collecting them.

To review, we define "things collection" as: *any collection of physical objects that serve a utilitarian purpose as tools, equipment, or goods; that circulate beyond the walls of the library; that provide a cost-savings benefit to patrons by supplying something for which they have an existing need; that have an inherent appeal to patrons; and that defy standard processes for acquiring, cataloging, and circulation.*

Proponents of the things movement know the following criticism all too well: "Why is the library wasting its time and money on [fill in the blank]? Libraries are for books." Patrons with this flavor of complaint have a valid point, given their obviously traditional notions about why tax and tuition dollars are funneled into library budgets. These are people with whom the "wow" factor has backfired. However, in trying to pinpoint the distinctiveness of things collections, we discover the perfect way to refute this complaint. Although their purposes and uses might be revolutionary, things collections in many ways are a continuation of what libraries have always done. Through the expenditure of common funds, libraries can select, collect, process, describe, and make available items that benefit a larger community of patrons, for both educational and recreational purposes, and by leveraging their assets, they can do so at a cost-effectiveness unattainable to average individuals. Things collections are another chapter in libraries' longtime missions to create community synergy.

# CULTURAL CONTEXT: UNDERSTANDING THE SUDDEN POPULARITY OF THINGS

As we elaborate in Chapter 1 of this volume, the things movement was preluded by many earlier, specialized things collections, including curriculum materials, tools, toys, and multimedia equipment. So, on the one hand, the lending of things is not revolutionary. On the other hand, the creation of things collections is unquestionably gaining steam and turning into a genuine movement, becoming more prevalent, visible, and creative. Because libraries have long been in the business of doing what they do, librarians and patrons alike might find themselves wondering, "Why are things collections becoming so popular *now?*" We identify three main drivers behind this movement: the rise of the sharing economy; the resurgence of the do-it-yourself ethic through the maker movement; and the desire among libraries to assert their value by delivering innovative services.

## The Sharing Economy

The term *sharing economy* is shorthand for the digital sharing economy, also sometimes called the peer-to-peer economy or the collaborative economy (Dillahunt & Malone, 2015). Because of recent innovations in computer technology, people are now able to share, sell, and exchange their assets and services in new ways, facilitated by websites and applications. Consumers needing a ride across town can use Uber, Lyft, Via, or numerous other ridesharing apps. Airbnb allows hosts to rent out their homes, apartments, or spare rooms, with more than two million listings worldwide (Benner, 2016). All this sharing is enabled by the technology that connects consumers with sellers, which only became possible with recent advances in information and communications technology (Hamari, Sjöklint, & Ukkonen, 2016).

The sharing economy encompasses many types of activity. Selling your old furniture on Craigslist is quite different from getting a ride from an Uber driver: although they both involve payment, one of these transactions involves a transfer of ownership, whereas the other is simply a temporary extension of ownership (Kennedy, 2016). Other sustainability-oriented sites, such as Freecycle .org, allow users to give away their possessions free of charge, to reduce waste. Additionally, another segment of the sharing economy is dedicated to microwork, or the crowdsourcing of a project by hiring laborers to complete small data-processing tasks, such as sites like Amazon Mechanical Turk (Irani, 2015). In our age of digital connectivity, sharing has come to have many connotations.

Perhaps the central pillar of the sharing economy is collaborative consumption. Belk (2014) defines collaborative consumption as "people coordinating the acquisition and distribution of a resource for a fee or other compensation" (p. 1597). This would include Airbnb, Zipcar, and any other services where ownership of an object is extended for a fee or exchanged for an in-kind trade. Truly free sharing, such as with Couchsurfing.com, and gift giving, such as through Freecycle.org, would not fit this definition.

Much of the interest in collaborative consumption stems from a desire for environmental and economic sustainability. Following the mass production and consumption of the 20th century, people view sharing as a less wasteful and more empowering alternative (Leadbeater, 2009, p. 240). Hamari, Sjöklint, and Ukkonen (2016) found that the perception of sustainability was the biggest factor shaping respondents' attitudes toward the sharing economy, and a positive attitude translated into participation (p. 8). Other motivating factors behind participating in collaborative consumption include enjoyment and economic benefits (p. 6). For many people, sharing is just fun, as it creates opportunities for new experiences. Also, the prospect of making money from lending out one's belongings, or of saving money through renting or purchasing second-hand, is alluring.

By building and circulating things collections, libraries are tapping into many of the same motivators as the sharing economy, such as economic benefit and enjoyment. Söderholm (2016) interviewed patrons of Berkeley's Tool Lending Library to uncover their reasons for using the collection. He found that patrons' borrowing was "decidedly needs based," with patrons making practical judgments about whether to purchase their own tool or just borrow one, weighing their need against the costs and burdens of ownership (pp. 145–146). Of course, to individual patrons, libraries provide an even greater economic benefit than the sharing economy by making their things available for free. Many borrowers also described how the tools enabled them to do new things, such as complete certain tasks and even find part-time work (p. 148). Just as the sharing economy brings economic benefits through cost savings and opportunities to expand one's horizons, so too do things collections. Because of their overlap in motivating factors, it is no surprise that the things movement and the sharing economy have both emerged side by side.

In building things collections, many librarians find inspiration in the values of social entrepreneurship. Social entrepreneurship supports using resources to produce economically, socially, and environmentally positive outcomes for a community or organization (Less, Filar Williams, & Dorsey, 2012). This bent toward social and environmental justice is visible in the work of many things collections, such as the community farming project described by Youngs in Chapter 4 and the seed libraries described by Tanner and Goodman in Chapter 5 of this volume. Notably, Söderholm (2016) found that although some patrons did mention ideological considerations, such as sustainability, in their reasons for using the tool library, most patrons were not motivated by such lofty goals. They simply wanted the convenience of tools without all the expense and hassle (p. 148). Although these findings might not be generalizable, librarians might have more success in promoting the practical and enjoyable aspects of their things collections, rather than the ideological.

Despite their similarities, things collections and collaborative consumption have some major differences. These differences give libraries many solid advantages. Collaborative consumption requires buy-in from users in order to work. Botsman and Rogers (2010) describe the four principles of the sharing economy as (1) trust between strangers; (2) idling capacity; (3) critical mass; and (4) belief in the commons. Participants must be able to gain enough information about a potential consumer or renter, such as through ratings or profiles,

*libraries have advantages over the sharing economy →

to entrust their belongings to them. In investigating why people in disadvantaged communities choose to participate in the sharing economy, Dillahunt and Malone (2015) found that safety was a large concern. If people were going to meet up with strangers, they wanted to do so in a safe, public place. Here, things collections provide a solution. Libraries are already viewed as safe spaces, and patrons seeking to borrow a tool or piece of equipment should feel less threatened by entering their public library than by approaching a stranger's house. Also, the position of libraries as builders of collections overcomes the challenge of gaining critical mass. The library has an established reputation and patron base, and consumers can trust that the library will deliver a high-quality service.

Things collections have another advantage over the sharing economy in terms of idling capacity. For collaborative consumption to work, some participants need to have excess stuff. Supply is constantly in flux, based on participants' willingness and ability to part with their belongings. Libraries do not face this problem. Things collections are cultivated for the express purpose of being lent, providing a more reliable supply. Even when something is already checked out, libraries have mechanisms for recalling an item and ensuring that the patron ultimately gets the needed resource.

## Makerspaces and Do-It-Yourself

Another factor driving the current proliferation of things collections is the maker movement and its revitalization of the do-it-yourself ethic in libraries. Do-it-yourself, or DIY, is defined as "activities in which individuals engage raw and semi-raw materials and component parts to produce, transform, or reconstruct material possessions" (Wolf & McQuitty, 2011). DIY has its origins in the post-World War II economic boom. Ramped-up production and consumer demand led to an unprecedented range of available consumer products, including hardware and tools. Access to this supply allowed homeowners to undertake their own home repairs, a fad that first coined the "do-it-yourself" term ("Do it yourself," 1954).

Libraries have been providing patrons with practical information since long before DIY was a concept. Writing in 1920, Morgan asserted the value of the public library in improving home life: "By the circulation of books on house-planning, building, and home decoration, impetus is given to the construction of improved houses. . . . Books on cooking make a contribution to the well-being of the home" (pp. 341–342). By the 1950s, libraries were collecting DIY books in significant numbers, supporting readers' attempts at everything from roofing to learning new sports and subjects (Kingery, 1958). The idea of "do-it-yourself" permeated book titles throughout the rest of the century, quickly expanding beyond the confines of home repairs to topics such as automotive maintenance, self-publishing, health, recreation, and finance. Libraries also supported DIY programming, usually as a way to attract younger patrons and fulfill their educational missions.

The present-day maker movement is a new manifestation of DIY programming. Makerspaces are now in hundreds of libraries across the country, offering patrons opportunities to collaborate, design, and build. As Moorefield-Lang (2015) notes, library makerspaces come in many forms: "some have a focus on crafting, painting, and more artistic endeavors, while others have an emphasis on technology with 3-D printers, laser cutters, music studios, and computer programming" (p. 107). Makerspaces are comfortably situated in the paradoxical position of embracing traditional arts and crafts (such as woodworking, embroidery, and crochet) and modern technologies (such as computer programming, robotics, and drones) at the same time. Libraries are setting up makerspaces as catalysts of creativity that use active learning to teach communication and collaboration skills (Hamilton & Schmidt, 2015, p. 3).

The start of the maker movement is traced to the establishment of *Make* magazine in 2005 and that publication's first Maker Faire in 2006 (Dougherty, 2012). It is worth pointing out that makerspaces did not originate in libraries but, rather, grew out of the technology start-up community, shepherded by leaders such as former TechShop CEO Mark Hatch and former *Wired* editor Chris Anderson (Hamilton & Schmidt, 2015, pp. 11–12). With its emphasis on using one's hands to create and manipulate physical objects, making is framed as a return to traditional human practices and values that were lost due to industrialization and the mass consumption that followed. In the opening line of his *Maker Movement Manifesto,* Hatch writes: "Making is fundamental to what it means to be human. We must make, create, and express ourselves to feel whole" (2014, p. 1).

The maker movement is driven by many of the same factors that are behind the things collection movement and the sharing economy. Environmentally sustainable practices and the self-sufficiency of local communities are certainly central tenets of all three. In our current media landscape, irrefutable scientific evidence of climate change and attention on finding policy solutions to curb carbon emissions are prominent issues. The urgency of sustainability has propelled the maker movement, the things movement, and the sharing economy forward. The maker movement is a rejection of conspicuous consumption in favor of the practical and locally produced (Hamilton & Schmidt, 2015, p. 11). Sustainable making practices might include mending clothing, repurposing old items, or creating a needed object using a 3-D printer rather than purchasing it mass-produced.

Makerspaces are also popular because they are enjoyable. *Make* magazine founder, Dale Dougherty, writes, "When I walk around a Maker Faire, the thing I notice most is how happy people are" (2012, p. 14). Making fosters learning, self-confidence, collaboration, connectedness, and other factors that people find intrinsically rewarding (Ryan & Deci, 2000). In this, making replicates the enjoyability offered by things collections and the sharing economy, which enable participants to expand their horizons.

Things collections have a great deal in common with library makerspaces. In fact, makerspaces might offer many of the same items seen in things collections, such as sewing machines and microcontroller boards. However, some important aspects distinguish them as separate phenomena. Although makerspaces typically are for in-house use only, things collections can leave the building. Makerspaces also place special demands on a library's facilities. They typically require a dedicated space that can support ongoing programs, that is tolerant of noise, and that is allowed to get messy (Hamilton & Schmidt, 2015, p. 17). Although things collections present their own challenges in terms of storage and display, they generally place less strain on a library's available space. Additionally, library makerspaces emphasize collaboration and making things together, often as part of workshops or other educational programming. Although many case studies in this book describe workshops hosted in support of things collections, group participation and educational programming are not as central to the things movement.

## Creatively Demonstrating Value

A final driver behind the things collection movement is the importance of innovation as a way for libraries to assert their value. To be sure, libraries have always been creative in meeting their patrons' needs, experimenting with emerging formats, developing resource-sharing services, and reconfiguring spaces. However, the financial crisis of 2008 and the years-long downturn that followed left many libraries, especially school and public libraries, with smaller budgets and fewer employees (Horton, 2013; Kelley, 2012). Faced with budget cuts and even closures, librarians find it more necessary than ever to be able to demonstrate our value to stakeholders (Oakleaf, 2010; Town, 2011).

Innovation is one such way to show our value. Designing creative services and delivering the unexpected form an approach that brings patrons in our doors, satisfies unmet patron needs, improves public perception of the library, creates goodwill, and provides us with a richer narrative for explaining our value. Things collections are one recent outcome of librarians' daring spirit of innovation.

# OVERVIEW OF THIS BOOK

This volume offers 14 case studies, from a combination of public, academic, and special libraries. Each case study describes a successful effort to build and maintain a things collection. Authors tell of the impetuses that gave rise to their collections, the challenges they faced, and how their services have grown and adapted. The authors present lessons learned and advice for readers who hope to develop things collections of their own.

The book begins with a historical overview of the things collection movement. We explore the histories of four types of specialized collections, which paved the way for the things movement and have led to the emergence of what we call the "limitless things collection."

The next section presents six case studies from public libraries. In Chapter 2, Broner tells the story of Berkeley's Tool Lending Library, one of the oldest continuously operating tool libraries in the country. In Chapter 3, Hill describes the Book-a-Bike program at the Athens County Public Libraries (Ohio) and the process of gathering input from a multitude of community partners. In Chapter 4, Youngs writes about the LibraryFarm at Northern Onondaga Public Library (New York), a community gardening project that circulates plots of land

and brings together community members from many generations. This chapter neatly complements Chapter 5, wherein Tanner and Goodman describe seed libraries and their role in preserving genetic diversity. Kirschner articulates the importance of toy libraries to early childhood literacy in Chapter 6, presenting a case study on the Toy Library at Cuyahoga County Public Library (Ohio). The final chapter in this section, from Alvarado, Azevedo, and Calhoun, tells the story of the Sacramento Public Library's Library of Things, which has attracted much attention and brought the things movement to new prominence.

The subsequent section provides seven case studies from academic libraries. In Chapter 8, Burns describes the all-inclusive things collections at Hampden-Sydney College's Bortz Library, which support various needs of undergraduate life, such as presentation equipment, photography, and computer technology. In Chapter 9, Harvey and Krueger discuss curriculum materials collections, offering advice for building, maintaining, and assessing them. Chapters 10 and 11 present case studies about multimedia centers in academic libraries. McCoy describes the development of the Student Multimedia Design Center at the University of Delaware and its day-to-day operations, and Shuldman describes the successful advocacy by the library's Division of Media Services at the University of Massachusetts Lowell to integrate video projects into the curriculum. In Chapter 12, Radniecki and Colegrove describe how a collection of technological gadgets, including virtual reality headsets, robotics kits, and Google Glass, has revived the DeLaMare Library at the University of Nevada, Reno. In Chapter 13, Robson, Parks, and Miller present a case study of the Media Library at University of North Texas's collection of tabletop and video games. This section concludes with Chapter 14, in which Johnson describes the "perception collection" at Virginia Commonwealth University's Cabell Library, including a microscope, telescope, GoPros, and an endoscopic camera.

Chapter 15 provides a perspective from a special library. Rozen, Woods, and Kazzimir tell the story of the Alaska Resources Library and Information Services' collection of animal furs, skulls, and mounts and the collection's use in local classrooms.

This volume concludes with a comprehensive list of best practices in building and maintaining things collections. We have culled these best practices from the wisdom and warnings presented by the authors. Some of this advice is specific to particular materials or settings, such as the types of boxes to use or where to buy equipment. Much of it, though—such as the importance of assessing your community's needs and considering your library's mission—should be useful to anyone wanting to start a things collection.

## A FINAL WORD ABOUT TERMINOLOGY

In describing things collections, we have been careful to avoid certain words. It might seem natural to use words like *nontraditional* or *unique* when talking about lending seeds, bicycles, and drones. However, each of these labels is problematic in its own way. Calling such offerings "nontraditional" is not necessarily inaccurate, but it sets up a false dichotomy between traditional collections and nontraditional ones. These categories are overly simplistic and ignore the fact that things collections have made their entrance gradually over the past few decades. This dichotomy assumes that there is such a thing as a traditional or typical library collection, whereas libraries have long been hybrids of various formats, for various purposes.

Similarly, labeling things collections "unique" is restrictive in its own way. Yes, these collections are distinctive. The average library does not have animal furs or a community garden. However, the term *unique collection* implies that these projects are not replicable, which would be self-defeating to this book. None of the collections described in this book are off-limits to imitation or adaptation. The ideas offered by these case studies are meant to inspire copycats, to spark conversations, brainstorming sessions, planning meetings, grant proposals, and the full force of librarians' innovation.

## NOTES

1. See the Special Collections' LibGuide at guides.library.duke.edu/history_of_medicine.
2. See the Library Special Collection's Heavy Metal Archive's LibGuide at: www.library.ucla.edu/special-collections/discover-collections/collecting-areas/lsc-heavy-metal-archive.

## REFERENCES

Alexander, J. (2009). Gaming, student literacies, and the composition classroom: Some possibilities for transformation. *College Composition and Communication, 61*(1), 35–63.

Apperley, T., & Beavis, C. (2013). A model for critical games literacy. *E-Learning and Digital Media, 10*(1), 1–12.

Belk, R. (2014). You are what you can access: Sharing and collaborative consumption online. *Journal of Business Research, 67*(8), 1595–1600.

Benner, K. (2016, April 20). Airbnb app offers guides to learn the neighborhood. *New York Times,* p. B6.

Botsman, R., & Rogers, R. (2010). *What's mine is yours: How collaborative consumption is changing the way we live.* New York: HarperCollins Publishers.

Carter, L. R. (2012). Articulating value: Building a culture of assessment in special collections. *RBM: A Journal of Rare Books, Manuscripts, and Cultural Heritage, 13*(2), 89–99.

Dillahunt, T. R., & Malone, A. R. (2015). The promise of the sharing economy among disadvantaged communities. In B. Begole, J. Kim, K. Inkpen, & W. Woo (Eds.), *CHI 2015: Crossings.* Paper presented at the 33rd Annual CHI Conference on Human Factors in Computing Systems, Seoul, South Korea (pp. 2285–2294). New York: Association for Computing Machinery.

Do it yourself. (1954). *Marriage and Family Living, 16*(1), 54.

Dougherty, D. (2012). The maker movement. *Innovations, 7*(3), 11–14.

Hamari, J., Sjöklint, M., & Ukkonen, A. (2015). The sharing economy: Why people participate in collaborative consumption. *Journal of the Association for Information, Science and Technology, 67*(9), 2047–2059.

Hamilton, M, & Schmidt, D. H. (2015). *Make it here: Inciting creativity and innovation in your library.* Santa Barbara, CA: Libraries Unlimited.

Hatch, M. (2014). *The maker movement manifesto: Rules for innovation in the new world of crafters, hackers, and tinkerers.* New York: McGraw-Hill Education.

Horton, V. (2013). Whither library consortia? *Collaborative Librarianship, 5*(3), 150–153.

Irani, L. (2015). The cultural work of microwork. *New Media and Society, 17*(5), 720–739.

Kelley, M. (2012). The new normal. *Library Journal, 137*(1), 37–40.

Kennedy, J. (2016). Conceptual boundaries of sharing. *Information, Communication and Society, 19*(4), 461–474.

Kingery, R. E. (1958). Review of the book *Know-how books: An annotated bibliography of do it yourself books for the handyman and of introductions to science, art, history and literature for the beginner and home student,* by F. Seymour Smith. *Library Quarterly, 28*(2), 164.

Leadbeater, C. (2009). *We-think: Mass innovation, not mass production* (2nd ed.). London, England: Profile Books.

Less, A. M., Filar Williams, B., & Dorsey, S. B. (2012). Librarians as sustainability advocates, educators and entrepreneurs. In M. Krautter, M. B. Lock, & M. G. Scanlon (Eds.), *The entrepreneurial librarian: Essays on the infusion of private-business dynamism into professional service* (pp. 183–201). Jefferson, NC: McFarland.

Moorefield-Lang, H. (2015). Change in the making: Makerspaces and the ever-changing landscape of libraries. *TechTrends, 59*(3), 107–112.

Morgan, J. E. (1920). The library and the home. *Education, 40*(6), 340–342.

Oakleaf, M. (2010). *The value of academic libraries: A comprehensive research review and report.* Chicago: Association of College and Research Libraries.

Ryan, R. M., & Deci, E. L. (2000). Intrinsic and extrinsic motivations: Classic definitions and new directions. *Contemporary Educational Psychology, 25*(1), 54–67.

Sanford, K., & Madill, L. (2007). Understanding the power of new literacies through video game play and design. *Canadian Journal of Education, 30*(2), 432–455.

Söderholm, J. (2016). Borrowing tools from the public library. *Journal of Documentation, 72*(1), 140–155.

Town, J. S. (2011). Value, impact, and the transcendent library: Progress and pressures in performance measurement and evaluation. *Library Quarterly, 81*(1), 111–125.

Wolf, M., & McQuitty, S. (2011). Understanding the do-it-yourself consumer: DIY motivations and outcomes. *AMS Review, 1*(3), 154–170.

# Part I

## History

# 1

# A History of Things Collections: From Specialized Precursors to Present-Day Diversity

*Mark Robison and Lindley Shedd*

Collections of things—such as seeds, bicycles, teaching aids, power tools, multimedia equipment, and sewing machines—demonstrate libraries' ingenuity in meeting the needs of their patrons and in reinforcing their positions as community resources. But they also challenge many traditional notions about the role of libraries. Some question whether libraries should spend taxpayer or tuition dollars on materials other than books, magazines, and other media. In recent years, the things collection movement has gathered momentum and reached new heights of participation and visibility. However, these successes did not develop overnight; the movement's way was pioneered by earlier specialized collections. In this chapter, we elucidate the origins of the things movement by providing historical overviews of four specific types of specialized collections: curriculum materials, tools, toys and games, and multimedia equipment. These histories reveal the changes in public expectations of libraries over the past century and provide documentation of how these specialized collections developed. This chapter concludes with a summary of the current things collection landscape, including the emergence of the limitless things collection.

## CURRICULUM MATERIALS IN CIRCULATION

Curriculum materials centers were undoubtedly the earliest things collections. As Jennifer Harvey and Rochelle Hunt Krueger elaborate in Chapter 9 of this volume, curriculum materials centers (CMCs) are collections of materials maintained to aid in the training of preservice teachers. In addition to the predictable textbooks and juvenile literature, today's CMCs typically offer a range of things that teachers might use in a classroom, including board games, puzzles, puppets, flash cards, models, manipulatives, and kits.

According to Attebury and Kroth (2012), who provide a thorough history of these centers, the movement for educational colleges to create specialized curriculum libraries started in the 1920s. Originally dubbed "curriculum laboratories," the precursors to today's CMCs began at universities with strong education programs, such as Western Michigan and Columbia, as spaces where teachers-in-training could design and test curriculum. A growing number of institutions and school systems created such laboratories during the 1930s, against a backdrop of larger changes in the American education system, including an increase in the number of students attending public schools due to compulsory education laws, and a push toward—and backlash against—the standardization of curriculum and use of textbooks (Attebury & Kroth, p. 51). Scholarship suggests that "things" beyond the printed word had not yet made a prominent entry into these laboratories. In 1938, Wood outlined a list of "essential materials for the average curriculum laboratory." This list of essential material types was limited to paper-based resources: courses of study, lesson plans, bulletins, books, pamphlets, term papers, indices and bibliographies, textbooks, and tests. In the same issue of *Curriculum Journal,* Leary (1938) described the results of her survey of the 107 curriculum laboratories then in existence. She noted that "maps, posters, charts, and other display materials . . . and collections of enrichment materials were the exception rather than the rule" (pp. 352–353).

Nine years later, the number of curriculum laboratories had ballooned. In his national survey, Drag (1947) found the presence of no fewer than 353 curriculum laboratories across the United States, maintained by city and county school systems, state departments of education, and universities and colleges. The majority of these laboratories had been established in the period from 1935 to 1944. Drag's survey showed a diversity of materials available in these curriculum laboratories, including many of the paper-based materials Wood suggested, such as textbooks, standardized tests, workbooks, and bibliographies, but also a newfound prevalence of "display materials" (p. 33). "Display materials" meant such items as films, slides, pictures, maps, posters, "science paraphernalia," manipulatives, globes, kits, and fine arts materials, like easels (p. 135). Thus, at least by the 1940s, curriculum laboratories were already collecting nonprint "things" in support of teacher development, although it should be acknowledged that less than half of the respondents to Drag's survey noted having display materials.

The intensification of the Cold War through the space race, and particularly the Soviet Union's launch of the satellite Sputnik in 1957, led to anxieties about the insufficiencies of the American educational system. This event sparked a decade of unprecedented federal involvement in, and aid for, education (Dyer, 1978). One result of this involvement was an even greater standardization of math, science, and language curricula in public schools (Attebury & Kroth, 2012, p. 53). Accompanying these changes was an urgency for teachers to incorporate more audiovisual materials in their instruction, and for colleges and universities to do a better job of preparing teachers to use this equipment. Several national accrediting agencies for teacher education began requiring the establishment of curriculum centers as part of accreditation. Thus, this period saw another explosion in the number of curriculum materials centers, along with a wider array of "things" being offered in them. Between 1957 and 1969, surveys showed that the number of teacher education institutions that had curriculum materials centers rose from 46 percent to 92 percent (p. 48). Along with this growth came a proliferation of the types of nonprint "things" offered, including games, models, audio recordings and record players, slides and projectors, and even tape recorders and cameras (p. 54).

Today it might seem natural that higher education institutions and even school systems would make educational objects available to preservice and inservice teachers. However, the idea has not been without its resistors and identity crises. Particularly in the domain of schools, which often had their own collections of curriculum materials available for teachers, the idea of "library" as "place for books" was persistent and complicated the development of nonprint curriculum collections. Sleeman and Goff (1967) provide an illustrative piece. These authors describe what they call "instructional materials centers" (IMCs) and how such centers, in their mission to support teachers and to provide a variety of materials, spark a "controversy of location" (p. 161). The controversy lay in the tension between librarians and audiovisual specialists over who had ownership of such centers, which offered both library and audiovisual materials. The authors put a fine point on the matter with their declaration that, "[b]y its nature, the IMC is not a library" (p. 161).

Miller (1961) noted that, in many schools an "artificial division of materials" existed between printed materials and audiovisual services, creating a "no man's land" of responsibility (p. 366). The establishment of instructional materials centers could fix this problem by creating a coordinated effort of all curricular materials; however, he warned, "Some librarians may be fearful of the rapidly growing audio-visual field" (p. 367).

By the late 1960s and early 1970s, this divide between librarians and school media specialists—and consequently between print and nonprint materials in schools—was closing. In 1969, the American Association of School Librarians (AASL) coauthored a set of standards with the National Education Association's Department of Audio-Visual Instruction. These standards called for cohesive media programs in schools, which would be overseen by media specialists responsible for selecting materials and consulting with teachers (Joint Committee, 1969). These standards sparked conversations and meetings about the future of media services in schools among educators, librarians, and media specialists across the country. The standards were updated a mere six years later by new guidelines outlined in the publication *Media Programs: District and School,* a joint project of AASL and the Association for Educational Communications and Technology (1975). In reacting to the guidelines, Harper, Rosenfeld, and Eshelman (1975) remarked, "[I]t is evident from the draft copy of the revised standards that the years from 1969 to 1975 have seen a change from the predominantly book-oriented school library to the actively media-oriented center" (p. 362).

Realignment within the profession was accelerated by administrative changes. During the 1970s, many state departments of education undertook reorganizations in how they oversaw school libraries and media support, combining these units for efficiency. For example, prior to reorganization, the Georgia Department of Education had separate units for school libraries, school film libraries, and instructional television. In the 1970s, the department combined these duties, giving school librarians responsibility for supporting all instructional materials. School libraries were accordingly renamed "media centers" (Kirby, 1989). In Michigan, the fictitious character Marian the Librarian was the center of a campaign to educate the public about librarians' new roles as media specialists (Saks, 1977). Kies (1978) described the challenges and opportunities inherent in shifting from "school librarian" to "media specialist," including uncertainty among students, teachers, and librarians about what a media center looks like or what materials it offers. Noting the integration of functions, she wrote, "The new school media specialist is trained to be a part of the school's total curriculum development and execution function" (p. 179). Ultimately, librarians, teachers, and administrators shifted their views on the role of the library in providing items beyond the printed word in support of developing teachers and curriculum.

## TOOL LIBRARIES AND COMMUNITY EMPOWERMENT

Tool libraries were another type of specialized collection that was indispensable in ushering in the things movement. In Chapter 2 of this volume, Broner tells the story of the Berkeley Public Library's Tool Lending Library, which began in 1979 with funding from the U.S. Department of Housing and Urban Development. Berkeley's Tool Library is often cited as the largest, but it is by no means the oldest. The Grosse Pointe Public Library in Michigan has a tool library that has been in continuous operation for over 70 years. This collection was created in 1943 with funding from the local Rotary Club, to make tools available to citizens amid the scarcities of World War II (Grosse Pointe Public Library, 2016; Stellin, 2004).

The 1970s saw a spurt of new tool collections, such as the Cohoes Tool Library (New York) in 1970 and the East Orange Small Tool Library (New Jersey) in 1971 (Faber, 1974; Rejnis, 1976). Despite their names, many of these earliest tool collections were not associated with formal libraries. Rather, they were administered by local housing authorities or city planning departments, often with federal grant money. The Cohoes Tool Library was overseen by the city's Office of Planning and Development and was housed in the basement of a church (Faber). The East Orange Small Tool Library was run by the city's Model Cities Department ("Model Cities Lends Tools," 1971). In each of these cases, local agencies made creative use of special funding to support urban renewal by circulating useful objects to the public.

Several other tool libraries originating during this time were operated by nonprofit agencies with a goal of urban redevelopment. A notable example is the tool library at Rebuilding Together Central Ohio, the Columbus-based affiliate of the national nonprofit that performs repairs and remodels for low-income homeowners. This tool library was started in 1976, making it likely the second-oldest continuously operating tool library still in existence (Rebuilding Together Central Ohio, 2016). In Oklahoma City, the nonprofit Neighborhood Development and Conservation Center started a tool library in 1979. It purchased its tools using federal grants, and neighborhood organizations paid the dues money. In being interviewed, then-executive director of the program, Linda Ivins, explained that the collection existed to "provide tools for people who want to fix up their homes and don't have the money to buy a tool for a one-time use" ("Oklahoma City," 1981).

Many additional tool collections created during the 1970s, such as Berkeley's, were partnerships between public libraries and larger city initiatives, using federal funding. Other examples include Takoma Park, Maryland, which created its tool library with funds from the Community Development Block Grant program (Reece, 1978) and Atlanta's Mobile Tool Library van ("Atlanta Library Routes," 1978).

The diversity of models for implementing tool libraries shows the national emphasis on urban renewal during the 1970s. It also reveals the debt that the things collection movement owes to non–library players. These early models demonstrated proof of the concept that "things" could be lent to the public at large. They also consistently attached the label "library" to their programs, creating an important association in the public's mind between libraries and useful tools. In his chapter, Broner describes the new momentum that tool libraries are currently gathering.

## TOYS AND GAMES

Other specialized collections also served as forerunners to the present-day things movement. As Sue Kirschner explains in Chapter 6 of this volume, the first toy library was established in 1935, through a collaboration between a shop owner and local school officials. The idea reemerged in the 1960s with the creation of the Head Start program, which works to prepare children from low-income families to attend school. Many local Head Start programs created toy libraries, which made toys available to teachers to borrow and use in their class-rooms (Moore, 1995, p. 10). The number of toy libraries continued to grow throughout the 1970s, spurred by new federal assistance for children with disabilities and for subsidized day care.

From the start, toy libraries were seen in terms of educational value. Hoffman (1981) credits day care centers and preschool programs with originating the idea of using toys in the learning process, which libraries later adopted (p. 87). Many contemporary researchers and educators saw great potential for toy libraries to benefit low-income, preschool-aged children. The Far West Laboratory for Educational Research and Development, based in Berkeley, developed the "Parent/Child Toy Library Program" (Nimnicht, 1971). This program consisted of a course for parents in the use of toys for educational purposes, a toy library from which parents could borrow, and materials for librarians. The Utah State Board of Education experimented with implementing this program in many of its school districts (Utah State Board, 1972).

Professional organizations soon took an interest in toy libraries. The Children's Services Division (now the Association for Library Service to Children) of the American Library Association (ALA) created the Toys, Games, and Realia Evaluation Committee in 1974 (Moore, 1995, p. 13). This committee sought to establish guidelines for evaluating toys and other realia and raised awareness among librarians of toys' educational potential (Hoffman, 1981, p. 88). This committee was disbanded in 1984, coinciding with the establishment of the USA Toy Library Association (Moore, p. 17). Today, toy libraries number in the hundreds, offering toys, puppets, story kits, and other items in support of play and its connection to early childhood literacy.

As with curriculum materials, the collecting and lending of toys was not always self-evidently a good idea and required justification by its proponents. The first ALA publication about the toy library phenomenon was titled *Toys to Go: A Guide to the Use of Realia in Public Libraries* (Hektoen & Rinehart, 1975). An entire chapter, written by Peggy Abramo, is spent justifying the purposes of realia (specifically toys) in fostering children's development. Another chapter, authored by Patricia Boyd, explains how toys can be used as gateways for introducing children to books, such as the suggestion that a child who played with a toy steam shovel could then be told about Virginia Lee Burton's classic, *Mike Mulligan and His Steam Shovel* (p. 10). The contents of this trailblazing edition suggest that toys defied contemporary notions about library collections.

Games have always been an important component of toy libraries. Interestingly, probably because of their educational value, games have an even longer history in U.S. libraries than toys. Board games were indispensable to curriculum collections by the 1960s (Attebury & Kroth, 2012, p. 54). However, board games showed up in libraries as early as 1910, when the public library in St. Paul, Minnesota, acquired more than 700 games to circulate to local children (but only on Saturdays) with assistance from a local women's club. The games included chess, checkers, and dominoes, puzzles, and a variety of historical and literary games, intentionally including a mixture of educational games and those "for fun only" ("Circulation of Games," 1910).

Libraries have supported gaming not only through collections but also through programming and the use of their spaces. In his thorough history, Nicholson (2013) writes that the roots of gaming in American libraries go back to the 1850s, when the Mechanics' Institute Library in San Francisco became host to a chess club, which is still in existence (p. 344). Over the past century, gaming in libraries has benefited from a shift in attitudes, for libraries to serve as places not only for education but also for recreation. Nicholson notes that some libraries, such as New York Public Library, have even offered programs where patrons could design their own games (p. 348). Game creation could be seen as a precursor to today's makerspace movement. Although board games have a longer affiliation with public libraries, many academic libraries are now beginning to see the value these games have for their university communities. In Chapter 13 of this volume, Diane Robson, Sue Parks, and Erin DeWitt Miller provide a case study of successful board game lending at the University of North Texas, in the context of a larger gamification campaign involving video games.

## AUDIOVISUAL AND MULTIMEDIA EQUIPMENT

Although curriculum materials, tools, toys, and games were some of the most prominent early models for collecting and circulating "things," they certainly were not the only ones. We would be remiss not to broach the long, circuitous history of audiovisual and multimedia materials and equipment in libraries. As with games, these materials have their library roots in curriculum materials' collections. Drag's (1947) survey of curriculum laboratories found that many offered films and slides for circulation to teachers. Although some of these laboratories had equipment such as opaque and filmstrip projectors and record players, this equipment was largely for in-house use only (p. 50). Most librarians were slow to adopt these materials. In 1947, Hoyt R. Galvin wrote a piece in the *Wilson Library Bulletin*, urging librarians to recognize the informational value of audiovisual materials, such as films, slides, and audio recordings:

> It is the business of libraries to provide and circulate all classes of material used for recording and transmitting knowledge, and you must agree that the film and other audio-visual materials are major vehicles for this purpose. For years libraries have been accustomed to providing the book, the magazine, the newspaper, the pamphlet, the chart, the map, and even still pictures, but we have been slow to adopt and supply the moving picture. (p. 423)

As described earlier, the Cold War produced anxieties about the educational system, resulting in a new emphasis in audiovisual training for preservice teachers. Thus, as the number of curriculum collections expanded throughout the 1960s, so too did their offerings of audiovisual materials and equipment. Records, record players, opaque projectors, filmstrip and slide projectors, tape recorders, and even cameras became common in curriculum libraries (Attebury & Kroth, 2012, p. 54). For many librarians, these items were unfamiliar territory. In 1967, William Quinly offered advice on selecting, processing, and storing nonprint library materials and equipment, such as films, records, and videotape recorders. He predicted the growing influence that educational media would have on librarianship and called on librarians to assert responsibility for the curation of these materials, rather than media specialists: "the librarian is armed with comprehensive book lists, definitive bibliographies and a wealth of experience, while new media specialists often appear lost in an uncharted wilderness" (p. 275).

The role of the library in providing media services was revolutionized with the popularization of the personal computer in the 1980s. Libraries began making "microcomputers" available for in-house use and providing gateway software for patrons to conduct searches of abstracting and indexing databases (Boulanger, 1987). Libraries also started circulating resources, such as encyclopedias and periodicals, in the new CD-ROM format. Other technological developments around this period gave rise to additional types of circulating material, such as VHS cassettes and audio CDs (Julien, 1988). Unlike CD-ROMs, these formats had much more potential to satisfy recreational needs, not just educational.

Advances in, and the growing affordability of, digital recording equipment and video editing software during the 1990s and early 2000s led many libraries, especially school and academic, to begin developing services specifically for digital multimedia production. Many students and faculty members came to see multimedia projects as a vital component to coursework, and libraries rose to meet these expectations. Although it was not unheard of for libraries to support video production in the analog days of film, an explosion in the availability of recording equipment and editing software in libraries occurred the 1990s and 2000s (DeVillez, 1997; Mitchell, 2005).

Although the number of media formats mentioned here is impressive, most do not fit the definition of "things" used in this book. Because they are utilized as information media, audiovisual materials have a great deal in common with traditional print resources. But along the way, to support the creation and use of these materials, many libraries also began circulating equipment—from projectors and record players in the earliest days to today's digital cameras, lenses, tripods, and other recording equipment. Even laptops and tablets, which are certainly more common in libraries, would qualify as things collections. The availability for patrons to borrow these items from their library reflects the shift toward the library as facilitator for the creation of new information, rather than just passive consumption.

Today, a large swathe of libraries' things collections consist of circulating digital cameras, video cameras, audio recorders, and the accessories of multimedia production, such as green screens and light kits. Several chapters in this volume tell the stories of academic library multimedia centers, including Shelly McCoy's description of the University of Delaware Student Multimedia Design Center (Chapter 10), Mitchell Shuldman's chapter on the library's support for student video projects at the University of Massachusetts Lowell (Chapter 11), and Eric D. M. Johnson's description of Virginia Commonwealth University's Innovative Media Department (Chapter 14).

## DIVERSE AND LIMITLESS COLLECTIONS

The things collections landscape is becoming increasingly more diverse each year. Librarians are co-opting elements of the specialized collections that paved the way, remixing and adapting them to create unique collections that benefit their communities. Many libraries, such as the Charles County Public Library in Maryland[1] and the North Haven Memorial Library in Connecticut,[2] are circulating impressive collections of cake pans. These pans allow patrons to bake thematic cakes, such as in the shapes of trains and cartoon characters, for which patrons might have only an occasional or one-time need. Telescopes are another flourishing trend in libraries. Several societies of professional astronomers, such as the New Hampshire Astronomical Society[3] and the Aldrich Astronomical Society in Massachusetts,[4] have developed programs to purchase and donate telescopes to local libraries.

We are also witnessing a rise of more comprehensive things collections. In serving their communities, these collections are not limited to any specific format or area of focus. These "limitless things collections," as we are calling them, offer a little bit of everything, from fishing poles and sewing machines to guitars and art supplies. The Sacramento Public Library, which launched its Library of Things in 2015, is a prominent example of a limitless things collection. As Michelle Coleman Alvarado, Justin Azevedo, and Amy Calhoun explain in Chapter 7 of this volume, Sacramento's Library of Things offers musical instruments, crafting supplies, board games, GoPro cameras, and much more. The library made its purchasing decisions after collecting extensive community input. Sacramento Public Library's project has garnered significant media attention and contributed greatly to the visibility of the things collection movement. Many other libraries have or are developing comprehensive things collections. The Ann Arbor District Library has an extensive list of "Unusual Stuff to Borrow,"[5] which includes art prints, games, tools, science kits, and even museum passes. As Brian Burns explains in Chapter 8 of this volume, the Bortz Library at Hampden-Sydney College offers a diverse collection of items for the benefit of its undergraduate students, including graphing calculators, camera equipment, projectors, and even umbrellas and a bicycle tire pump.

The emergence of limitless things collections in recent years demonstrates how far patrons' and librarians' expectations have shifted in just a few decades. Most of the items in these collections would have had no place in the library of the mid-century, when even audiovisual materials challenged traditional notions about the library's role. The successes of curriculum materials, tools, toys, and multimedia equipment collections provided models for how libraries could meet the needs of their communities in new ways, beyond information services. As libraries continue to explore innovative ways to engage their patrons, the number of both specialized and limitless things collections is certain to grow.

## NOTES

1. The Charles County Public Library's cake pans are visible through their online catalog, at ccplonline.org.

2. See the North Haven Memorial Library's cake pan collection at northhavenlibrary.net/children/cake-pans-2/.

3. Details about the New Hampshire Astronomical Society's Library Telescope Program are available at www.nhastro.com/ltp.php.

4. Details about the Aldrich Astronomical Society's Adopt-a-Library Telescope program are available at aldrich.club/adopt-a-library-telescope.

5. See www.aadl.org/catalog/browse/unusual.

## REFERENCES

American Association of School Librarians & Association for Educational Communications and Technology. (1975). *Media programs: District and school.* Chicago: American Library Association.

Atlanta library routes handy man's tool van. (1978, Dec. 25). *The Atlanta Constitution,* p. 9B.

Attebury, R., & Kroth, M. (2012). From pedagogical museum to instructional material center: Education libraries at teacher training institutions, 1890s to 1970s. *Education Libraries, 35*(1–2), 48–58.

Boulanger, M. E. (1987). Online services at the reference desk: New technologies vs. old problems. *Reference Librarian 6*(15), 269–277.

Circulation of games by the library. (1910). *Public Libraries, 15*(10), 430.

DeVillez, S. (1997). Video production in the media center. *Indiana Media Journal, 20*(1–2), 19–21.

Drag, F. L. (1947). *Curriculum laboratories in the United States: A research study.* San Diego: Office of the [San Diego County] Superintendent of Schools. Retrieved from HathiTrust website: http://hdl.handle.net/2027/mdp.390150 70542413.

Dyer, E. R. (1978). Forces affecting educational change and school media centers. *Peabody Journal of Education, 55*(3), 184–192.

Faber, H. (1974, July 1). Upstate public library lends tools, not books, to residents. *New York Times,* p. 33.

Galvin, H. R. (1947). Practical aspects of audio-visual services. *Wilson Library Bulletin, 21*(6), 423–426.

Grosse Pointe Public Library. (2016). Tool collection. Retrieved from www.gp.lib.mi .us/tool-collection.

Harper, P., Rosenfeld, H., & Eshelman, W. R. (1975). The new standards. *Wilson Library Bulletin, 49,* 362–363.

Hektoen, F. H., & Rinehart, J. R. (1975). *Toys to go: A guide to the use of realia in public libraries.* Chicago: American Library Association.

Hoffman, F. W. (1981). Toys, games, etc. (realia). In A. Kent, H. Lancour, & J. E. Daily (Eds.), *Encyclopedia of library and information science* (vol. 31, pp. 84–104). New York: Marcel Dekker.

Joint Committee of the American Association of School Librarians and the Department of Audiovisual Instruction of the National Education Association. (1969). *Standards for school media programs.* Chicago: American Library Association.

Julien, D. (1988). Evolution of a project: Experimenting with videocassettes. *Public Library Quarterly, 8*(1–2), 101–107.

Kies, C. (1978). Shifting school relationships: How people react when organizational functions change. *Peabody Journal of Education, 55*(3), 178–183.

Kirby, E. (1989). 25 years of state media services. *Georgia Library Quarterly, 26*(1), 19–21.

Leary, B. E. (1938). Survey of curriculum laboratories. *Curriculum Journal, 9*(8), 350–354.

Miller, W. C. (1961). Role and function of the instructional materials center. *Educational Leadership, 18*(6), 364–367.

Mitchell, G. A. (2005). Distinctive expertise: Multimedia, the library, and the term paper of the future. *Information Technology & Libraries, 24*(1), 32–36.

Model Cities lends tools. (1971, Aug. 28). *New York Amsterdam News,* p. C3.

Moore, J. E. (1995). *A history of toy lending libraries in the United States since 1935* (master's thesis). Retrieved from ERIC database (ED No. 390414).

Nicholson, S. (2013). Playing in the past: A history of games, toys, and puzzles in North American libraries. *Library Quarterly: Information, Community, Policy, 83*(4), 341–361.

Nimnicht, G. P. (1971). *Parent/child toy lending library: A report on evaluation.* Berkeley, CA: Far West Laboratory for Educational Research and Development.

Oklahoma City tool "library" caters to homeowners. (1981, Sept. 25). *Los Angeles Times,* p. C4.

Quinly, W. J. (1967). The selection, processing and storage of non-print materials: Aids, indexes and guidelines. *Library Trends, 16*(2), 274–282.

Rebuilding Together Central Ohio. (2016). Our programs. Retrieved from www .rtcentralohio.org/about-us/our-program.

Reece, B. (1978, May 6). Takoma Park's sense of place. *The Washington Post,* p. E35.

Rejnis, R. (1976, Aug. 22). Tool libraries. *New York Times,* p. 209.

Saks, L. (1977). Marian the Librarian smiles and tells all. *Audiovisual Instruction, 22*(2), 43–45.

Sleeman, P., & Goff, R. (1967). The instructional materials center: Dialogue or discord? *AV Communication Review, 15*(2), 160–168.

Stellin, S. (2004, Nov. 4). Library science, Home Depot style. *New York Times,* p. F10.

Utah State Board of Education & Utah State Department of Public Instruction. (1972). *Implementation of the toy lending library in the state of Utah: Summary Report, 1971–72.* Salt Lake City, UT: Office of the State Superintendent of Public Instruction. Retrieved from ERIC database (ED No. 076255).

Wood, H. B. (1938). How to organize a curriculum laboratory. *Curriculum Journal, 9*(8), 345–349.

# Part II

## Things Collections in Public Libraries

# 2

# Measure Twice, Cut Once: A Long-Lasting Tool Lending Library in Berkeley

*Adam Broner*

## PREFACE: AN ARGUMENT FOR LOANING "THINGS"

From the scrolls of Alexandria to Benjamin Franklin's intrepid "Library Company," the concept of library has always been fluid and provocative, a balancing act between the rights of ownership and the needs of scholarship. Libraries are thought of as the hallmarks of constancy, but that constancy includes a curious malleability. That fluidity is quite visible in the last 30 years, the "information age," as a deluge of information in a new electronic landscape caused changing patterns of patron usage. As book content became increasingly mobile, many public libraries and librarians have had to redefine themselves as aides and organizers for online information, and as a center for access to this new online world. There has been a slow shift away from libraries' core values of education and community center and into that electronic realm, and a corresponding shift away from librarians' traditional roles as guides to physical resources. Indeed, as online databases have exploded, those physical resources have been shrinking in response to changing patterns of patron use.

Swedish library scholars Söderholm and Nolan (2015) discuss the concurrent economic shift from mass markets to globalization: "To frame current Western society as a post-Fordist era is to emphasize how we do things rather than what we do. By this token, the development of public libraries is defined by profound structural and professional change and not merely by shifting focus from paper to information. . . . [It is a shift away from] proactive, close involvement with community development" (pp. 246–247). They were, however, optimistic about reshaping the outcome of those changes, ". . . the potential of merging the ideas of place, collection, and community to bridge the social-societal gap" (p. 245). And indeed, in the last 10 years there has been a countermovement, again thanks to the fluidity at the center of the concept of library. Unusual collections of physical objects, as well as books, have in some places reasserted the strength of community and helped to reverse the diminished role of the branch library.

In their process of redefining their functions, many nonacademic libraries have reached out to communities, seeking to understand and answer the needs of their patrons. Interestingly, the changing landscape has not affected the desire for a physical place that acts as a resource for communities. And many nonacademic libraries are expanding into those directions, regaining focus on their earlier core role of encouraging young readers and offering classes that are outside those of pure literacy. From beer making to quilting, from tax help to cinemas, these classes and events have become the means by which libraries have shouldered their way back into societal relevancy. Some have even become a forum for their communities.

That responsiveness to community needs has been at times a little surprising to libraries themselves, particularly in their expanding arena of unusual collections. Through them, libraries have been tasked with embracing collections of objects outside those focused on reading to build bridges to their constituents; collections such as toys, tools, pets, kitchen gear, and musical instruments have found their way into the library's domain. Concurrently, we have seen the rise of do-it-yourself, or DIY, classes and programs, and the growth of a movement toward an economy that emphasizes sharing (Tabor, 2013). Serving this newly conscious community is an opportunity for libraries to have "things" to reflect the rise of fresh social partnerships and the culture's increased awareness of the benefits of a sharing economy. It is an apt fit for libraries, which have long pioneered varied forms of sharing.

## HISTORY OF AN EARLY EXPERIMENT

Berkeley Public Library's Tool Lending Library (TLL) has garnered much praise, along with solid lending statistics, and has often been cited as a model for this new paradigm. It has been successfully lending tools, providing basic technical instruction for tool usage, advising library patrons on home repair and maintenance issues, and acting as a nexus of informational flow and community connections for over 35 years. Opening its doors in January 1979, Berkeley's TLL is one of the oldest continuously operating tool libraries in the United States.

Berkeley's experiment is a vivid symbol of the independent and boldly pragmatic idealism of a small West Coast city with an outsized cultural impact on national and international culture. Beginning modestly with $30,000 of U.S. Department of Housing and Urban Development (HUD) funding from the federal Community Development Block Grant (CDBG) program, the TLL has grown into a model of sustainable lending and healthy community development that draws inquiries and attention from people, publications, and institutions around the United States and abroad.

Originally organized and staffed by Peter McElligott, Berkeley's TLL was funded by HUD as part of its projects to rehabilitate low-income housing. Housed in a portable trailer (on loan from the city of Berkeley), the library began with approximately 500 tools. Now the collection stands at over 4,000 tools, and it has its own 1,000-square-foot facility attached to the larger Tarea Hall Pittman South Branch of the Berkeley Public Library (BPL). The entire building—both the book and tool wings—was rebuilt and expanded in 2012 and reopened its doors in 2013. Today the TLL is comprised of a main room of nearly 800 square feet, including tool storage and counters. The repair room is 175 square feet. And there are two dedicated parking spaces for short-term pickup and drop-off of tools. Above the TLL portico is a fresh sign saying simply "TOOLS" in large block letters, and below it a cautious adage for an unusual service: "Measure twice, cut once."

The primary objective of the project was to provide easy access to tools and repair information for residents of South and West Berkeley, which have historically lower-income, working-class, and marginalized neighborhoods. The TLL would provide free, convenient access to tools (some of which are prohibitively expensive) so that residents could improve their homes. The benefits were many: low-income families would be able to borrow tools for free that they could not otherwise afford; personalized building instruction and advice would be available to young householders, women, the elderly, and others less inclined to ask for it; and the subsequent improvements in neighborhood housing would promote community pride and self-esteem. Community meetings were held to determine what services, tools, and supporting books and materials the community wanted, and $2,000 of the original seed money was used to purchase books, pamphlets, and other instructional items.

Applications to the original HUD grant could fall under two categories: projects that would better a neighborhood (and potentially raise the property values), and projects that would increase opportunities for its inhabitants through skills development. As access to tools fit both categories, the library was able to consistently win those grants. But the funding required two more hurdles. First, a rubric had to be devised to measure the outreach success of the project. To comply with this requirement, the government asked for questionnaires that included income for every single borrower. Instead, the BPL was able to substitute general demographics on the economics of each potential ZIP code served and accordingly made the cost of borrowing free for the lowest-earning zip codes, while borrowers from wealthier zip codes would pay a nominal fee of $0.50 to $3.00 per tool.

The second requirement was that a local panel would distribute the monies, but that granting panel had other agendas and its own favored projects. This arrangement meant that, every year after the government awarded the funding, McElligott had to go before a local board (the Housing Advisory and Appeals Board) and argue for the merits of a tool library. One year the panel decided to cut the funding in half. The BPL system was able to temporarily find sufficient money to keep McElligott employed and the tool library doors open. However, after this loss of federal funding, the BPL made it a priority to have the TLL budget, and that of the whole BPL, taken out of the city's general fund and funded separately from the city in the property tax. After some years, Library Director Regina Minudri wrestled the necessary measure for changing the source of the funding onto the ballots, and this university town, with its much-loved book library and increasingly popular tool branch, was able to muster a two-thirds vote in favor of that measure. After the passage of that 1988 measure, the tools were loaned for free in all ZIP codes.

McElligott was conversant with several trades: a gardener with an encyclopedic knowledge of local flora; a builder who did much of his own home maintenance, using a range of tools from snakes to scrapers and pipe threaders to seed spreaders; and a self-taught mechanic familiar with automotive tools, having rebuilt his Volkswagen bus engine more than once. That knowledge of a variety of trades helped him build the early collection.

McElligott worked alone out of that trailer for 10 years before a more substantial addition was built onto the former South Branch Library, after which one and then two half-time positions were created, and the TLL's hours were increased. The BPL hired me in 1990 for a half-time position. I had been a carpenter for 15 years and running jobs for 10 and therefore brought with me a solid knowledge of the building trades. I had little experience in tool repair, however, and watching McElligott tear apart and rebuild demolition hammers and belt sanders was an education. I have continued to do most of the tool repairs in the 15 years since he retired.

McElligott's dry wit and photographic memory made those first 10 years rewarding, and he continues to come into the TLL (most recently to borrow power snakes and reciprocating saws) and still finds the right *bon mot* for the occasion. One example of his cagey humor was when he was interviewed by a TV personality for local television Channel 7. The coifed and lacquered host asked Pete what his favorite tool was. He replied that it was a garden fork and a shovel. Afterward I asked him why, and he replied that the question was ridiculous, but because he was hungry at that moment, his favorite tools were a fork and a spoon.

Working at the TLL is a job that touches the public in a unique and personal way. More than funding or the coincidental growth of a social movement, I suspect that the intent behind the project and its staff's very human qualities have made this tool library popular (Gray, 2008).

## INVENTORY AND COLLECTION DEVELOPMENT

Choosing inventory is not a simple task. Just as librarians handling book collections have to balance factors such as popularity, availability, cost, and literary merit, tool librarians need to balance many of those same factors, especially popularity, availability, and cost. But they also need to evaluate manufacturers, how well the tool is designed, how well it stands up to constant use, how much power it has, and how much available parts for replacement cost. Sturdiness is always first when considering a tool that will be lent to a thousand strangers with differing levels of expertise. Each manufacturer has different strengths,

**FIGURE 2.1**   Long-Handled Tools at the Berkeley Public Library's Tool Lending Library (Photograph by Marina Parrera Small).

and one cannot simply choose a line of tools. For example, the SKILSAW 77 is an impressively solid circular saw, but Skil also makes a line of homeowner tools that are not up to the challenge of professional or continuous use. Confusingly, Porter-Cable makes an excellent 4-inch belt sander, but Makita makes a better 3-inch belt sander. Besides that bewildering range of quality, the industry does change, and frequently I have found that even after reading consumer articles in *Fine Homebuilding* or researching on the Internet, the only way to road test a tool is to take it in my hands and use it.

That became apparent when I was trying to replace the TLL's ⅜-inch drills. Over the last decade, ⅜-inch corded drills have declined in use with the rise of better and better cordless drills, with greater power, longer battery life, and the advent of drivers. I can no longer find the sturdy Porter-Cable corded drills that I relied on for years in the field, and Makita dropped its best 5.2-amp model in exchange for a less powerful version.

After years of not offering cordless drills, we decided to take the plunge in June 2013, and the results have been gratifying. We started with 10 drills, 10 impact drivers (that is, a drill designed for driving screws), and 10 chargers, and every weekend the shelves emptied out. We increased those items over the following two years and now have 16 cordless drills, 18 drivers, and 20 chargers, and they all circulate once or twice a week. In fact, the cordless drills circulate 83 times per year, and the drivers over 68 times per year. That adds up to around 6,000 satisfied patrons in not quite three years, with the only additional costs being four batteries that no longer sustained a charge and two drivers that needed repair. On a lively Google Group for tool libraries[1], some have discussed whether the ongoing cost of those batteries is sustainable. It depends on the rate of failure and cost to society of recycling. Because the average drill sold commercially is used under 10 times in its life and TLL's drills have circulated over 180 times each in just under three years, this effort is an unqualified success.

Some tools are too hard to maintain. Finding the right balance between the price of the tool and repair versus the cost to the individual is delicate. We have moved away from some tools and will not currently consider floor sanders or paint sprayers (although the Columbus Tool Library does have two much-loved floor sanders). Those tools are just too much trouble and investment for the return, or for the possibility of only going out once or twice and getting stolen. Additionally, after a five-year experiment, we have given up on tile saws. Sooner or later someone will try to cut a brick with it and quickly ruin an $80 diamond blade and the alignment of a $450 tool. Other tool libraries continue to offer tile saws because of their popularity and manage to keep up the repairs.

Sewer snakes are our bread and butter, so to speak. When winter rolls around, it is definitely snake time in the Bay Area. Those members of our community who can least afford the cost of hiring a plumber would be most at risk if we did not carry these items. But snakes require a lot of maintenance. As for the risk of snakes being biohazards, that is just a matter of washing up (otherwise, plumbers would be quarantined and have those yellow three-lobed biohazard symbols on their lunch boxes). I spray the snake cables with WD-40 before sending them out and let them air-dry when they return, and that seems to do it. But also I wear disposable gloves when handling them, and have a bottle of disinfectant lotion on the counter, which I also offer to patrons returning the snakes.

To keep sewer snake maintenance affordable and the cables from becoming kinked or fouled, education is a must. Often I will draw a tub trap for patrons or show them an illustration from a plumbing book, so they can see that they need to snake through the overflow. The TLL used to have a sink trap under the counter that we would pull out to show patrons the several pieces and washers. With power snakes we warn patrons to be hypercautious when using reverse, and to choose the right cutter head. And paramount, we make sure we are giving patrons the right cable: toilet augers for toilet clogs, hand snakes for tubs and sinks and washing machines, ⅜-inch power snakes for 2-inch cleanouts, and half-inch power snakes for three- to four-inch main lines. About 15 years ago, we got rid of the ¾-inch self-feeding snake, as that was too much for most of our patrons to handle and too expensive for us to maintain. When patrons need to cut larger roots, they need to rent that snake from an equipment rental company.

The return on the library's investment in snakes is huge. I retired a hand snake recently and saw that it had gone out over 400 times. Polling our patrons, their success in using these snakes is around 70 percent, so an investment in one $70 snake saved our patrons $42,000 (assuming that plumbers charge around $150 per visit). The TLL has eight snakes on the shelf, with half of them having the double-down head for tub traps. We also currently carry five motorized snakes (General Mini-Rooter at $620), and in the winter they are often on hold. Roto-Rooter typically charges $300 to clean out a sewer, so borrowing that snake for free or for a modest fee is pretty significant for our patrons. I understand the reluctance to carry snakes, and some people seem to be allergic to the things, but it is no worse than changing diapers.

## CATALOGING

As tools are collected, they must be cataloged for tracking and loaning. The TLL switched from a paper system about 20 years ago, integrating into the software that the BPL was adopting, the Millennium system from Innovative Interfaces Inc. (III). This program is somewhat cumbersome for tools, as it is primarily designed for the needs of book lending, and those are increasingly aimed at self-checkout (and at the TLL, patrons do not check out their own tools). Part of the awkward fit is due to the very different loan periods, fine schedules, and hold treatments for tools, along with our need to visually inspect returned tools and to get feedback from patrons on how well they performed. Our larger items and power tools circulate for just three days, and the demand on them is heavy and continuous, unlike the three weeks that books circulate. At the TLL we phone patrons to tell them that their tool is ready and that we will hold it for them for 24 hours, unlike electronic book holds that are e-mailed automatically. Similarly, late notices require running searches at a high level, instead of being simply at hand.

But despite these difficulties, there are some key advantages to being more closely allied to a public library, and the software is what integrates us. Our patrons often have a history of borrowing from the BPL. They are familiar not only with the concept of sharing, but also with the system of cataloging and tracking, and they can look at our inventory in an online database along with the books. Or they may have book fines or unreturned materials, and that blocks them from borrowing our tools, which provides a system of double checks for both the BPL and TLL. Millennium software can send accounts into collections to recover tools.

The Millennium system was originally developed for UC Berkeley's Doe Memorial Library system, a very large academic library, but was adapted for us by Nayiri Bouboussis, an automation librarian who programmed our tool terminal log-in to recognize a four-digit bar code instead of the 13 digits that books require. Thus, we are able to have up to 9,999 tools, easily carve or inscribe that number on the tool, and then key the number in manually for checking items in and out. The Oakland Tool Lending Library also uses Millennium but has adapted to it differently, scanning bar codes out of a book for their checkouts.

Two other principal types of software are available, and a number of tool libraries are using these. One is Local Tools, created by Gene Homicki when he helped found the West Seattle Tool Library. Another is Tool Librarian, developed by E. Michael Brandt and the SouthEast Portland Tool Library. A number of libraries use both utilities, and they have replaced entry-level programs like Small Library Organizer Pro (or SLOP), which had limited abilities. Adam Jackaway founded the ReSource Tool Library in Boulder, Colorado, and developed his own software system based on a 10-digit cataloging of tools that is impressively organized. However, using 10 numbers requires bar codes instead of the

4 digits that we type into the computers at Berkeley, or the 5 digits that Local Tools requires. Tool Library circulation systems are still a growing area, and the source of much discussion in the National Tool Libraries Google Group.

# ESSENTIAL UPKEEP

A major focus of our endeavor is upkeep. A recent survey of the TLL's SKIL-SAWs revealed that all but two of them have had repairs, ranging from simple cord replacement to straightening out the frames on dropped tools. Similarly, demolition hammers (a 30-pound impact hammer capable of digging hard clay or breaking up a four-inch slab) have an extensive history of repairs, ranging from cord repair to complete rebuilds. Each demo hammer needs to be rebuilt every 150 to 250 usages, and several rebuild kits are kept on hand for the slower winter months when most of the TLL's upkeep is done. Without this upkeep, only one or two SKILSAWs out of the dozen on the shelf would be usable, and only one demo hammer out of eight. That is a shockingly real statistic, and flies in the face of book library practices, where upkeep is minimal. Over the years we have learned how important it is to keep a small stock of tools moving in and out of repair every week.

Similarly, it is necessary to sharpen garden tools often. Years of construction have taught me that dull tools are inherently dangerous, because a dull tool must be forced to do its job. Besides the extra wear on tool and user, force versus guidance is the basic problem of tool use. Force requires using large muscle groups for fine motor control, with an accompanying lack of accuracy, instead of letting the tool do its job. For ease, to avoid accidents, and to lessen liability, regular sharpening is a must.

The repair facility at the TLL is a narrow back room with a long bench and the essentials for repair: a bench grinder, a vise, and a bearing press. The grinder is truly a machine of many uses, and we use it for sharpening chisels and plane blades and for all of our light machining needs. The vise is substantial, and I use it to hold things securely for drilling or to bend and straighten metal. And the bearing press is necessary to replace bearings, which have a tight friction fit. All electric tools have bearings, which can be replaced as they wear out. With miter saws, table saws, and belt sanders, this can double the life of a tool. With smaller tools it may be necessary to balance the increased usage against the price of a bearing, but palm sanders are almost always worth that investment at least once, because of the ease of replacing the bottom bearing, which is the one most exposed to dust.

There are also some must-have hand tools, namely bearing pullers, various retaining ring pliers, dental picks, multimeter, and tap and die sets. Also, a supply of lubricants is essential, including heavy and medium greases such as M6 and M3 that are stable when a tool heats up, regular lithium grease (and grease gun, preferably) for wheelbarrows, 3-IN-ONE oil, WD-40, which we buy by the (literal) gallon, thread cutting oil, and snake oil. That last item is a deodorized heavy oil for sewer snakes, not the hard-to-find cure-all.

To give a better idea of the ongoing nature of upkeep, a list of our most common off-desk tasks is appended at the end of this book (see Appendix A).

# EXPANDING INTO NEW TERRAIN

Physical collections create their own rules, and librarians that handle such collections may find that they need to offer advice to go with their "things." That is a step librarians have long shied away from, preferring to point out resources rather than advise directly on usage. It can be an explosive issue, after all, one that directly confronts the question of accountability and liability. Nonetheless, those issues are resolvable through judicious limits.

Building and gardening tools in particular require a different approach, and cannot be treated like media. SKILSAWs require the regular changing of blades and inspection of guards and cords. Demolition hammers require extension cords of the proper gauge, and drills need sharp bits. Lopping shears, and indeed many tools, need frequent sharpening and oiling to do their job, to remain effective and safe. Maintenance is an expected requirement of this sort of collection, though somewhat unusual compared to needs of a traditional library.

What is unexpected, however, is when a borrower asks if this is the right season to prune their pittosporum or Japanese maple with that lopping shears. It would be entirely understandable if a librarian were to point to a text on gardening or an online link for that borrower, but often patrons need advice for specific and differing tasks. This fact makes the tool library job more intensively interactive with patronage. For example, perhaps a patron has a door that sticks and asks for a hand plane, another tool that needs to be sharpened or honed every other time it is lent out. The tool librarian needs to ask if the patron is going to plane the top of the door or the side of the door to provide the right tool. A jack plane is for the side of the door, and a low-angle block plane cuts across the grain on the top of a frame-and-panel door. Usually the librarian also demonstrates how to use and adjust the plane, followed by an admonition that "less is more" to prevent chip-out, a reminder to watch out for nails and to rasp the paint off first, and perhaps a discussion on how much to bevel back the lead edge where the door first meets the jamb. Doors are the carefully engineered parts of a shelter that are responsive to air movement and the boundaries of temperature change, sound, and the safety of inhabitants, and they have to be able to work efficiently to allow egress in fires. They are tricky, as any carpenter would tell you, and have to be coplanar with the jamb in order not to bind. Any change in their performance heralds a swelling or shrinking of the door or jamb or a movement in the structure or underlying soil.

Such advice is necessary to keep patrons safe and tools in good working order. Giving that advice, it becomes clear that this kind of library works to educate the perceptions of patrons and to midwife budding engineers in the public. Succinct advice for laypeople helps foster the success of their tasks. And the patrons' expectations are realistic: They are not asking whether they should invest in a Roth IRA or if a mole looks suspicious. They just want to know how regular blokes deal with the challenges of the physical worlds of construction and gardening. These are worlds where common sense rules, worlds in which the staff of the tool library helps its patrons engage. We encourage patrons to realize that they truly are the experts of their own homes, because they know them most intimately. Impenetrable municipal codes have made residential structures too complicated for common folk to create and build their own homes.

Our mission has been to reverse that process and give back to our patrons the power to shape their own homes and neighborhoods. Between library patrons that are ready to borrow and return items and a community that now can log on to online plans, advice, encouragement, and access to free or low-cost tools— the bar for building has dropped considerably. When also associated with gardens or community classes and reuse facilities, tool libraries complete a triumvirate of instruction, materials, and tools.

## CREATING A SENSE OF PLACE

After 35 years, Berkeley's experiment has proven to be so popular that it can hardly be called experimental. Although no longer edgy or provocative among today's plethora of lending libraries, the TLL's endurance has woven the library deeply into the fabric of the community. I have offered tools to a number of second-generation borrowers, having watched them come with a parent and then grow up and borrow tools on their own. But in a city like Berkeley, with its high turnover and yearly influx of students, that is more the exception.

The success of Berkeley's Tool Lending Library rests not just in its collection, but also in the process of educating its borrowers. This worthy goal is in line with the book lending of the library next door, the Tarea Hall Pittman South Branch Library, and creates overlapping goals and pools of patrons. There is a healthy cross-fertilization between the two libraries. Some book patrons find their way to the TLL's door when, on a whim, they decide to do some gardening or put up a shelf, and then become more deeply invested in borrowing from our wide range of tools, which far exceeds that of average homeowners. We also urge patrons to visit next door and check out gardening books and plumbing primers, or DIY manuals that will guide them through their intended jobs with a word or two about materials and codes.

Our hands-on approach to patronage has established the tool library as a community resource, not unlike the saloons and salons of a mostly bygone era, a place where members can come together and share concerns outside of a particular job. And like the bartender of old, I have often been surprised at the roles I have been asked to assume, from weatherman to psychologist. Before the practice of online cataloging of information, libraries gave more prestige to "place," honoring the idea that the library was a physical place of inquiry and study. The physicality of a tool collection requires that sense of place, and that in turn has engendered the same kind of patina that libraries have, a sense that here one will find tools and learn how to use them, and that this is a place where questions can be asked.

A few months ago one of my coworkers asked a new patron how he had heard of us. He answered that he just knew about us. "Everybody knows about you," he explained, puzzled. Our community access and distribution was explored in an early study by Wei (2008), who reported, "[r]egistered users number about 10,000 (about 10% of the city population) with an active membership estimated at 300–500 users."

Five years ago, two graduate students at UC Berkeley interviewed a number of our patrons, along with nonpatron members of the community and then told us that the TLL was sometimes mentioned as "the spiritual center of the city." This unexpected ascension is most probably a translation of the life-affirming value of being part of a community that shares.

In the summers of 2011 and 2012, we received a visitor from Sweden, Jonas Söderholm, who was working on his doctorate in library science and specializing in unusual collections. He focused on Berkeley because of our successful duration and conducted lengthy interviews on 22 of our patrons, culminating in the publication of a paper on the motivation of borrowing (Söderholm, 2016). He spoke often of that "sense of place."

Creating a sense of place follows a simple recipe: We connect with our patrons on a visceral and pragmatic level, and then we empower them. That connection often begins with their homes, but touches central aspects of their lives. They may be young students needing to put up shelves or repurposing pallets to make a bed frame, and they will ask us about how to find studs in the wall or design their bed. Or they may need a snake to clean out their drain and cannot wash their dishes until they fix it. Or perhaps they want a deck or need to expand, or want garden boxes, or are elderly and need handholds in the shower. We encourage them, believe in them, and take the time it takes to help them achieve success. Presto!

**FIGURE 2.2** Chapter Author, Adam Broner, Beside a Chicken Coop Built with the Help of a Beginning Carpentry Class He Taught at the Oakland Tool Library (Photograph by Christiane Broner).

One long-time patron rushed into the TLL one day and said, "I need everything!" I replied, "Yes, I heard your wife is expecting again. Congratulations." He answered, "Baby, shmaby. My mother-in-law is coming!"

## FINDING A LARGER COMMUNITY

When its growing popularity led to inquiries from across the country, the Berkeley TLL mailed out packets of information with inventory and forms to encourage other groups to start their own tool libraries. It also answered many questions over the phone. Some interested parties sent out delegates to tour our site and to see how our model functioned.

In the 1990s the Oakland Public Library (OPL) was also interested in starting up a tool library. When their Temescal Branch needed to be earthquake-retrofitted, they designed a tool library to fit in the building's lower level. The OPL chose Ty Yurgelevich to create and run its program, and unusually, he was hired first in Berkeley for six months to work with McElligott and me because the BPL needed a part-time tool librarian. He opened the Temescal Tool Library in January 2000 and retired recently after running it for 15 years.

Willie Brown, then mayor of San Francisco, also approached the Berkeley TLL when gathering information on how to create a tool library that could run under the aegis of the San Francisco Public Library. This San Francisco-based tool library was first administered by a community garden group, the San Francisco League of Urban Gardeners (SLUG), and later run by Gia Grant of the SF Clean City Coalition when it moved into the city's Bayview district. I was hired to go in once a week to help with setup, to repair tools, to write safety documents (which we laminated and attached to many of the power tools), and occasionally to teach safety classes.

As is evident, we have had local success at spreading the idea of a tool library, and interest from farther afield accelerated with the help of the online world. West Philly opened its doors in 2007, Northeast Portland in 2008, and Boulder and Seattle in 2010. Michael Froelich of the West Philly Tool Library began a Google Group for tool libraries in 2010, and it blossomed into a popular online discussion group, tapping into a burgeoning list of communities that were opening tool libraries. In its pages is a repository of information on topics such as funding, software, fiscal sponsors for nonprofits, waiver forms, lending periods and fees, and repairs. Those intent on starting this sort of venture would do well to read through its discussion threads carefully. Another project that became an online resource was the webinar, "How to Start a Tool Library," filmed and published by the Center for a New American Dream (2012). Several people interested in founding their own tool libraries have mentioned that video to me.

Adam Jackaway, founder of the tool library in Boulder's Community ReSource Center, organized a conference call between tool libraries, which took place on August 10, 2011, and was considered a successful forum. However, although I continued to greet visitors in Berkeley, a larger meeting of tool librarians did not happen for five more years, when Piper Watson and the Station North Tool Library of Baltimore, Maryland, hosted the first International Lending Library Symposium in March 2016. Forty participants came from across the United States, Canada, and Europe. The second symposium is planned to take place in Toronto, Canada, in 2017. There were half a dozen tool libraries in 2000, and 15 years later that number has grown to over 60, a sure sign of the success of this type of borrowing.[2]

## SUMMARY

Today, the 35-year-old Berkeley Tool Lending Library is flourishing, with heavy usage by patrons from all walks of life.[3] It is a long way from the scrolls of Alexandria to Berkeley's Tool Library, but those ancient Egyptians who inspired the Ptolemaic librarians and geometers would have been pleased to see our transit and our laser levels, which produce a level line of red light at the click of a button. In 4000 BC, they engineered a level surface upon which to build their pyramids by cutting a trench through the sandstone on all four sides of the intended construction and filling it partway with water. As water always seeks its own level, the waterline gave them a perfectly level line to mark and then laboriously chisel. We actually used to have water levels (a reservoir and a transparent tube), but I retired those when we got the lasers.

Although libraries are indeed fluid and provocative, their essence appears to have changed little. Indeed, the new "sharing economy" may be one of the oldest of human concepts.

## ACKNOWLEDGMENTS

I would like to thank the Berkeley Public Library, and particularly James Moore, manager of the Tarea Hall Pittman South Branch Library, along with the thousands of intrepid users of the Berkeley Tool Library, who have inspired me for many years.

## NOTES

1. https://groups.google.com/forum/#!forum/toollibrary.
2. A directory of tool libraries is available at http://localtools.org/find/.
3. Its inventory of over 4,000 tools can be found online at the Berkeley Public Library website: www.berkeleypubliclibrary.org/locations/tool-lending-library.

## REFERENCES

Center for the New American Dream. (2012, Aug. 9). How to start a tool library (Webinar). Retrieved from www.newdream.org/resources/webinars/webinar-start -a-tool-library.

Gray, J. (2008). Interview with Peter McElligott of Berkeley Tool Library. Retrieved from www.jonathangray.org/2008/07/08/interview-with-peter-mcelligott-of -berkeley-tool-library.

Söderholm, J. (2016). Borrowing tools from the public library. *Journal of Documentation, 72*(1), 140–155.

Söderholm, J., & Nolan, J. (2015). Collections redux: The public library as a place of community borrowing. *The Library Quarterly: Information, Community, Policy, 85*(3), 244–260.

Tabor, N. (2013). *Evaluating the success of tool-lending libraries and their contributions to community sustainability* (Undergraduate thesis). Lincoln, NE: University of Nebraska-Lincoln.

Wei, M. (2008). *A study of utilization in consumer goods* (Independent report). Berkeley, CA: University of California-Berkeley.

# 3

# Book-a-Bike: Increasing Access to Physical Activity with a Library Card

*James Hill*

## INTRODUCTION

In the fall of 2012 our library system had been struggling to implement a wellness plan for the staff, a challenge for seven far-flung branches with anywhere from 1 to 15 employees. The administrative team started brainstorming ideas about what we could do as a library system to reach our staff in even the smallest villages. The director said, "Bikes!" Bikes. Bicycles. Why not? And why keep them just for the staff? Why not let patrons borrow them?

A quick Internet search did not turn up any results of other public libraries checking out bicycles. As a library system, Athens County Public Libraries (ACPL) has a reputation for firsts. We were the first public library system in the United States to switch to an open-source Integrated Library System (Koha) (Breeding, 2002) and we were the first public library system to host free summer lunches (Watkins, 2002). Bicycles could be another first.

We studied bike rentals and sharing programs that we could find information about, like CitiBike kiosk system in New York. The librarian mind starts racing: How does one check out a bicycle? What about storage, helmets, repair, and upkeep? How long is the loan period? Do you need a deposit? Fees, liability, safety, age limits, training? We knew we had a lot to figure out.

Athens County is a mix of rural and small cities in the Appalachian foothills of southeastern Ohio with a population of about 65,000 people (U.S. Census Bureau, 2016). ACPL has seven buildings throughout the county. Of our seven libraries, three branches are located within close proximity to the Hockhocking Adena Bikeway, a paved trail of over 22 miles that follows the Hocking River and traverses wonderful landscapes of woods and open areas, including parts of the campus of Ohio University, a historic mining town called Eclipse, past canal ruins, through the Wayne National Forest, and across Hocking College in Nelsonville, Ohio (Athens County Visitors Bureau, 2015). A bike-lending program that took advantage of that resource was a natural fit for the libraries.

## COMMUNITY INPUT

Because this was going to be a truly new program, however, we wanted to judge the interest and practicality of such an effort. We decided to call a community meeting of anyone and everyone we thought might have insight, advice, and warnings. Thanks to a new local nonprofit, Live Healthy Appalachia, and the ongoing efforts of the city/county health department, Athens County was recently abuzz with information and programs about health, wellness, and exercise. The library wanted to capitalize on that momentum and contribute our part.

We sent 32 invitations to our local hospitals, bike shops, schools, police departments, city officials, the health department, and other nonprofits. At our first meeting in November 2012, we had about 20 attendees, including a school nurse, a city council member, the county and city planners, the director of the Convention and Visitor's Bureau, the city's DARE officer, the health department's education director, and a handful of representatives from other businesses and nonprofits.

Even if the library decided not to pursue bicycles, the meeting brought together the right people and advanced the conversation about bikes and safety and the desire to get our community outside more. We discussed the need for a bike-lending program and what types of bicycles and other equipment might be included. Potential funding sources were considered. Could the program run on donations? The county's and city's planners both pointed out that it dovetailed perfectly with their respective long-range comprehensive plans of improving alternative transportation access and increasing access to resources such as the paved bike path, rural parks, and preserves.

The school nurse discussed the obesity problem in the local district and was a great help alleviating concerns about lice in helmets. As a parasite, lice need a host to survive. The nurse recommended simply placing helmets in rotation. If left unused for 24 hours, any parasites should die; a visual inspection inside the helmet after the dormant period would suffice.

A local bike cooperative, ShadeTree Bike Works, also detailed their past problems with attempts at a bike share program in town and shared lessons learned from their efforts. ShadeTree Bike Works' approach was to repair donated bicycles, paint them yellow, and leave them around high-traffic areas for people to use. If you saw a yellow bike uptown, for example, you were welcome to take it to use, then simply leave it in a visible place for the next person. In a college town, however, where bicycles are often rounded up en masse by fencers, most of the bikes quickly disappeared. The quality of donated equipment was also a barrier. With different brands and types of bicycles, constant maintenance was needed.

Buoyed by the positive energy of the meeting, the library started research in earnest. What other bike-loaning models are out there outside of libraries? Do these models charge, and how can we offer ours for free? What is the liability if someone wrecks and is injured? Is there an age limit? What about children's bicycles? How many different sizes of bikes do we need? Where do we keep the bicycles? And how do you catalog a bicycle?

The two most common models we found were the kiosk systems used in larger cities and rental programs usually offered by a bike store or, in some cases, by a local business like a winery trying to promote tourism.

The kiosk systems were too complicated and expensive for our purposes. Our capital city, Columbus, had just announced its kiosk system called CoGo starting up summer 2014 (CoGo Bike Share, 2016). Along with the ability to use credit cards to unlock bikes, they have built-in computers to monitor usage, GPS navigators, and various other antitheft devices. We simply wanted to make bicycles available to our patrons as easily and cheaply as possible.

One of the local bicycle shops had offered rental equipment for a short time, but abandoned this program after it found the bikes coming back damaged and dirty. The shop was renting mountain bikes, and the temptation for inexperienced riders to try to do more than they were capable was too great, apparently. Because of the shop's experience, we decided to use a heavier cruiser bike that cannot be easily taken off road.

In that first community meeting, it was suggested that we conduct an online survey on our website to gauge public interest. We asked questions about current bike usage habits, roadway availability, and respondents' perception of safety. We wanted to know how far people typically rode and their destination or reason for riding. Most respondents reported an average ride of 20 to 40 minutes, traveling 5 to 10 miles at a time. They ran errands, visited friends, went to work or school, took picnics, or visited the library. The majority thought the idea of borrowing a bike was appealing and agreed that they or someone they knew would check one out if available.

The survey also helped us hone in on what was needed. We found that most children had a bicycle, but not the parents. If they were transporting bikes to use the paved path, they only had room for the smaller kids' bikes. Having adult bikes available would mean that families could more easily ride together. For that reason, we opted for adult-size bicycles only.

## FUNDING

Because Athens County consistently ranks as one of the poorest counties in Ohio (Frohlich, 2015), ACPL does not charge late fines. We do not want a few dollars to be a barrier to the valuable services we provide. In keeping with that philosophy, we knew this new program had to be free. As a library system, we were willing to absorb the risks of theft and maintenance if it meant making bicycles available to more people. We settled on a program that simply required a valid library card and a "hold harmless" waiver for all users.

Initially, we thought this program might be eligible for a grant from the State Library utilizing Library Services and Technology Act (LSTA) funds, but unfortunately, due to a government funding impasse that year, those monies would not be available (Millane, 2013). We researched a few other ideas, but finally found a potential funder closer to home. The O'Bleness Foundation funds programs nationally, but also focuses on regional projects, and prefers to fund start-up programs focused on health and disabilities. It has no budgeting or matching fund requirements and a simple application process. It was a perfect fit. The application deadline, however, was quickly approaching.

*had to price out everything they needed. pick appropriate bikes, accessories think of storage space*

## EQUIPMENT AND BUDGET

In early January 2013, we held another community meeting with the same stakeholders as the first meeting. We shared our research and outlined the direction we were thinking of heading with the Book-a-Bike program.

We asked ShadeTree Bike Works and a local bike shop to help us put together an equipment list and budget for the grant proposal. We have three bikes shops in the area, but only one, Athens Bicycle, attended our meetings, so ultimately it received our business. This has become a continuing partnership, and we relied on their expertise heavily as we evaluated a variety of bicycles. We settled on a three-speed internal hub commuter bike. It has the benefits of being low-maintenance with no derailleur or rear brake pads to maintain. We chose two frame sizes, a 15- and a 19-inch. With a quick-release adjustable seat, it is comfortable for most people and not a bike currently sold in Athens. If you see a black Trek Cocoa, you know it is a library bike! Additionally, it is a heavy, low bicycle. Three speeds are enough for the relatively flat bike path, and there is very little concern of it being used as an off-road bike. Even the most expert riders will have a hard time bunny-hopping these bikes.

We also wanted trailers that could double as strollers and tagalongs for younger patrons. A tagalong turns a regular adult bicycle into a tandem; the adult rides the regular bike while a child rides a smaller attached bike. It is a fun way for kids learning to ride to feel like they are on a bigger bike.

We also priced out a few specialty bikes to round out the program. Because of the O'Bleness Foundation's interest in disabilities and adaptive equipment, we requested a hand trike, a three-wheeler that operates with a rowing motion and only requires use of the upper body. We also added a regular adult-sized trike that has a hauling platform on the back. Our Nelsonville Public Library is located near the food pantry, and on distribution days, it is not unusual to see the yellow cargo bike being used to carry a box of canned goods home.

Additionally, we asked for a heavy-duty three-wheeled recumbent for those patrons who maybe had not ridden a bike for a while or who might have balance issues. It continues to be one of the most popular items simply because it is so much fun to ride. The total requested budget for 21 bicycles was $11,709.84. Athens Bicycle agreed to purchase the bikes for us at wholesale cost and assemble them for free.

After much thought, we decided to keep all of the equipment on the floor inside the three library branches that would have Book-a-Bike. We considered the possibility of outside storage but were concerned about theft and weather. We also considered adding small storage-type sheds near the library, but decided it would ask too much of the staff to leave the building to facilitate a bicycle transaction. By keeping the bikes inside, we could protect them and stay near the circulation desk for the checkout process.

In our grant, we asked for carpet protection for the area we planned to use as an equipment-holding location. Large plastic floor mats (like those used at a desk to make rolling chairs move more easily) were perfect. We found an online distributor for helmets and bike safety flags. We priced bells, baskets, and locks through the bike shop, again at wholesale. Our budget request for miscellaneous equipment was $4,444.45. Additionally, ShadeTree Bike Works provided a list of common tools needed for basic repairs and upkeep. From wrenches to bike stands, we compiled a comprehensive list. The total cost of tools for three buildings was $1,162.00. We did not request monies for staffing or salaries. Our total estimate for bicycles, equipment, and tools to be included in the grant request came to $17,316.29.

*applied for a grant*

# GRANT WRITING

*insurance considerations – if someone is injured using it – bike stolen*

One of the first questions asked at the community meetings was, "What is the libraries' potential liability if someone is injured while riding a library bike?" Anticipating that question from the foundation, too, we talked to our insurance company about the risks. Although we are not a municipal library, our property insurance is considered a municipal plan, similar to those cities carry. When our broker contacted the insurance underwriter, the company quickly dismissed our concerns. As bike kiosk systems have become ubiquitous across the country, the big questions and issues have been solved. As long as we had a standard "hold harmless" clause on file for each user, the library assumed no additional responsibility. The insurance company did request that we make helmets available, which was already planned. As a result, the Book-a-Bike program did not increase ACPL's overall liability premium, though we did add additional rider coverage for the replacement cost of the fleet. So, if a bicycle was stolen, we could submit a claim. That annual premium increase was less than $100.

Writing the actual grant application gave us the opportunity to flesh out how the program would function. With input from our board of trustees, we drafted the necessary policies and procedures. Users would need to have a valid library card, have the necessary paperwork on file—including the lending agreement, parental permission, and the hold harmless consent (see Appendix B and C). ACPL's general circulation policy applied: there would be no fines or late fees for using Book-a-Bike; however, bikes and equipment not returned by the agreed-upon time would be treated as theft. Locks would be provided by request.

To highlight the community interest in our proposal, we gathered letters of support from those who attended our planning meetings. Our grant application included six letters from various agencies and organizations. We also included a letter from our insurance broker alleviating any concerns about the institution's liability and policy protections we would put in place.

We submitted our grant application on February 15, 2013. In March, we were notified that the project was funded in its entirety. On April 4, we called a final community meeting and announced the award. The Athens city planner commented that over the years he had attended several meetings to discuss bike lending. No one, until now, had successfully pulled it off. From start to finish, Book-a-Bike took about six months to put in place.

We had our official rollout on May 5, 2013, with test rides, a safety town (an area for safety demonstrations), a Maypole dance, music, and refreshments. We sent a press release announcing the program and created fliers inviting the community to come and inspect the fleet. The local bike club donated kids' helmets left over from an event, which we were able to give away for free. It was a big party that resulted in a lot of media attention, including the local newspapers and an NPR affiliate.

## THE MANAGEMENT DETAILS

All of the Book-a-Bike equipment is bar-coded and cataloged (helmets, locks, lights, bikes, even tools). A quick search of our Online Public Access Catalogue (OPAC) will pull up the entire collection. The catalogers used standard Anglo-American Cataloguing Rules (AACR2) language to design the original Machine-Readable Cataloging (MARC) record. For added equipment, they simply revise the necessary fields. Most importantly, we just needed a way to check out the various equipment so we knew who the responsible party is. Each piece is scanned to the patron's record just like a book or a video.

For the first few months, we asked users to fill out an evaluation form so we would have some ideas for improvements to the process. Almost immediately, we extended the checkout period from two hours to three, we relaxed the requirement for a parent to be present for those under age 13 in favor of letting any responsible adult assume the liability (that is, grandparents and older siblings), and we loosened the tedious inspections of the bikes.

At the start of the program, the bike shop owner presented a mini-workshop to the staff about what to look for when inspecting the bikes for safety and what could be catastrophic to a rider. Initially, we were checking the bikes thoroughly before each checkout. Each piece of equipment has a folder with an ongoing inspection checklist; ideally, if a bike comes back with a scratched fender, the damage is noted and kept with the bicycle so the next user is not blamed. That process, however, was taking too long, especially on busy days. Now, staff gives the bike a cursory once-over (air pressure, brakes, handlebars, bell), but assumes everything else is functional until we hear otherwise from a user (see Appendix D). We ask everyone upon return if they had a good trip and if everything worked as expected.

Because our bikeway is paved, we have very little issue with mud. We keep a rag nearby to wipe off any rain. We store our helmets in bins under the front desk and rotate them out after each use. As suggested by the school nurse, they sit for 24 hours before being reused. We also keep the other add-ons (lights, baskets, locks) at the front desk, but only check those out when asked. In keeping with the insurance company's request, we require everyone to check out (or have) a helmet. We cannot make adults wear them, but we do require anyone under the age of 18 to have the helmet on when they leave the building.

After our first summer, we purchased headlights and taillights. We thought the bikes might be mothballed for the colder months, but even during the long winter, our patrons want to get outside many days. Because it gets dark so early during those months, we wanted to be able to allow equipment to continue to go out and meet Ohio state law: cyclists must use front and rear lights a half hour before sunrise and a half hour before sunset.

After three years, aside from a few new tires and tubes and brake adjustments, we are still using our original fleet. Quality goes a long way. We still keep the bicycles on the floor at all three libraries. They are visible from the front desk and serve as conversation starters for new patrons and visitors: "I can check out a bike?!"

There have been incidents. We have not had any thefts, although we have had late returns and warnings. The front desk staff have barred a handful of patrons from borrowing due to consistent lateness. One bike was destroyed when struck by a car, but the patron was uninjured. Another time, a patron rode a cargo bike into the river; again, no injuries. Mostly, the incidents have led to funny stories.

## IMPACT BEYOND THE LIBRARY

Since its inception, Book-a-Bike has continued to be a popular service and has been the model for other libraries. At least once a month, a library calls to ask how we did it. I share our story and even send them all of our collateral via a shared file in Google Drive. I have talked to libraries and consortia from Kansas to Florida, and closer to home. Based on our success, Meigs County Library, an adjoining county to our south, partnered with its health department to make bicycles available for free (Meigs County District Public Library, 2016). It even (with our permission, of course) used the name. Its health department used grant funds to pay for the bicycles, and the library makes them available with a library card. Like Athens, Meigs County has a paved path near the library. They were even able to use the same bike shop for their equipment.

In Stark County, Ohio, which has a much larger population than Athens, the library system partnered with a kiosk company to make bicycles available at six of its buildings (Stark Library, 2015). With BikeSmart, bicycles can be borrowed for a fee with a credit card, or for free with a valid library card using a mobile phone app, Zagster. In each case, the library is looking at what works best for its community and its budget.

In the summer of 2015, the city of Athens was designated a bronze-level Bicycle Friendly Community by the League of American Bicyclists. Book-a-Bike and the availability of free bikes helped make that possible. The designation makes Athens even more well known across the country and further distinguishes our community as a great place to visit and live. Book-a-Bike has been well received in the communities and is often asked about at community events and festivals. Our patrons have come to expect innovation from the Athens County Public Libraries.

# REFERENCES

Athens County Visitors Bureau. (2015). Hockhocking Adena Bikeway. Retrieved from athensohio.com/wheretoplay/hockhocking-adena-bikeway-2.

Breeding, M. (2002). An update on open source ILS. *Information Today, 19*(9). Retrieved from www.infotoday.com/it/oct02/breeding.htm.

CoGo Bike Share. (2016). Retrieved from www.cogobikeshare.com.

Frohlich, T. C. (2015, Jan. 10). The poorest county in each state. Retrieved from www.usatoday.com/story/money/personalfinance/2015/01/10/247-wall -st-poorest-county-each-state/21388095.

Meigs County District Public Library. (2016). Book a Bike. Retrieved from meigs.lib .oh.us/node/639.

Millane, E. M. (2013). *LSC Redbook: Analysis of the Executive budget proposal.* Retrieved from Ohio Legislative Service Commission at www.lsc.ohio.gov/fiscal /redbooks130/lib.pdf.

Stark Library to loan bikes at six locations. (2015, June 5). Retrieved from www .cantonrep.com/article/20150605/news/150609602.

U.S. Census Bureau. (2016). QuickFacts: Athens County, Ohio. Retrieved from www.census.gov/quickfacts/table/PST045215/39009.

Watkins, C. (2002). Free lunch now feeds the minds of future readers. *American Libraries, 33*(4), 15. Retrieved from www.questia.com/read/1G1-84722546 /free-lunch-now-feeds-the-minds-of-future-readers.

# 4

# The LibraryFarm

*Jill Youngs*

Imagine a warm summer breeze full of fragrance and bees, a patchwork quilt of dirt and greens, tomatoes, flowers, and the rustle of leaves and a wind chime. Did you imagine that this would be part of a library? This scene actually describes the LibraryFarm in the month of July, a quarter-acre square of fertile property on the grounds of the Northern Onondaga Public Library (NOPL) at Cicero, four miles south of Oneida Lake in the very center of New York State. This region is designated 6b by the United States Department of Agriculture (USDA): a climate with a robust but relatively short growing season similar to Pittsburgh, Pennsylvania, and Detroit, Michigan. The town of Cicero is named for famous Roman orator Marcus Tullius Cicero (106–43 BCE), and his picture-perfect quote adorns the welcome sign to the LibraryFarm: "If you have a garden and a library, you have everything you need." Cicero's quote continues to be an inspiration to everyone who is involved with this successful linking of a mid-sized public library with an organic community garden.

The LibraryFarm is a quarter acre of land surrounded by fields on two sides, a low-volume town street on the north side, and the library building on the east. One-half of the garden area is sectioned into roughly 4-by-8-foot plots that are worked by individuals; the original dozen plots have been expanded to 58 plots involving dozens of community members; they call themselves "plotters." The other half of the garden is three 4-by-100-foot-wide rows that are labeled the Pantry Garden. Plotters and volunteers tend this area, and as the name indicates, the produce from this side of the LibraryFarm is grown, donated, and delivered to three local fresh food bank pantries throughout the growing season.

# GERMINATION OF THE LIBRARYFARM

The NOPL at Cicero has one very valuable asset that most libraries do not have: vacant land. The vacant land was a natural opportunity for constructing a garden on library property. When the idea was first discussed by library staff and administration, it was agreed that it would be vital to ascertain interest, to get a better idea of who would support the project and how many people would want to actually garden at the library. Turning a barren field into a garden is no small endeavor. The community was surveyed to determine interest in creating an organic learning garden on library property, with individual plots that could be "checked out" by members. Then, by working together, the library and the LibraryFarm participants would learn and share organic practices and experiences with each other, and with the entire Cicero community. The response was small; many people were interested and supportive, but only a dozen people actually stood shovel ready on the other side of Knowledge Lane (a local street) when the area was first turned over in the spring of 2010. Their enthusiasm would contribute to an effective and manageable good start.

The first growing season flourished with a dedicated group of participants who found the location convenient and the soil and climate remarkably productive. Five years later, many of the original participants are still gardening in the LibraryFarm, trading plots, sharing tools, and enriching the highly compactable clay soil with amendments, including local United States Composting Council (USCC)–certified compost from the county waste and recycling agency, the Onondaga County Resource Recovery Agency (OCRRA).

The original size and shape of the area has grown as additional plotters "check out" more plots each year. In addition to the plotters' area and the Pantry Garden, the LibraryFarm now houses other features in various stages of completion, including a demonstration garden, a vertical garden, a container garden, a children's five senses garden, and raised beds.

# LIBRARYFARM VARIETIES

The LibraryFarm plotters enjoy trying out new varieties of produce, including brilliantly colored chard and heirloom tomatoes. Unlike at the seed libraries that are gaining popularity around the country, LibraryFarm plotters provide all their own seeds for planting. The plotters also test new styles of mulching, ground covers, and growing techniques. The plotters themselves are as diversified as the gardens they tend; some are experienced and have landscaped yards at home, and others are apartment dwellers or absolute beginners who appreciate the guidance and encouragement fellow members offer. Our plotters represent many age groups, families, cultures, culinary tastes, and differing opinions about organic gardening and practices. To till or not to till is a common conversation, as is sharing opinions on the merit of hardneck garlic and whether the area will experience tomato blight in any given year.

In turn for using the property to grow produce for their own consumption, the LibraryFarm plotters agree to help plant and tend the Pantry Garden, then harvest and deliver the produce to local food pantries. Plotters also give back to the library and the Cicero community by taking part in practices and programs that support learning about food equity and literacy. At the beginning of the season, the plotters design a sign for their plot. The signs are original, personal descriptions of each garden plot: its contents in Latin or possibly an explanation of a special growing technique or plot theme being used. The plotters give back to the LibraryFarm when they share what they have learned designing their plots and signs. The LibraryFarm has been home to all-purple plots, habitat plots, squash on sweater-drying frames, kale in barrels, potatoes in baskets, a five senses garden, and a three sisters garden, to mention a few. Every plot is unique—unlike its neighbor by crop, by orientation to the sun, by composting and mulching methods and ornamentation. The LibraryFarm is already full of a visual variety of inspiring people and plants before the added bird feeders and whirligigs, garden quote signs, painted stones, and every kind of frame, trellis, cage, and chime.

## THE LIBRARYFARM ATTRACTS ATTENTION

The LibraryFarm generates a good deal of interest, and not just from pollinators and toads. The LibraryFarm is one of many new approaches that libraries are employing to adapt to the interests of their communities and to the opportunities their location might uncover. The LibraryFarm has been referred to in numerous library school and library conference presentations, as well as in local newspapers and larger publications, including the *New York Times, GOOD* magazine, TakePart, *Nonprofit Quarterly,* and in publications of the American Community Garden Association and the American Library Association. The LibraryFarm receives frequent inquiries from other librarians nationally and internationally. In fact, the LibraryFarm was recently described as one of an increasing number of public libraries that are more rooted in the "brick-and-mortar" world than traditional brick-and-mortar libraries, or trending book-free libraries with enviable cutting-edge technologies. "Public libraries, by their very nature, are public spaces conducive to gatherings, interactions, and community engagement," observed Mike Scutari in a recent article for *Inside Philanthropy,* in which the LibraryFarm helped earn the Northern Onondaga Public Library (NOPL) at Cicero a mention as one of the country's most innovative public libraries. "Technology may be important, but it's not necessary to the existence of a public space and its practical uses" (Scutari, 2015).

It is fairly natural that if a library has land, then a library farm is simply an obvious extension of library resources. A garden area coupled with a library provides an interactive, multipurpose learning space that just happens to be outside the four walls of our library. The LibraryFarm has a mission and vision; Holt (2014) appreciates the larger community benefit and thinking behind the LibraryFarm, stating: "The LibraryFarm is part of a growing trend in which public libraries redevelop their role as a community center and a place to borrow books. Many of these libraries are finding that whether they're planting vegetables or teaching new gardeners, promoting local food is often in line with their mission." Steering existing library assets, including space and acquisitions, to answer the needs, interests, and expectations of the service population is what practical libraries have always done. The NOPL at Cicero also lends bicycle pumps, croquet sets, and thermal leak detectors. Neighboring public libraries successfully lend cake pan collections and ukuleles. Another branch library, NOPL at Brewerton, offers a fully equipped preservation studio where patrons convert aging media to digital storage. The LibraryFarm is just one more example in the long tradition of libraries using resources creatively to meet their communities' needs.

## MAKERSPACE, LEARNING CENTER, LIBRARY BRANCH, PROGRAM, AND COLLECTION

The LibraryFarm has often been referred to as a makerspace. However, it has also been listed as a learning center, a subbranch, a library program, and a unique library collection—and it fits neatly into all five categories. The Library-Farm is certainly a makerspace when considering the seasonal harvest of organic bounty: peppers, zucchini, garlic and onions, kale, chard, beans, peas, and insistent tomatoes. The food pantry plots alone produced or "made" nearly 175 pounds of organic fresh food in 2014. The LibraryFarm is a superb location for Boy Scouts to produce and build Eagle Scout projects. The LibraryFarm also houses a Certified Wildlife Habitat butterfly garden constructed as a service project for a Girl Scout silver badge. "Libraries are looking for ways to become more active places," said Kate McCaffrey, director of the Northern Onondaga Public Library. "People are looking for places to learn, to do and to be with other people." McCaffrey considers the garden "a maker lab that happens to be outdoors."

The LibraryFarm also "makes" new relationships every season with local non-profits and local business. The LibraryFarm draws volunteers from local non-profits and schools, and seeks out corporate gifts to purchase hoses and sprinklers and raised bed supplies. Recently, the LibraryFarm hosted a community service project day for one of our local banks; many hands made fast work of building raised beds out of donated materials, including old library shelving.

The LibraryFarm is also a learning place. The learning takes place through relevant programming with knowledgeable presenters, and learning also takes place between the plotters, from each other in the garden and at our meetings. Recently, at the soup meeting in January, our new and established plotters perused seed catalogs and shared advice, garden tales, and recipes: from sharing a learning experience with bucolic celery too bitter to eat, to an absolute failure of growing Brussels sprouts in a straw bale garden, to marveling at the ease of success with growing potatoes in a half barrel. At the soup meeting, plotters sign up for committees, including the open house committee, the steering committee, and the new "pest and dirt" committee. We will depend upon the pest and dirt committee to be active learners and teachers. Our plotters come from many educational and gardening backgrounds, but everyone enjoys sharing their knowledge with anyone who wants to learn.

The LibraryFarm has also become a fun learning place for our Summer Nature Camp, a six-week library program that engages kids from ages 8 to 13 in many topic areas of environmental education. Early summer mornings, these young people learn and participate with gardening and plant identification, explore nature science, and practice upcycling. They have the opportunity to do everything from gaining hands-on experience by watering and weeding to sampling raw beans from their communal plots, all while journaling about their experiences. The library is fortunate to have STEM (science, technology, engineering, and mathematics) knowledge and environmental dedication from the entire staff. Even the staff lunchroom has a kitchen compost bin.

The LibraryFarm could also be considered a subbranch of the library, uniquely situated outside the library building, physically involving library staff, board members, and volunteers, yet wholly dependent on the Cicero branch and the NOPL administration for support in every respect. This vital support includes many types of resources, including staff engagement, promotions, water, and assorted supplies like yard bags and pallets. Similar to a unique branch of the library, the LibraryFarm has its own modest budget line, dedicated programming, and a Facebook page. The LibraryFarm is also the inspiration for green and sustainable print resources and media at the NOPL at Cicero.

Is the LibraryFarm a program too? This is a bit more difficult to determine. For traditional library programs, we measure success by program attendance and feedback. For the LibraryFarm, attendance at meetings and committees is counted; attendance at the annual open house and group workdays is collected as well. We count the number of registered plotters and measure pantry garden produce weight, but it is nearly impossible to measure individuals in the garden or how many visitors we have. So, the LibraryFarm relies on positive affirmations from our participants and visitors to confirm its success and vitality.

Whether or not the LibraryFarm is a program, it certainly generates a cornucopia of green and sustainable programming that is popular among the plotters as well as among like-minded homesteaders throughout the area. The NOPL at Cicero, the physical home of the LibraryFarm, often fills the community room with programs on preserving harvests, organic pest management, extended growing with hoop houses, and many hands-on garden "make" events like upcycled trellises, building hypertufa containers, backyard chickens, and home solarization. Through program presentations, the LibraryFarm has developed valuable partnerships with similar groups, agencies, and businesses, including the Cornell Cooperative Extension, the Onondaga County Resource Recovery Agency, Habitat Gardening in Central New York, Syracuse Grows, Syracuse University, and the SUNY College of Environmental Science and Forestry, with whom we share a mutual interest in sustainability and green practices. All of these agencies have presented programming at the library, often multiple times. Some of the programs these partners have presented include the rain barrel construction class "Save the Rain," a three-part composting class, and classes titled "Attracting Butterflies to Your Yard," "Preserving the Harvest," "Community Gardening," "Getting to Know Our Local Farms," "Greening Your Business," "Low-Water Gardening," and "Organic Pest Management," to name just a few. The Cicero Public Library is also an organic Community Supported Agriculture (CSA) drop site for another partner, Freedom Rains Farm, and now hosts the seasonal Cicero Farmers Market partnered with the town of Cicero in the library parking lot.

In addition to these other classifications, is the LibraryFarm also a unique collection? Today's library collections contain everything from books and guitars, to human libraries and digital intellectual capital. In any format, a library's individual collection is still a tangible and significant piece of a library's identity. At the NOPL at Cicero, when coupled with a trending local interest in sustainable practices, the LibraryFarm as a collection serves that goal. In a recent Pew Internet article, Zickuhr (2013) listed the LibraryFarm under a "Unique Library Collections" category. So it seems the LibraryFarm is an uncommon library collection with many unique parts.

## THE LIBRARYFARM COLLECTION

The following is a list of noncirculating collection components that together make up the LibraryFarm:

**Certified Wildlife Habitat Butterfly Garden**. This colorful spot was created as part of a Girl Scout project and was also the LibraryFarm's first raised bed.
**Children's Garden**. Our children's librarian commented that when having fun, children can weed very fast! The Children's Garden is home to a five senses garden and Bomber, the toad.
**Communication Board**. Installed in 2015, this board is important for exterior communications. It also holds maps to our emerging nature trail.

**FIGURE 4.1**  The Northern Onondaga Public Library LibraryFarm, Summer 2016.

**Compost Bin**. This standard three-part bin was constructed for the LibraryFarm as an Eagle Scout project.

**Compost Passes**. Two shared passes to the county compost site (OCRRA) are available for circulation. With this pass, users are eligible to load and transport local certified compost to their own gardens.

**Container Garden**. This is a newer demonstration garden of donated pots and barrels, making use of an unusable area.

**Demonstration Garden**. In past years, this plot has been the scene of unusual repurposed trellises and kale-filled planters created from donated soda barrels.

**Food Pantry Garden**. Nearly 200 pounds of fresh food are grown here for our local food pantries, all with donated plants and volunteer labor.

**Insect Hotel**. Aging recycled pallets stacked five feet tall, with an assortment of cups, colorful stones, moist crevices, and escape routes.

**Little Free Library**. Another Boy Scout project created from donated materials, this is now home to garden information, yard bags, and organic white fly spray, as well as items you would find in other Little Free Libraries, like paperback romances and thrillers free for the taking.

**Pallet Trellis**. Upcycled from refuse from a local maintenance company, these pallets were reconstructed into vine trellises.

**Platform with Benches**. Another Eagle Scout Project; a comfortable place to rest.

**Raised Beds**. Raised beds are much easier to tend for gardeners with physical limitations. Each year we fundraise to add a few more.

**Raspberry Bramble**. This spot holds five raspberry bushes. Although they are more prolific every year, curiously, this produce never makes it into the library.

**Shed**. For storage of tools and materials.

**Straw Bale Garden.** As an alternative to planting directly into the soil, these bales of straw serve as excellent containers for growing plants.

**Water Spigot**. Installed from a grant by the Central New York Community Foundation, easy water access has completely changed the comfort and convenience of gardening at the LibraryFarm.

**Additional Accessories**. These include a variety of shared-use hoes, hoses, watering cans, shovels, sprinklers, stakes, watering cans, wheelbarrows, and other donated gardening tools.

## CHALLENGES AND LESSONS LEARNED

Having a LibraryFarm on the property is not without difficulties. The weather is an important player, of course. Two years ago our area received too much snow and rain in the early spring, only to dry up like a moonscape in June and July. In addition to being ready for the changeable central New York weather, we also need to be creative with the "opportunities" for learning that voles, raccoons, and other garden adventures like tomato blight, cutworms, and ground bees bring our way. The LibraryFarm has rocks; we are always battling weeds and sometimes the garden smells like manure from the fields nearby.

One of the biggest challenges of the LibraryFarm, however, has been communication between the plotters and the library. General information about the LibraryFarm is on the library website. The LibraryFarm has a Facebook page and distributes e-mail newsletters. However, some of the plotters do not have Internet in their homes, and it is difficult to keep in touch if not directly in the garden. There is a notebook inside the library at the service desk, and we use the Little Free Library and the Nature Trail communication board at the entry of the garden to post notes. However, it is not a perfect system. Communication about the LibraryFarm events is not as important as reaching out plotter to plotter when help with watering or harvesting is needed. This season we will be placing an increased emphasis on the importance of scheduled workdays, so plotters will be able to plan when they will meet, learn, and share with other plotters in the garden, rain or shine.

Another challenge for the LibraryFarm is staying organizationally flexible. Although the LibraryFarm is a very real place in the sun (and in the snow), the LibraryFarm is really all about people. From a physical and management point of view, the entire LibraryFarm community needs to be able to redefine priorities and goals sometimes very quickly, according to the interest, resources, and capabilities of the ever-changing events and participants. People become involved with the LibraryFarm but may move away, have an unexpected family, health, or employment issue, and leave abandoned plots that need to be tended. Agencies become involved with the LibraryFarm and have plants or cardboard or a truck of compost to donate that will be delivered, that same day. Flexibility is a challenge, and the LibraryFarm relies on the good nature of the plotters, the library staff, and the board of trustees.

The LibraryFarm has changed dramatically since its inception, and will certainly continue to change five years from now. Any account of the LibraryFarm would be incomplete without a thankful acknowledgment to the enlightened administrative and trustee leadership of the NOPL branches who support and take great pride in the LibraryFarm. Special gratitude is also extended to the people, mostly plotters, who invest their weeknights and Saturdays, and—quite literally—their knees, backs, and vehicles into making the LibraryFarm a successful innovation for our library.

# REFERENCES

American Library Association. (2014). Libraries and community engagement. *State of America's Libraries Report 2014*. Retrieved from www.ala.org/news/state-americas-libraries-report-2014/community-engagement.

Brown, P. L. (2015, Sept. 14). These public libraries are for snowshoes and ukuleles. *New York Times*. Retrieved from www.nytimes.com/2015/09/15/us/these-public-libraries-are-for-snowshoes-and-ukuleles.html.

Casey, A. M. (2015, July 21). Little green thumbs. *Eagle Star-Review*. Retrieved from www.eaglestarreview.com/news/2015/jul/21/little-green-thumbs/?lifestyle.

Central New York Community Foundation. (2015, Dec. 11). Northern Onondaga Public Library grows a greener community with its LibraryFarm program.

*Central New York Community Foundation News*. Retrieved from cnycf.wordpress
.com/2015/12/11/library-farm.

Holt, S. (2014, March 19). There's no shushing at this library—and you'll want to
bring a trowel. *TakePart.com*. Retrieved from www.takepart.com/article/2014
/03/19/going-library-bring-trowel.

Johnson, C. (2012, Oct. 10). Libraries reinvent themselves as labs of creativity. *The
Christian Science Monitor*. Retrieved from www.csmonitor.com/World/Making
-a-difference/Change-Agent/2012/1010/Libraries-reinvent-themselves-as
-labs-of-creativity.

McCambridge, R. (2014). Library usage soars as libraries get madly innovative. *Nonprofit Quarterly*. Retrieved from nonprofitquarterly.org/2014/03/10/library
-usage-soars-as-libraries-get-madly-innovative.

Peters, A. (2013, Feb. 17). LibraryFarm: Check out a garden plot with your books.
*GOOD Magazine*. Retrieved from www.good.is/articles/libraryfarm-check
-out-a-garden-plot-with-your-books.

Schrier, B. (2014, Sept. 12). How to get your hidden collections online—Digitizing
for access. Retrieved from agblog.auto-graphics.com/how-to-get-your-hidden
-collections-online-digitizing-for-access.

Scutari, M. (2015). Behold the library of the future: A place where technology is an
afterthought. *Inside Philanthropy*. Retrieved from www.insidephilanthropy
.com/libraries-literacy/2015/10/30/behold-the-library-of-the-future-a-place
-where-technology-is.html.

Zickuhr, K. (2013, Jan. 29). Innovative library services "in the wild." *Pew Internet
& American Life Project*. Retrieved from libraries.pewinternet.org/2013/01
/29/innovative-library-services-in-the-wild.

# 5

# Seed Libraries: Lend a Seed, Grow a Community

*René Tanner and Betsy Goodman*

**"It's like checking out a book, except that you've added a chapter when you return it."**

**—Rebecca Newburn, Richmond Grows Seed Lending Library, Richmond, CA[1]**

## INTRODUCTION

Heirloom fruits and vegetables have been valued over generations and their seeds have been passed from one caretaker to the next, but these precious plants can be lost in as little as one season without seed saving. This chapter gives a brief history of seed saving and sharing from colonial times to present, an introductory "how-to" for those who would like to start a seed library, and a summary of the progress and continued work to change current state-level seed laws to enable a broader sharing of heirlooms and open-pollinated plants. The purpose of this chapter is not to explain the intricacies of seed saving, as there are many publications on this somewhat complicated art; instead, we hope to propel you to start a seed library in your community or support an existing one.

# A HISTORY OF SEED SAVING

## An Earlier Time

As people settled in new regions, they brought seeds with them. These seeds—precious items that can be contained in small spaces—were extremely valuable when moving to a new homestead. Early European settlers brought seeds for a variety of crops to what would become the United States. However, many British crops were unsuccessful at first, and two-thirds of the settlers in Jamestown, Virginia, died of starvation in the winter of 1609–10. Survivors turned to locally grown corn and Native American farming practices while working to adapt their transplants to the new climatic conditions. Through trial and error and saving and replanting grain from the plants that produced seeds, they acclimated many British crops, including English wheat, to the New World (Rasmussen, 1975).

Traditionally, families passed seeds from one generation to the next, creating what we call heirloom varieties. Neighborhoods and towns came together for seed shares and swapped seeds in an effort to increase the genetic breadth of edible plants, introduce new cultivars, and keep genetic lines strong through outbreeding (Ray, 2012).

Recognizing the importance of crop diversity, in 1819 Secretary of the Treasury William L. Crawford requested that the foreign consuls and naval officers assist in the collection of useful plants for a growing nation. Crawford understood that it would take many experimenters to discover successful crops and adapt germplasms. Collection activities increased under the guidance of Henry Ellsworth, Commissioner of the U.S. Patent Office, who in 1839 was successful in securing funding from Congress for the collection and distribution of seeds and plants. The Patent Office continued to mail small packets of seeds through members of Congress to increase distribution and cultivation of foreign plant materials. By 1855, over a million seed packets had been distributed to farmers (Kloppenburg, 2005, pp. 55–56).

Through the U.S. Patent and Trademark Office, the government handed out free seeds to increase genetic crop diversity and to establish stable communities across the country. Under management by the U.S. Department of Agriculture (USDA), established in 1862, the flow of seeds reached its highest volume in 1897 with the distribution of 1.1 billion packets of seeds (Kloppenburg, 2005, pp. 63–64). Once the seed industry began to form, lobbying to eliminate the free seed program was persistent, and in 1924 the program was eliminated (p. 71).

With passage of the Morrill Acts of 1862 and 1890, the land-grant universities were established, and the public sector began to play a dominant role in agricultural research and development (R&D). This role continued until roughly the 1930s, when the availability of commercially viable hybrid corn and subsequent changes in property rights (the Plant Patent Act) led to an economic incentive for private investment in agricultural R&D. As a result, private industry invested heavily in plant breeding (Fernandez-Cornejo, 2004, pp. 41–42).

## Recent Reductions in Diversity

For 12,000 years, humans saved seeds and freely shared them. However, change in the last 100 years, and in particular over the last few decades, has shifted our dependence from small seed suppliers to large commercial seed companies (Fernandez-Cornejo, 2004, pp. 30–40), which has decreased the availability of genetically diverse, open-pollinated plant materials. There was a time when it was common for families to have their own varieties and to share this abundance freely (Ray, 2012). Now we have many food deserts in low-income areas and a growing trend of food insecurity (Camp, 2015), with a dramatic loss of heirloom varieties (Fowler, 2009; Fowler & Mooney, 1990). One solution is in the seed. Try saving seeds from your favorite lettuce or tomato, and soon you will find that you have enough to share with all your family and friends.

# THE PURPOSE OF A SEED LIBRARY

A seed library can provide an easy means for people to try growing a variety of edible plants in their yards and on their balconies, including locally adapted and rare varieties. When we asked speakers at the First International Seed Library Conference in Tucson, Arizona, what the purpose of a seed library was, we received the following responses:

> I believe that our main purpose is to create and encourage unobstructed access to seeds and information so that the most members of our community can become acquainted with and empowered by growing. On the big-picture scale and at the root of it all, every seed library is serving the grand purpose of contributing to global, long-term, food security.
> —Kelly Wilson, Librarian, Pima County Public Library, Tucson, AZ (personal communication, December 9, 2015)

> The purpose of a seed library is to get seeds into the hands of as many people in a community as possible. Ideally, many of those people will grow them out and return seeds to the library, building the supply of seeds that are acclimated to that particular area and ultimately building a resilient food/seed supply within the community.
> —Cindy Conner, author and permaculture educator, living near Ashland, VA (personal communication, November 7, 2015)

> The purpose of a seed library is as varied as the communities they serve. Our intention is to provide food security through sharing and saving unusual varieties, with a focus on crops that have cultural significance to our community. In doing so we are able to preserve and celebrate genetic and cultural diversity. When seeds are shared that have a face, place, and story attached to them, folks are not just getting seeds, they are getting connections. In this era of Big Ag, we have lost a connection both to the foods we eat and the people who grow them. We want to honor our ancestors by sharing seeds while we also breed the heirlooms of the future and with these shared seeds nourish our bodies, minds, and souls.
> —Rebecca Newburn, educator and founder of Richmond Grows Seed Lending Library, Richmond, CA (personal communication, November 9, 2015)

The themes that run through these statements vary in terms of their emphasis, yet they share an understanding of the purpose and opportunity that a seed library provides, which is to encourage the sowing, harvesting, and sharing of seeds. Each of these individuals sees the patrons, the collection of seeds, as well as books and other materials about gardening all working in concert to preserve rare seeds and keep unique varieties in the hands of growers. Although these efforts have the potential to preserve existing rare varieties, they also have the potential to create new varieties with adaptations specific to the locale in which they are grown.

## PUBLIC LIBRARIES: IDEAL FOR SEED LIBRARIES

Libraries help us remember that we have a shared history. Libraries link their communities to stories, information, and knowledge that provide life enrichment, personal growth, social engagement, and self-directed learning. Libraries remind us that we believe in the value of these opportunities not only for the few, but for the many.

Library systems also hold integrity. With longevity, the systems are in place to add additional materials to the catalog, including those needed for a seed library. Also, the staff is resourceful in supporting its patrons. Specific staff members specialize in areas such as programming, marketing, tracking usage, and organizing volunteers. With many hands collectively assisting with unique aspects and a strong structure in place, public libraries can support a seed library fairly easily.

Libraries are places where the public can access free information. The service that a public library provides to its community is unprecedented in its benefit to the nation. Thomas Jefferson's broad interest influenced the evolution of public libraries with the addition of his personal library to the Library of Congress (Murray, 2009). Jefferson was also an avid gardener and made free seeds and cuttings, collected from his Monticello gardens and from around the world through consuls, available to other gardeners (Cornett, 1993; Raver, 2010). Still to this day, the Monticello garden is disseminating seed through the Thomas Jefferson Center for Historic Plants (Thomas Jefferson Foundation, n.d.). In the spirit of our founding fathers, we continue to add diversified content to public libraries across the nation. ". . . Agriculture . . . our wisest pursuit, because it will in the end contribute the most real wealth, good morals, and happiness" (Jefferson, 1787).

Seed libraries are a modern spin on the tradition of sharing seeds with one another. Housed in public spaces, seed libraries allow patrons to check out seeds just like checking out a book, except there is no need to return anything. Although there is no requirement to return seed, there are often educational resources available to encourage the practice of seed saving with the hope that patrons will save some for themselves and bring back a portion of the best seeds to share with others.

In its basic setup, a seed library has a bin, storage cabinet, mason jars, or former card catalog to store seeds.

**FIGURE 5.1**   Rebecca Newburn, Co-founder of Richmond Grows, at the Seed Lending Library Cabinet (Photo by Michelle T. Sixta).

When it comes to organizing the seed collection, like so many structures, there is more than one way. If your collection is small, a simple alphabetical organization of seeds by common name may work best. Another option is to organize your collection into three distinct sections: flowers, herbs, and vegetables, and then alphabetize the seeds by common name in each of the three sections. If your collection is more extensive and you want to focus on seed saving and seed deposits, you could organize your seeds by level of seed-saving difficulty with regard to producing true-to-type seeds,[2] which means that the seed grows out to be what the label reads.

Easy, medium, and advanced or super easy, easy, and difficult are both common designations for seed labels with regard to the level of seed-saving skills required to collect true-to-type seeds. For other helpful tips regarding how to organize a seed library, you could visit the guide from the Seed Libraries network on how to start a library.[3] As with any organizational structure you choose, you can modify as needed to fit your particular collection.

The checkout system can be tailored to meet your library's needs as well. Seeds can be "checked out" by signing them out on a sheet of paper and indicating what was taken and in what quantity. Alternatively, in a more sophisticated system, seeds can be added to the online catalog, and the seed packets can be scanned at the desk or the self-checkout machine. This process is very similar to checking out a book, except there is no expiration date for the material.

**FIGURE 5.2** Inside the Seed Cabinet at the Pima County Public Library Seed Lending Library (Photo by the Pima County Communications Office).

When seed is returned to the library, it needs to come back with a slip that has as much information as possible regarding the common name, variety, and the measures that were taken to prevent cross-pollination (see Appendix E). This form is important for redistribution purposes. It aids in determining the suitability of seeds for the collection and gives a way to track the seeds in case they do not come back true to type.

One practical reason to house a seed library in a public library is the cataloging system. Cataloging is important for keeping an inventory of seed stock. Public libraries already have the cataloging system in place and staff to manage the online catalog. For example, two library branches that the authors have a personal connection to are the Omaha Public Library in Nebraska and the Pima County Public Library in Tucson, Arizona, which both use cataloging systems helpful to libraries with many branch locations because it makes interlibrary lending easy and user-friendly. For instance, in Omaha or Tucson, the closest library branch may not have an old card catalog filled with seeds, but you are able to get seeds transferred from another branch that has a seed library. Transferring small quantities of seeds from one library to another is yet another reason to consider repackaging seeds from bulk jars into individual packets with bar coding. Although it takes more time and resources, such as purchasing small envelopes and making labels, repackaging seeds allows for easy usage tracking. This extra processing also conserves seed resources because patrons are less likely to take more than needed if seeds are prepackaged.

Other seed libraries housed in academic libraries, rural towns, or smaller library systems may use a simple piece of paper rather than adding the seed library to their cataloging system. This is the structure for the seed library at the Noble Science Library at the Arizona State University in Tempe. This system is based on trust. Patrons are responsible for taking only the number of seed packages they need and for recording their names and varieties chosen on the checkout sheet. Sometimes seed libraries with this honor system find that

**FIGURE 5.3**  Seed Packet Labels Showing the Seed-Saving Designations of Easy, Medium, and Advanced (Photo by the Pima County Communications Office).

people take more seed than necessary, and therefore the library goes through more seed. In addition, more consistency is needed to monitor this type of system because no online database is used to track the inventory. Another option that can help is to have dedicated volunteers manage the seed library and limit the hours to when volunteer staff are available.

## IT ALL STARTS WITH THE SEED

You can take a variety of approaches for your seed library collection. The collection can focus on plants that are easy to grow, container garden–sized plants, local seed stock, or plants for which growers new to gardening will have high success collecting true-to-type seeds. Although the collections can vary, it is imperative that seed libraries only distribute open-pollinated, viable seeds with high rates of germination. Seeds that are hybrid, have plant variety protection (PVP), Plant Patent Act (PPA), genetically modified organism (GMO), or utility-patented varieties should not be disseminated by seed libraries because gardeners will not be able to successfully or legally save the seed from them, which contradicts the primary purpose of a seed library and the goal of moving toward a secure, locally adapted seed system.

Garden-variety seeds can be open-pollinated or hybrid. The difference between open-pollinated and hybrid seeds is that one will grow true to type if you save the seed, and the other most likely will not. When you plant an open-pollinated carrot seed, allow the plant to flower, collect the seed, and replant it, you will get a carrot. Open-pollinated generally refers to seeds that will produce a plant similar to the parent plant, or "breed true." When open-pollinated varieties self-pollinate, or are pollinated by a plant from the same variety, the resulting seeds will be true to type. Plant an open-pollinated carrot, take precautions to avoid a cross with another variety, save the seeds from the best plants, and you will get seeds that produce a very similar-looking carrot to what you originally harvested (Conner, 2014).

In contrast, hybrids have two genetically different parents. The plants have been crossed, and the cross has not stabilized. In general, it can take seven years for them to stabilize. On seed packets, the label could indicate a hybrid variety with "F1," meaning first generation. In contrast, open-pollinated plants have been stabilized over generations (Conner, 2014, p. 9). In addition, sometimes the seeds from a hybrid are sterile and will not produce fruit (Best, 2013, p. 163), and other times the fruit may be inedible.

To illustrate this last concept, we share a situation on the farm where author Goodman worked for six years. Bloomsorganic Farm, in Crescent, Iowa, produces a diversity of herbs, vegetables, and flowers.

In the spring, the farm sells small starter plants for backyard gardeners and then grows excess to sell to local restaurants. With any given crop, many varieties are grown, both open-pollinated and hybrid. In a high tunnel, which is similar to a greenhouse without electricity, the farm seasonally grows one of its favorite hybrid cucumbers, the Harmonie F1 cucumber. One season, a few of the Harmonie F1 cucumbers grew to maturity and fell off the vine. When a

**FIGURE 5.4**  Betsy Goodman on the Bloomsorganic Farm in Crescent, Iowa (Photo by Emily Beck).

cucumber grows to maturity, it becomes much larger than the size picked for eating, turns deep yellow, and adopts a hard outer skin. In the fall, while turning in the rye grass cover crop, workers inadvertently incorporated the Harmonie cucumber seeds into the soil. That winter was untypically mild for the region, so the seed survived and began growing once the soil warmed the next year. The farm crew recognized that it was a cucumber, and curious to see the fruit from the second generation (F2) of their favorite hybrid cucumber, they let it grow. The fruit from the second generation was furry and inedible. This experiment was a reminder that it is not worthwhile to save seed from hybrids unless you are an aspiring plant breeder.

Although seed libraries should avoid hybrid seeds, it is important to note that hybrid cultivars have many benefits, which is why commercial growers often prefer them. Hybrids may have more vigor and disease resistance, and may outproduce the open-pollinated varieties. Hybrids are usually bred to have desirable characteristics that a previously open-pollinated ancestor did not. One example is the famous Big Boy tomato bred by plant breeder and geneticist, Dr. Oved Shifriss, for W. Atlee Burpee & Company in 1949 (Shattuck, 2004). This tomato is an American favorite whose ancestry still remains a trade secret (Klingaman, n.d.).

In her book, Conner (2014) talks about Romulus romaine lettuce and how she had grown it for years because the restaurants she was supplying liked it for its open head, which made it easy to clean. She did not realize it was a "PVP," meaning that it was protected under the Plant Variety Protection Act, until she went to buy more. When it was not available from the seed company that year, she planted the remaining seeds she had and harvested the seeds from those plants. The following year she learned for the first time that it was PVP when another company picked it up and labeled it as such. PVP varieties allow gardeners to save seeds for replanting, but not for seed swaps or for sale. As Conner states in her book, labeling seed packets to indicate PVP is required, but she has seen other cases where it is missing as well (p. 10). If ever in doubt, one can check the PVP database,[4] which is maintained by the USDA.

Hybrids can occur naturally or with human assistance. However, unlike hybrid seeds, genetically modified seeds (genetically engineered, genetically modified, or transgenic) are developed by inserting DNA, often from a completely different organism, such as an animal, bacterium, or fungus. This type of breeding would not occur in nature. Some of these seeds are covered by utility patents, as established by the 1980 Supreme Court decision in *Diamond v. Chakrabarty*. Utility patents provide broader protections for breeders than both the Plant Patent Act of 1930 and the Plant Variety Protection Act of 1970. Utility-patented seeds cannot legally be saved or shared (U.S. Congress, 1989).

The takeaway is that seed libraries should only distribute open-pollinated seed. Why? Because we want people to remember how to save seed! The only way to preserve and evolve open-pollinated seed varieties is to keep them in production. Also, in time, the hope is that each seed library will be self-contained, with no need to purchase seed or ask for donations because members are returning seed. Although returning seed will likely never be a requirement of a seed library because it could be in violation of a state's laws, it is the goal to create a resilient, locally adapted seed system in each community. We want to empower people to successfully save seed that they check out from the library. The way to empower patrons of seed libraries to perpetuate seed abundance is by starting with open-pollinated seed, which is genetically rich and true to type.

## WHAT KIND OF SEED LIBRARY SHOULD YOU START?

There are a variety of options when it comes to starting a seed library. You may find that a focus on growing food and giving seeds away is best for your community. Alternatively, you may discover that seed saving and sharing are vital for the financial sustainability of your seed library and match the interests of the community. If you decide that accepting seed donations and sharing seeds is best for your library, you could start by consulting the seed law in your state. The Seed Law Tool Shed is a state-level seed law wiki that provides a collaborative space for interested parties to link to their state's seed law, make updates, add clarifications regarding application of the seed law language, and to ask questions of the community about seed law interpretations. The Seed Law Tool Shed was initiated by Sustainable Economies Law Center (Johnson, 2014). To find your state, visit the Seed Law Tool Shed website.[5]

Once you have your state seed law in hand, you could contact your state agriculture partner to discuss your plans for a seed library. You may discover that organizing a seed swap is legal, but that legislative changes are needed to accept donations and redistribute seeds through your seed library. Be encouraged: progress to allow for the free and legal exchange of seeds is being made, and you may have an opportunity to be a driver in this change for your state. In the end, even if you decide to distribute only commercially purchased, open-pollinated seeds, you are still making a significant contribution to your community by encouraging gardening and an appreciation for food.

## HOW TO START A SEED LIBRARY?

The key to building a community of successful seed savers is giving them the best possible seed and setting them up for success with plenty of educational resources. The following steps for starting a seed library were adapted from Richmond Grows[6] and presented by librarian and Common Soil Program Coordinator, Carol Erkens, and author, Betsy Goodman at the 2015 Healthy Farms Conference (Erkens & Goodman, 2015).

### Get Your People Together

Who can you reach out to for help? You'll find many potential partners, including a permaculture guild, transition town initiative, a local garden club, the cooperative extension master gardeners, or local community center. Also, check to see if any sister seed libraries are located nearby or with similar climatic conditions. They may have seed-saving tips and library materials and policies that will fit your needs. Check online communities such as Seedlibraries .org or the Seed Libraries Facebook community for supporters. Community building is an underlying principle within the seed library movement. Collaboration is key to success, so find out who is interested in supporting this project. Who are your funders? Who in the public library is willing to take on this project? What are some already established community organizations that could help build support and awareness for the seed library? Who are your seed savers and farmers? Who are your educators (Erkens & Goodman, 2015)?

## How Much Will It Cost?: Decide on What Type of Seed Library You Want

The cost is dependent on what type of seed library you want. The cheapest option is to have a library that is run by volunteers with donated supplies that need periodic replenishing. This model could be housed in a public library but maintained by community members rather than a responsibility of the library staff. The Ely, Iowa, Seed Lending Library is one example of this.[7] The costs associated with this model are minimal, but the challenges in maintenance will need to be overcome with strong community support. Without careful curation by skilled personnel, well-meaning donors may give hybrid seed. Additionally, patrons may take much more seed than necessary and supplies may dwindle quickly (Getzschman, 2014). One way to curb overconsumption is to offer a suggestion about the number of seeds needed. Have a sign that reads, "Take three seeds for each plant you intend on growing. For example, if you want five tomato plants, take 15 seeds" (Erkens & Goodman, 2015).

A more sustainable option is to have paid staff and a budget for maintaining the seed library. The budget required is unbelievably small in comparison to the population served. For example, Common Soil's 2013 budget was $2,000. This grew to $2,500 in 2014 with plans to open seed libraries at two new branches. The funding enabled staff to order supplies and pay for educators to teach free classes to community members (Landgraf, 2015). A portion of the budget allowed for the purchase of seed based on what grows well locally and what patrons will be able to successfully regenerate if they choose to do so (Getzschman, 2014). Between the opening of the seed library in 2013 and early 2015, Common Soil distributed over 5,000 seed packets (Cook, 2015). Library staff members helped with marketing, outreach, cataloging, and education. A useful element in cataloging is bar-coding seed packets. Bar coding integrates the checkout into a computer database so that the library can more easily maintain inventory and track distribution amounts (Erkens & Goodman, 2015; Landgraf, 2015).

Once again, there may be hybrid seed donations, so the staff would have to discard donated seeds that were not identified on the seed-return form as open-pollinated (Peters, 2015). The seed-return form requests that people supply the following information about the seeds: common name, scientific name, variety, harvester, location of harvest, year, population size, isolation distance, and other details of cultivation (see Appendix E).[9]

Many free downloadable seed-saving guides are available on websites such as SeedMatters.org and RichmondGrowsSeeds.org. Including seed-saving resources in your library will help patrons know which species are good to start with as a novice seed saver and which species they can aspire to save once they have sufficient skills and knowledge. For example, some species have a high likelihood of producing true-to-type seeds without much care. These species include tomatoes, beans, and lettuce (Page-Mann, 2014). Conversely, corn is an example of an advanced seed to save because of the vulnerability to inbreeding depression[8] and outcrossing (Janson & Carlson, 2013).

## Acquire Library Materials

A successful seed library will be an organized operation with clearly defined roles. Libraries will need envelopes, seeds, signage, labeling materials, record-keeping materials, policies for borrowing and returning seeds, a seed storage file (DVD storage box or index card cabinet), as well as money to pay presenters and make needed purchases, planting calendar, and most importantly a staff member who manages all of this.

A database or cataloging system is extremely helpful because the collection could otherwise turn into a chaotic mess. People like to plant many different vegetables in their garden; there may be 10 to 50 varieties of each vegetable available at the seed library. Add in flower and herb seeds, and a library has hundreds of different seed packets to track. A good cataloging system is necessary if you want to attempt to maintain a stable inventory. Most public libraries already have a cataloging system in place as well as a person in charge of cataloging, which is extremely helpful. Alternatively, some free options are available, including the WordPress-Seedbank plugin.[10]

Seed offerings can change over time or be set from the beginning. Most likely, you will find that patrons have favorites ("A Growing Expansion," 2015; Erkens & Goodman, 2015). This process is all about trial and error. That said, if the library uses a bar code cataloging system, the staff member who continually has to add new cultivars of tomato varieties will not be happy. The seed library can choose to catalog items by strict name or by description and then make a gene pool. For example, hundreds of varieties of red slicing tomatoes exist. Rather than label Rutgers, Campbell's, or Brandywine, the library could choose to just call them "Red Slicers" and create a grab bag of seeds. Besides saving indexing work, this system could result in a new, unique landrace of tomatoes reflecting the climatic conditions and preferences of the local community.[11]

To gain additional insight into the types of seeds to acquire for a new seed library, we interviewed Kelly Wilson, one of the librarians who works with the seed collection at the Pima County Public Library. She identified wildflowers, tomatoes, peppers, lettuces, and herbs as seeds that "seem to fly out of the drawers." She also notes that there is not one particular type of seed borrower. Wilson notes, "I meet every type of person imaginable at the seed library cabinet. There are many new gardeners, many seasoned gardeners, children to grandparents. It is a very diverse group of users." Although the library does not keep statistics on the number of repeat borrowers, she can confidently say that "we do continue to grow our circulation every year, so I know that we are getting new people all of the time. It seems like once they begin using our seed library, they continue to come back again and again" (Kelly Wilson, personal communication, December 9, 2015).

In addition to seeds, you can also offer a variety of seed screens to help sort seeds based on size.[12] For more advice about what to collect for your seed library, you could consult a number of library webpages. The Common Soil Seed Library maintains a guide about gardening and seed saving that is full of tips, book recommendations, and advice.[13]

## Recruit Volunteers

Once you are set up, it is time to contact the people you reached out to initially. That includes your small-acreage farmers, avid and new gardeners, teens and tweens, permaculturalists, or anyone who wants to help! Oftentimes the library has volunteers already lined up, and they can be assigned to package or label seeds. Seed libraries need volunteers to educate the public about gardening and seed saving through workshops and public speaking, to grow seed, and to advocate for the library in general and for the seed library specifically (Erkens & Goodman, 2015).

## Create Signage, Advertise, and Promote Programs for Your Library

Posters, fliers, general advertising materials, a logo, deposit slips, seed-return forms, and instructions for staff and users are all items to consider for your seed library. Good marketing brings people to the seed library, and proper signage empowers people to use it. Richmond Grows has downloadable templates and other resources to create a seed-sharing library.[14]

Seed libraries are a community resource because they support food equality by providing access to free seeds for everyone. Marketing can be the biggest challenge because, just like any resource, if the library is not used, it becomes marginalized. You may have a great program, but the idea has to catch on for it to be successful. Never miss an opportunity to ask people if they are aware of the seed library (Erkens & Goodman, 2015).

There are many ways to promote your seed library and to create interest in growing food and sharing the genetic diversity of plants. The seed library at the Pima County Public Library advertises a variety of events in support of the seed library, including a book club with selections themed around food, sustainability, and harvesting. They also display a monthly "Now Sowing" flier on the seed cabinet that lists seeds to sow that month and general gardening tips. This information is also available on Pima County's Seed Library webpage[15] and library blog,[16] which includes other special events.

## Talk About It . . . to Everyone!

Your seed library is a huge community resource. Getting the word out can be the most challenging part. Networking with other seed libraries, community members, long-standing community organizations, farmers, and gardeners will help to spread the message. Get on the news, in the news, and be the news. Tell everyone all the time to the point where your friends and family think you are a broken record. "Did you know that you can get free seeds at the public library?" Word-of-mouth communication is very powerful, and once again it is all about community building, so don't be shy (Erkens & Goodman, 2015)!

## Expect the Unexpected

If you are asking for seed donations, expect that some donations may not grow in your climate. Your community's gardening IQ may not be as vigorous as you expect, so be prepared to teach the basics of soil building, planting, and starting seeds. To raise the proficiency of gardeners, seed libraries often have classes, books, and online educational resources. These educational aspects need not focus on seed saving solely, but can include such topics as gardening, composting, raising chickens or bees, and food preservation.

Seed donations may very well contain patented seeds and hybrid seeds, so make a plan to discard these donations when discovered and maintain the collection's integrity. Examining the donation form for completeness and an indication of the collector's seed knowledge is an important step in the process of determining whether to add or discard the seed. Rachel Steiner, manager of the Benson Library in Omaha, estimates that her library rejects about 30 percent of donated seed received (Peters, 2015).

Lastly, become educated about the seed laws in your state. A visit from the Agriculture Department may ensue if the seed laws have yet to be reformed in your state or county to include an exemption for "noncommercial seed sharing." There is more on the seed law in the paragraphs that follow.

## SEED LAWS: ISSUES AND OPPORTUNITIES

The Federal Seed Act (enacted August 9, 1939) was crafted to protect farmers and give them assurance that the seed they purchased was held to quality and integrity standards, which had been lacking. With its passage, a seed company must affirm that the seed in each packet is, in fact, the variety that the label reads and has acceptable germination rates. The seed law also enforces noxious weed standards and sets limits on their presence among the desired seed. Specific labeling requirements are outlined in the Federal Seed Act (USDA, 1998).

Beyond the provisions of the federal law, each state independently adopts its own seed laws. The American Association of Seed Control Officials (AASCO) and American Seed Trade Association (ASTA) work together to maintain uniformity and overlap between the states (ASTA, 2016). Some ASSCO members are the USDA officials who oversee seed trade on the state level. Every year at the AASCO annual meeting, changes are made to a living document called Recommended Uniform State Seed Law (RUSSL), and states can choose to adopt those changes (AASCO, 2016).

Nebraska Seed Control Official, David Svik, presents the legal situation in Nebraska:

> The definition of "sale" as cited in the Nebraska Seed Law states its variant forms include barter, exchange, offer for sale, expose for sale, move, or transport in any of their variant forms or otherwise supplying. Therefore, public libraries that loan out or donate open-pollinated seed to individuals would fall under the definition of sale in the Nebraska Law and be required to test all seed and obtain an annual seed permit to distribute seed. (David Svik, personal communication, November 17, 2015)

Like Nebraska, many other states have adopted the RUSSL language and face the same challenge. In states across the country, the definition of "sale" includes exchange, barter, and trade. Seed libraries fall under this definition, so it could be interpreted that the traditional ways of freely exchanging seed are illegal in such states. Thus, seed libraries could be presented with the expenses associated with maintaining the same standards as any seed company. "Noncommercial seed sharing" is language that defines seed dissemination that is not selling in nature, such as seed exchanges and seed libraries. There are currently efforts to incorporate this language into RUSSL, a widely adopted model for state seed laws, to exempt noncommercial seed sharing from state law (Johnson, 2015).[17]

In Pennsylvania, the Cumberland County Library System opened a seed library at the Simpson Library in 2014 and planned to offer the public free seeds, as well as accept seed deposits. Because the seed library at Simpson Library would collect, supply, and distribute seed to the public at large, they were classified as seed distributors and fell under the regulatory hand of the state's seed laws. In June 2014, the library received a letter from the Pennsylvania Department of Agriculture informing them that its plans to collect seeds and redistribute them classified them as seed distributors under the regulatory language of Pennsylvania's Seed Act. Thus, they would be required to perform germination tests on the seed (Creason, 2014) and label the seed in accordance with the Pennsylvania Seed Act (Zook, 2014).

Neil Thapar, staff attorney with the Sustainable Economies Law Center (SELC), affirms that Pennsylvania and other states "have misapplied the law entirely," and Pennsylvania's Seed Act "does not actually authorize the state agriculture department to regulate noncommercial seed sharing through seed libraries" (Cook, 2015). Thapar argues that because seed sharing is a noncommercial activity, applying state seed laws to the libraries is inappropriate and was not the intent of the seed laws. "Seed laws were created solely as consumer protection laws to protect farmers from unscrupulous seed companies in the marketplace" (Cook, 2015).

As attention to the situation in Pennsylvania grew via the media and additional routes, organizers in states such as Nebraska and Minnesota took a look at their laws and began to take preemptive action requesting that legislation be refined (Johnson, 2015).

In Nebraska, Goodman and others approached a Nebraska state senator, who introduced a bill to exempt seed libraries from testing and permitting requirements (Peters, 2015). The bill was incorporated into Legislative Bill 175 and approved in May 2015. With this amendment, the definition of "seed library" cited in the law and its functions were defined to cover only the exchange of seed between the library and individuals free of any charge or consideration, and seed libraries can facilitate the donation, exchange, preservation, and dissemination of open-pollinated, public domain plant varieties (L.B. 175, 2015). A similar bill was signed into law in 2015 in Minnesota that specifically exempts noncommercial seed sharing from commercial seed laws (Johnson, 2015).

After a year, the Pennsylvania Department of Agriculture resolved to agree that, because seed libraries do not sell seed, they do not qualify as distributors. In a response to questions from Brian Snyder, then executive director of the Pennsylvania Association for Sustainable Agriculture, the Department of Agriculture (DOA) stated that seed libraries "do not meet the definition of a 'Distributor' as defined in the seed law" and "the edicts of the Seed Law do not apply" to seed libraries (Public Interest Law Center of Philadelphia, 2015).

The work continues with a group of seed-sharing proponents gaining assistance from the Oakland, California-based Sustainable Economies Law Center (SELC). The SELC is spearheading an effort to change the status of the Recommended Uniform State Seed Law to adapt to the ever-increasing prevalence of seed libraries and seed shares (Cook, 2015; Johnson, 2015).

When Pat Miller with the American Seed Trade Association was asked for his understanding of seed libraries, he stated, "The seed industry sees seed libraries as a positive thing. They serve as an important resource to help people understand the glories and woes of food production . . ." (Pat Miller, personal communication, December 2, 2015). Thus, people on all sides—industry, government, and public sector—are beginning to agree that it shall remain a freedom to share open-pollinated, nonpatented varieties of seed with one another, just as we have for the last 12,000 years.

If the right to share and exchange seeds were taken away, it could negatively impact the survival of heirlooms and the integrity of the food system. This change in the interpretation of seed laws would give seed companies excessive control over the food system and take away the ability of gardeners and citizens alike to share and exchange seeds. Although most people currently do not practice seed saving, it would be beneficial if they did. More seed saving and sharing would make the current food system more secure and give the public more options when it comes to taste, nutrition, and plant viability.

Above all, how are we to ensure that our favorite varieties stand the test of time? The best insurance is in our own two hands. In gratitude for the thousands of years of plant breeders who have worked to create such an abundant food system, exercise your freedom by saving seed from a favorite plant, lest it disappear forever. The following quote from Archibald MacLeish, poet and one-time Librarian of Congress, provides some inspiration: "What is freedom? Freedom is the right to choose: the right to create for yourself the alternatives of choice. Without the possibility of choice and the exercise of choice a man is not a man but a member, an instrument, a thing" (Peter, 1977).

Many people are critical of the current industrial food industry; however, they appreciate the ease of processed foods. Growing all the food one family needs is not convenient and not possible in many cases. Even more challenging is the process of saving seeds. That said, if you are concerned about the current food system so easily available at the grocery store, you could try growing more of your own food and saving seed to supplement your diet. A person does not need an acre of land or even a large garden plot to participate—a pot on the patio can produce an abundance of fresh herbs.

## CONCLUSION

Libraries can create new, lifelong readers and support people's quest for literature and information. Giving away seeds is another way libraries can nurture curiosity about gardening and an appreciation for human knowledge and tradition. Every tiny seed is a genetic library within itself. The seed contains the genetic code detailed within each of the DNA strands for what has come before it and the blueprints for what is possible. Allowing a plant to complete its life cycle and produce seed integrates the environmental circumstances of the season in which it grew into its genetic code. In times of climate change, regional adaptation of our food system is crucial.

Heirloom seeds are often full of variability, which makes them wonderful sources of genetic diversity and also difficult to farm on a large scale. For instance, heirlooms may mature at varying rates, producing a variety of heights, shapes, and sizes, which do not fit well in a uniform box size or travel to market easily. Fruits or vegetables may ripen too quickly or at different times. That is why preserving seed diversity lies in the hands of the gardeners and small-scale farmers. Libraries can be a piece in the puzzle to sustaining seed diversity. Not only can libraries offer seeds, but they also can provide a reminder that seeds and gardening are available to us all.

Many more of us can play a role in preserving edible plant diversity or creating pollinator gardens full of flowering plants for hungry bees, other insects, and hummingbirds. Imagine the possibility proposed by Greg Peterson (the Urban Farmer): "What if all libraries had seed libraries? What would that look like? That's the goal" (Greg Peterson, personal communication, November 9, 2015).

Pat Miller, Director of State Government Affairs with American Seed Trade Association, shared, "Ask any gardener and they will tell you that gardening is much more than an individual putting a seed in the ground, and feeding and watering it to produce food. Gardening creates a sense [of] community. Seed libraries provide a needed forum for like-minded individuals to share a common passion, while exchanging information and providing a source for learning" (Pat Miller, personal communication, December 2, 2015).

Also, new ideas are forming for seed collections that go beyond those designed to grow fresh produce. Goodman and Newburn see the potential for a seed library special collections that could highlight native seeds, dye and fiber collections, pollinator collections (that is, bee-friendly plants), and medicinal plants. These collections could also address pressing issues such as the decline in monarch butterflies by providing native milkweed seeds along with information about planting and other ways to support monarch butterflies. There is also a desire to offer seed library information in a variety of different languages to expand access and engagement.

In summary, Kelly Wilson, librarian with Pima County Public Library, offers the following to those thinking about starting a seed library: "The most important thing that I like to pass on to new seed librarians is decide what your mission is and don't lose sight of it. Every seed library serves a different purpose, and if you forget your purpose, it is easy to get scattered and lose your effectiveness. By knowing and sticking to your mission, the questions/issues that will inevitably arise day after day will be much easier to answer and solve" (Kelly Wilson, personal communication, December 9, 2015).

# NOTES

1. Personal communication, November 24, 2015.
2. See seedlibraries.weebly.com/how-to-organize-your-seeds.html.
3. See www.seedlibraries.weebly.com.
4. See www.ars-grin.gov/cgi-bin/npgs/pvp/pvplist.pl.
5. See hackpad.com/collection/BdawSUkxAQE.
6. See www.richmondgrowsseeds.org.
7. See elyfarmersmarket.blogspot.com/p/seed-library-information.html.
8. See the Omaha Public Library's guide on seed saving for more advice: guides .omahalibrary.org/commonsoil.
9. See the Seed Library of Los Angeles' guide to advanced seed saving: slola.org /learn-about-seed-saving/advanced.
10. See wordpress.org/plugins/wp-seedbank.
11. For more information, see the Vegetable Seed Saving Handbook's page on breeding new varieties: howtosaveseeds.com/breeding.php.
12. See the Pima County Public Library's page on seed cleaning screens: www .library.pima.gov/blogs/post/seed-cleaning-screens-check-them-out.
13. See guides.omahalibrary.org/commonsoil.
14. See www.richmondgrowsseeds.org.
15. See www.library.pima.gov/browse_program/seed-library.
16. See www.library.pima.gov/blogs.
17. The authors encourage you to reach out to state seed control officials as well as state legislators and ask them to amend the definition of sale to make an exemption for "noncommercial seed sharing" in your state.

# REFERENCES

American Association of Seed Control Officials (AASCO). (2016). What is AASCO? Retrieved from www.seedcontrol.org.

American Seed Trade Association (ASTA). (2016). State. Retrieved from www .betterseed.org/the-issues/state.

Best, B. (2013). *Saving seeds, preserving taste: Heirloom seed savers in Appalachia.* Athens, OH: Ohio University Press.

Camp, N. L. (2015). Food insecurity and food deserts. *The Nurse Practitioner, 40*(8), 32–36.

Conner, C. (2014). *Seed libraries: And other means of keeping seeds in the hands of the people.* Gabriola Island, BC, Canada: New Society Publishers.

Cook, C. D. (2015, Feb. 11). Seed libraries fight for the right to share (Blog post). *Shareable.* Retrieved from www.shareable.net/blog/seed-libraries-fight-for-the -right-to-share.

Cornett, P. (1993). Monticello's seeds of the past. *Thomas Jefferson's Monticello.* Retrieved from www.monticello.org/site/house-and-gardens/monticellos -seeds-past.

Creason, N. (2014, July 31). Department of Agriculture cracks down on seed librar- ies. *The Sentinel.* Retrieved from cumberlink.com/news/local/communities /carlisle/department-of-agriculture-cracks-down-on-seed-libraries/article _8b0323f4-18f6-11e4-b4c1-0019bb2963f4.html.

Erkens, C., & Goodman, B. (2015, Feb.). *Common Soil Seed Library staff training.* Presentation at the annual Healthy Farms Conference by the Nebraska Sus- tainable Agriculture Society, Omaha, NE.

Fernandez-Cornejo, J. (2004). *The seed industry in U.S. agriculture: An exploration of data and information on crop seed markets, regulation, industry structure, and research and development* (Agriculture Information Bulletin No. 786). Washington, D.C.: U.S. Department of Agriculture, Economic Research Service.

Fowler, C. (2009, July). Saving seeds: One seed at a time (Video lecture). Lecture delivered at TEDGlobal 2009 Conference, Oxford University, Oxford, England. Retrieved from www.ted.com/talks/lang/en/cary_fowler_one_seed_at_a_time _protecting_the_future_of_food.html.

Fowler, C., & Mooney, P. R. (1990). *Shattering: Food, politics, and the loss of genetic diversity.* Tucson, AZ: University of Arizona Press.

Getzschman, E. (2014). Omaha Public Library's Common Soil Seed Library. *Nebraska Libraries, 2*(2), 4–8. Retrieved from digitalcommons.unl.edu/cgi/viewcontent .cgi?article=1007&context=neblib.

A growing expansion. (2015, Winter). *Edible Omaha.* Retrieved from edibleomaha .com/2015/a-growing-expansion.

Janson, T., & Carlson, S. (2013, Dec. 9). Preventing GMO contamination in your open-pollinated corn (blog post). *Seed Savers Exchange.* Retrieved from blog .seedsavers.org/blog/preventing-gmo-contamination-in-your-open-pollinated -corn.

Jefferson, T. (1787, Aug. 14). (Letter to George Washington). In J. P. Boyd (Ed.), *The papers of Thomas Jefferson, 7 August 1787–31 March 1788* (Vol. 12, pp. 36–38). Princeton, NJ: Princeton University Press (original work published 1955). Retrieved from National Archives' *Founders Online,* founders.archives.gov /documents/Jefferson/01-12-02-0040.

Johnson, C. (2014, Nov. 21). SELC celebrates victories and launches seed library campaign (Blog post). *Shareable.* Retrieved from www.shareable.net/blog/selc -celebrates-victories-and-launches-seed-library-campaign.

Johnson, C. (2015, June 15). Seed sharing movement wins big with new legislation (Blog post). *Shareable.* Retrieved from www.shareable.net/blog/seed-sharing -movement-wins-big-with-new-legislation.

Klingaman, G. (n.d.). Origin of Big Boy tomato hybrid. *Walter Reeves: The Georgia gardener.* Retrieved from www.walterreeves.com/food-gardening/origin-of-big -boy-tomato-hybrid.

Kloppenburg, J. R. (2005). *First the seed: The political economy of plant biotechnol- ogy.* Madison, WI: University of Wisconsin Press.

Landgraf, G. (2015, Jan. 5). Not your garden-variety library. *American Libraries.* Retrieved from americanlibrariesmagazine.org/2015/01/05/not-your-garden -variety-library.

L.B. 175, 104 Leg., 1st Sess. (Feb. 2015). Retrieved from nebraskalegislature.gov /bills/view_bill.php?DocumentID=24729.

Murray, S. (2009). *The library: An illustrated history.* New York: Skyhorse Publishing.

Page-Mann, P. (2014, April 7). Four easy seeds to save this season. *Small Farms Quarterly.* Retrieved from smallfarms.cornell.edu/2014/04/07/four-easy -seeds-to-save-this-season.

Peter, L. J. (1977). *Peter's quotations: Ideas for our time.* New York: Morrow.

Peters, C. (2015, Feb. 24). Omaha lawmaker wants to rid seed libraries of outlaw status. *Omaha World-Herald.* Retrieved from www.omaha.com/news/legisl ature/omaha-lawmaker-wants-to-rid-seed-libraries-of-outlaw-status/article _d3f5f42b-c1ea-5fe6-909d-8c5cbdfeab82.html.

Public Interest Law Center of Philadelphia. (2015). Victory for PA seed libraries. Retrieved from www.pilcop.org/law-center-supports-seed-libraries-and-prom otes-local-food-systems.

Rasmussen, W. D. (1975). Experiment or starve: The early settlers. In U.S. Depart- ment of Agriculture (Ed.), *That we may eat: The yearbook of agriculture, 1975* (pp. 10–14). Washington, D.C.: US Government Printing Office.

Raver, A. (2010, June 30). At Monticello, Jefferson's methods endure. *New York Times.* Retrieved from www.nytimes.com/2010/07/01/garden/01monticello .html.

Ray, J. (2012). *The seed underground: A growing revolution to save food.* White River Junction, VT: Chelsea Green Publishing.

Shattuck, K. (2004, July 11). Oved Shifriss, 89, a plant breeder and geneticist, dies. *New York Times.* Retrieved from www.nytimes.com/2004/07/11/us/oved -shifriss-89-a-plant-breeder-and-geneticist-dies.html.

Thomas Jefferson Foundation. (n.d.). Thomas Jefferson Center for Historic Plants. *Thomas Jefferson's Monticello.* Retrieved from www.monticello.org/site/house -and-gardens/thomas-jefferson-center-historic-plants.

U.S. Congress, Office of Technology Assessment. (1989). *New developments in bio- technology: Patenting life—Special report* (Publication No. OTA-BA-370). Wash- ington, D.C.: U.S. Government Printing Office.

U.S. Department of Agriculture. (1998). Federal Seed Act. Retrieved from www .ams.usda.gov/rules-regulations/fsa.

Zook, J. (2014, June 12). (Letter from Pennsylvania Department of Agriculture to Simpson Library). Retrieved from Cumberland County Library System website at  www.cumberlandcountylibraries.org/sites/default/files/SIM/Documents /Misc/2014_PADeptAgriculture_Letter.pdf.

# 6

# The Real Toy Story: A Toy Lending Collection

*Sue Kirschner*

The findings of Friedrich Froebel (1889), G. Stanley Hall (1911), Immanuel Kant (1960), and others agree that play is a child's work and is the basis for literacy development. Toys are therefore natural and necessary tools for children (Huang & Plass, 2009). Who better to supply the tools of early childhood literacy than the public library? So when "Every Child Ready to Read" researchers Dr. Susan Neuman and Dr. Donna Celano (2010) supported the importance of play in the library, adding toys to a library's lending collection seemed quite natural. They cite Howes and Smith (1995), who report that children thrive both socially and cognitively in settings rich with play activities. However, it was not that long ago that toys and the happy sound of children at play were uncommon in our buildings. How then did this all start?

Moore (1995) identifies the first toy lending library as beginning in Los Angeles in 1935, when a dime-store owner, tired of youngsters stealing spools of thread to make wheels for their wooden toy cars, worked with the students' school principal and the probation officer involved in the situation to create a toy lending program (pp. 6–9). Thus, like the very core of public library outreach, a need was shown, a solution sought, tools were provided, and a problem was solved. This may sound like an easy fix but, just like public libraries, toy libraries have had their challenges and triumphs over the years.

With the formation of Head Start in the 1960s, an increase of educational toys and some toy libraries sprang up as a result, as did several after the Rehabilitation Act of 1973 (although funding did not materialize for over 10 years). A much greater impact occurred when the Lekotek movement arrived from Sweden in the 1980s, which successfully provided toys, information, and equipment to the families of children with special needs (Moore, 1995, p. 15). Toy libraries in the United States replicated this service by associating with other special needs agencies as these particular toys tend to be the costliest and hardest to come by for those who need them most. Funding for the initial purchases and then maintenance was, of course, the greatest challenge, although storage space and even getting the toys back could be difficult. Connecting a toy library to a public library solved many of these problems, as did the almost 60 intervening years.

## THE STORY OF THE BROOKLYN TOY LIBRARY: ESTABLISHING A WORKING MODEL

The Toy Library at Cuyahoga County Public Library was started at the Brooklyn Branch (Brooklyn, Ohio) in 1992. The story of its inception and how it morphed to its present-day operation will prove helpful to library systems of all sizes, in all locales, with all types of funding streams. Mayor John Coyne of Brooklyn was a forward thinker, so it was no surprise that when the Cuyahoga County Public Library administration approached him for a new branch building, he replied that he would be happy to help if it would house a toy library. The mayor had just come home from a visit to his niece in Rochester, New York. While there, she told her uncle she had some errands to do, including returning toys to the library. Well, that was something the mayor had to see, and a kernel of an idea was planted. Then, like so many of the mayor's innovative ideas, others saw the potential and the kernel sprouted. The library agreed with his design suggestion and Mayor Coyne's friend, George Zane, contributed $100,000.00. Donations from the Coynes and the Brooklyn Kiwanis Club resulted in a budget totaling approximately $130,000.00.

The branch was built and Branch Manager Cathy Monnin hired Donna Giannantonio to join the Children's Department as the public service assistant with the special role of putting together and running the Brooklyn Toy Library. It was to be a closed collection with the toys on 3-by-6-foot bakery-style racks with wire shelves. Seven racks lined each side of a 21-by-12-foot room with two rows of four forming an "island" in the middle. Adjacent to the room was an area large enough to contain a set of double cabinets above and below an extra-deep stainless steel sink, a stacked washer and dryer, and a shower stall. The shower was intended to rinse off oversized trucks and ride-ons that had been used outside, but early on it was found that those toys were easily hand-washed. Because of the popularity of the toys, more space was required to clean toys quickly and place them back in circulation so the shower stall was better utilized by holding a three-shelf drying rack. The rest of the drying took place on two rolling carts that could be loaded by the sink and then positioned under a ceiling-mounted dryer that was added later to blow hot air on the rack and speed the drying process. The washer/dryer unit was used to clean cloth toys, toy storage bags, and cleaning cloths.

As Ms. Giannantonio was setting up the operation, she knew the toys had to have a lightweight yet durable container to ensure all the pieces would stay together. Blue nylon mesh bags from the Janway Company were a good choice:

they were washable, with drawstring and toggle opening, mesh that allowed air circulation around the toy, and a gusset imprinted with the library name and logo. The toy bags would be stacked on the wire shelves, but how would they be organized and accessed by staff?

## Accessing the Toys on the Shelf

Much like Dewey, a numbering system would be used for toy identification on the shelf. Unfortunately, most of the toys would have fallen in the 700s, resulting in having to try and fit a very long Dewey number on a very small tag, so in the end, simplicity won out. First, 12 kid-friendly categories were created: Active Play; Art & Music; Baby/Toddler; Blocks; Explore, Discover, Learn; Games; Language; Let's Pretend; Puppets; Puzzles; Science and Nature; and Special Needs. Toys were assigned a category, an identification number, and a letter to distinguish the individual copy. Ms. Giannantonio went a step further and devised an ingenious system where children who could not read would be able to choose a toy and staff could tell at a glance if a toy was available for checkout.

To accomplish this, a toy sheet was printed for every copy of every toy. A template was designed and printed by the Graphics Department with space for the title, the category, appropriate age, and a warning that toys with small pieces were not safe for children under three years of age, the toy picture (which, in those days were cut out from toy company catalogs and duplicated on the black-and-white copy machine), the toy description, and a list of the toy pieces. The number of pieces reflected the uniqueness of the individual copy and influenced the checkout decisions of some grown-ups. The sheets were put into three-ring binders by category and the binders placed on slanted picture book tables on either side of the Toy Library checkout desk. Sitting on padded stools, anyone wishing to check out a toy could browse the toy notebooks. When they found what they wanted, the toy sheet was taken out of the notebook and handed to the toy clerk. The toy was located on the categorized shelf by matching the number and letter on the toy sheet to that on a sticker attached to each bag. On the front of the preprinted plastic tags were the library branch name, address, telephone number, and space for the bar code. On the back was the toy title and sticker with number and letter. The toy sheet would be placed in a Princeton file shelved right with the toys in that category so that when the cleaned toy was returned to its spot, the sheet would be pulled from the file box and put back in the correct binder. That was the genius of the Giannantonio system. No one, not a child, a recent immigrant, or adult new reader, would ever be disappointed looking through the notebook to find that the toy they wanted was checked out.

And the patrons, young and old alike, were not disappointed. Ms. Giannantonio selected multiple copies of approximately 350 toys from nationally known toy companies. She also joined the USA Toy Library Association[1] to broaden her education-based background by learning from others in the field, such as award-winning toy expert and author, Joanne Oppenheim. Independently reviewed toys and children's media are published in the annual Oppenheim Toy Portfolio[2], and their awards have become a benchmark of excellence with consumers, toy makers, and the media.

The National Association for the Education of Young Children (NAEYC) defines early childhood as the years from birth through age eight (2010, p. 3), which is the age range we set for our collection. The toys were chosen for quality, safety, durability, educational value, ability to be cleaned, and the all-important fun quotient. Once the toys arrived at the Brooklyn branch, each piece was marked with the three-letter BKL branch code, the bag and tags prepared, and the toy sheets filled out and placed in the binder. The grand opening ribbon was cut June 6, 1992.

## Day-to-Day Operations and Staffing

The Toy Library was up and running, but operating day to day would have been equally challenging had the Cuyahoga County Public Library administration not demonstrated its commitment to this endeavor by maintaining three part-time toy clerks. Their responsibilities included labeling the new toys, creating toy sheets and bag tags, checking toys out, inspecting, counting, and cleaning all pieces upon check-in, performing minor toy repairs, and maintaining the toy notebooks. In addition to managing the necessary tasks, our toy clerks would gladly answer interesting toy questions such as: "Does the door on the dollhouse count as a piece?" and "Yes, some children like to take it off but don't worry, it snaps right back on the front of the house."

To assist with these types of inquiries, whether in-person or by telephone, the toy clerks had two small file boxes for four-by-six index cards with the list of pieces and any quirks a toy might have to hinder a patron getting the count right. Those cards were especially helpful when a circulation clerk substitute would take a turn behind the desk and have to count the curved and straight train tracks in a returned toy bag. It was often found that after just one visit and a little training, all substitutes fell in love with working the toy desk and didn't mind the counting or cleaning.

This was such a great free service that toys would rarely go missing or come back broken or lacking parts. Being able to place a fine on a patron's library card eased collections instead of having to badger someone to return a toy or piece. The price of the toy was included in the bibliographic record and on the toy sheet. Fines were established at a late fee of 10 cents a day, a fee of the price of the toy for a lost or ruined toy, and $3.00 per piece for a lost piece (if the piece was crucial to the toy and could not circulate without it, like a puzzle piece; if half the pieces were lost, then the patron was charged half the price of the toy). Actually, like a disc being left in a car CD player, the missing piece fines tended to simply be placeholders on the card because the pieces eventually turn up. In the meantime, the toy would be marked damaged in the online catalog and the toy sheet moved to a "problem" file until resolved.

## Good Clean Fun

Once counted and checked in, each toy has to be cleaned. It is important to note that the time to be concerned with how difficult a toy will be to clean is prior to purchase. How will it be cleaned? Will it hold up to continued cleaning? All toys are cleaned and disinfected so only those toys that can withstand this process should be chosen. If you are not sure, do not buy it! Toys may be cleaned in one of three ways: (1) cloth toys go into the washer with regular laundry detergent; (2) plastic toys are scrubbed in a sink with a biodegradable cleaner; and (3) cardboard puzzle and game pieces are wiped with a biodegradable cleaner.

And here are two other things to remember about cleaning toys: "Foam is NOT our friend!" Soft blocks are cute and lightweight, but foam is a sponge, soaking up germs, and little ones can easily bite off chunks. A second, important cleaning tip is that despite what the ads tell you, bleach is not meant to be ingested, and it is difficult to know the exact amount that has been totally dissolved. With that in mind, here are a couple of good alternatives to consider. Disinfectant wipes work but may be cost prohibitive. A good rule of thumb is anything that is safe around food is safe to ingest so contact a restaurant supply house for what they use to clean their counters. Typically, only a capful of liquid concentrate will clean and disinfect a sink full of toys and more.

*Cleaning that is safe for the toys + the children*

Patrons may be concerned over how many strangers have borrowed the toy before them. It is quite gratifying to provide reassurance that the toy has been cleaned and disinfected. Another suggested precaution is to sign up for recall notices from the Community Outreach Resource Center, which is part of the Consumer Product Safety Commission. Recall information and news alerts can be received via e-mail from www.cpsc.gov.

Cleaning the toy bag also takes place at check-in. A toy tag, attached with an inexpensive and reusable nylon cable tie found at do-it-yourself stores or electrical supply warehouses, is cut off and set aside while the nylon mesh bag goes into the washer. Once cleaned, the toy can go into any clean bag with its tag reattached.

## Accessing the Toys in the Catalog

Access on the shelf helped staff connect a toy with a child at the branch, but what if you wanted to see what is in before coming to the building? Toys would be cataloged for online access even if they could not be requested. The cataloging rules of the 1990s still dictated original cataloging be done, so each toy purchased was routed through the Technical Services' Catalog Department so a complete record could be created. Because this was a new material type for Cuyahoga County Public Library, the cataloging process also included formulating local circulation rules. Like a book, CD, or movie, toys had a three-week loan length, but to prevent the decimation of the collection early on, circulation was limited to two toys per library card and they were nonrequestable and nonrenewable. The perceived benefit of restricting toys from being requested to be picked up at another branch would be the convenience of having a single pickup location for the community and Toy Library staff. The actual benefit of requiring all toys be borrowed at the Brooklyn branch was cheaper distribution, because toys rarely had to be brought back to the branch by the library shipping department. This meant that container costs could be lower, because the toys were packaged for families to carry out of the building. Keeping all aspects of the operation at the branch also helped ensure that no toys were lost, damaged, or possibly soiled more in transit. With the novelty of borrowing toys came enthusiastic borrowers, and total circulation hit 100,000 within five years.

### Staff Play Well with Others

Staff at all branches generously pointed patrons to the Toy Library at Brooklyn and started using toys in their programming. Gradually, the process of reserving toys for program use went from the toy clerks holding a toy for staff pickup to sending the toys through the library delivery system. Branch programs that utilized or centered on toys were made popular by Celia Huffman (then public services supervisor III) who saw an opportunity to help children learn through play at the Maple Heights branch.

With Huffman's endorsement, more and more county library staff took advantage of these wonderful literacy tools, and the toy clerks formulated a plan to reserve the toys in between patron loans. By this time, the Toy Library had been in operation for over 10 years, and Sari Feldman became the executive director of Cuyahoga County Public Library. Feldman, like Huffman, shared a strong background in early childhood and an understanding of the importance toys play in children's development. They also had in common the desire to serve all families across our service area. So, when Huffman became the manager of youth services in 2006, it was a natural progression to ask: How do we get these toys in the hands of children throughout our county?

# THE NEXT CHAPTER: BEYOND THE BROOKLYN BRANCH

Enter Youth Literacy and Outreach Manager Sue Kirschner (former early childhood specialist and Brooklyn toy librarian), who was tasked with centralizing and expanding the toy collection throughout the Cuyahoga County Public Library system by 2008. No longer would the collection be purchased solely from the Brooklyn Toy Trust Fund, however; to honor Mayor Coyne, a toy presence would be maintained at Brooklyn. Storage would be on open shelving and replenished by pages when the toys arrived from the new Youth Literacy and Outreach Department all checked in, inspected, and cleaned.

Kirschner began the migration of the collection to the administration building in June 2007. The Toy Library staff and all day-to-day operations of circulation, cleaning, repair, and storage moved to the same building in the autumn, and full service commenced in January 2008. Like the supplies and staff salaries, the toys would be part of the Cuyahoga County Public Library annual budget, which further demonstrated the commitment by the administration to toys in literacy development. Though still a closed collection, the toys would be requestable and renewable, and could be delivered to all 27 locations rather than just in and out of one branch. With delivery trucks crisscrossing the county twice a day, an available toy could arrive a day after being requested. Now that the toys were hitting the road, they needed to be outfitted for safe travel and the nylon mesh bags would not suffice. The Processing Department purchased and assembled boxes from U-Line and Demco because their clamshell style had attached lids. For oversized toys, custom canvas bags were ordered from a local company. But which toys made the "final cut"? If a toy fit in a bag or box, stayed clean and undamaged en route, and was not too heavy or cumbersome at patron pickup, then it was kept in the collection. These criteria still apply to choosing new toys today.

Keeping those toys clean and in the correct box was solved by the team from the Information Technology Division (ITD) whose solution was twofold: (1) a toy database was created for maintenance of all toy information, and (2) our Media Services Department would take a photograph of each toy and upload it to the database. The photos were then organized into a toy gallery for use by the Youth Literacy and Outreach clerks and the Cataloging Department to show the toys in the online catalog, similarly to the Brooklyn toy notebooks.

The ITD also produced a label for the outside of the box with a picture of the toy to discourage opening the boxes (for cleanliness and to avoid loss prior to checkout), a toy sheet listing pieces to be stored inside the box, and a second toy sheet to go in a new branch toy notebook with a sheet for every toy title. Even though the toy would be requested online, this was a close replication of the Giannantonio model that allowed nonreaders to browse toys by sight. The physical toy notebook and online searching were a nod to what successfully began at the Brooklyn branch 15 years previously and at that anniversary it was, of course, time to ask, "What will happen next in 'The Real Toy Story'"?

## TOYS: A REAL PAGE-TURNER

Libraries the world over are rapidly changing and so too are their special collections. Therefore, local decisions must be made. In the past, two copies of the same toy purchased from different toy companies had to have two different catalog records, such as in this favorite example: the "Color Slit Game" and the "Montessori Sorting Game." This toy is now titled "Sorting Box," which avoids confusion and original cataloging. The updated guidelines created by our Catalog Department also allowed for simpler, more uniform titles, streamlined fields, and the elimination of unnecessary fields. Within the Youth Literacy and Outreach Department, the addition of a "Processing Check List" (consisting of bar code, book/directions, box sheet, copy/laminate, box labels, pieces marked, and picture) facilitated the tracking of new toys and tasks done by our clerks or interdepartmentally.

The collection continues to grow, and access and efficiencies improve in response to patron and staff requests. Here are some of the most recent developments. Acknowledging the connection between toys and literacy, Kirschner added a book to every toy with a message about reading aloud. Select toys also have extra messages attached to the box lid. For example, the "Baby Variety Set" has a list explaining the contents ("What is a manipulative?") and how each relates to child development and the promotion of literacy.

Toy circulation averages 2,000 per month, including renewals (the highest toy circulation occurred in 2012, at 24,632 times). The Monday-through-Friday pull list averaged 44 items pulled and sent through delivery to 27 locations. And still the public wanted more, so the toy loan limit was increased in 2013, putting it at 50, just like books, CDs, and DVDs.

In 2015–16, the Marketing, Information Technology, and Youth Literacy and Outreach Departments worked together to revamp the electronic Toy Gallery and make toys immediately requestable through the gallery or the catalog. Toys can still be searched and sorted by category, but also by developmental age, toy tag, and title by either time in collection or an A-to-Z list. As part of the revamp, Kirschner added tags to over 1,000 toy titles for advanced catalog searching.

Toys for children with special needs have always been an important part of the toy collection, but recent purchases emphasize sensory needs (for example, tactile toys and those for mastering one's inner balance) and kindergarten-readiness skills. From using extra-large toy tweezers to sorting pretend fruit into a pie for prewriting, fine motor skills, and premath sorting and matching, to logic puzzles for spatial relations, toys remain the best tools children can use to affect their overall development, including cognitive, social and emotional, speech and language, and fine and gross motor skills.

As the collection grows, so do the creative uses for toys in branch use and programs that include toys, regardless of patrons' socioeconomic status. That being said, besides purchasing floor toys for branch Children's Departments, Kirschner came up with a pilot to supplement floor toys from the circulating collection for the Richmond Heights branch on a quarterly basis. It is hoped that the newness of the toys will increase visits and perhaps toy circulation by families in this at-risk neighborhood.

Families also have a chance to see samples from the collection at branch programs. All story times, from Baby & Me (birth to two years), Toddler (two to three years), Preschool (three to five years), and Mixed Age, include play and toys to promote the five principles of Every Child Ready to Read, be it a message to parents/caregivers, use of the toy as a prop, or as part of a special "stay and play" time afterward. Another branch program, Play, Learn, & Grow Workshops, are all about play and child development. As part of an Institute of Museum and Library Services grant, four branches have been designated as Family Place Libraries and hold workshops to enable families time for interaction with speakers from community health organizations while they play with their zero- to three-year-old children. For three- to five-year-olds, Exploration Station programs utilize the discovery learning model. Children move about science, math, art, or music stations with their adult caregiver acting as a "reading assistant," giving the child control over what, when, and where they will learn during the program through play.

Age-appropriate play is a valuable component in programs for school-age children, too. Kindergarten Readiness and Kindergarten Club reflect the growing necessity in many of our communities to help children enter school ready to learn. To that end, school preparation information and practical life activities are incorporated into the program series, and toys from the collection are available for immediate checkout. Staff may reserve toys, whether for after-school or program use, in advance of their program by contacting the Youth Literacy and Outreach via telephone or e-mail. Unless on hold for a patron or reserved for another branch program, all toys are available for immediate checkout.

## TIME FOR A HAPPY ENDING

Happy? Yes! Ending? Definitely not! The uses of toys are becoming as varied as the toys themselves with more and more special populations borrowing them all the time. Libraries are far from obsolescence, and toys are living proof because toys can breathe fresh air into a building. It may take someone with creativity and tenacity, but anyone can start a single toy library or collection serving a larger, multibuilding system. How? Here are some topics for you to consider.

- Budget: Grants, community organizations, and generous individuals are out there if your system desires help with funding.
- Space: Toys have been stored and lent from spaces as small as a closet and as large as a former grocery store. If there's no room in your building, perhaps there is space to borrow/rent. Access can be closed or open.
- Age: The National Association for the Education of Young Children (2009) defines birth through age eight as the age for early childhood. However, community demographics may warrant targeting additional special populations or the expansion to developmental age, so that senior citizens and families of children with special needs of all ages can feel that something is available for them.
- Scope: Decide what type of toys to lend. Many toy libraries are connected to charitable nonprofits wanting to help differently abled and/or at-risk children, so some of those libraries lend cribs, swings, or useful equipment along with toys.[3] The categories may change (ours did). Assess the needs of your community and the support you will receive to help shape your start-up collection.
- Size: Initially, the Brooklyn Branch Toy Library totaled 1,100 toys, but a much smaller number would still be an excellent core collection. Maybe you start with one category (for example, baby/toddler or toys for children with special needs), then add more categories as able, or choose more categories and spread your funding across all of them.
- Staffing and Procedures: All of the previous determine how many people are needed and the necessary tasks that are vital for a new collection to reach optimum effectiveness, but determine you must, as this will be a critical component to your project proposal.

## WRITE YOUR OWN ADVENTURE

As you can see, toy lending collections come in all shapes and sizes, but so does the joy; that's the beauty of play. Easy or hard, this may be one of your most enduring endeavors . . . for you get to choose the game and in the end everyone is a winner!

# NOTES

1. See www.usatla.org/USA_Toy_Library_Association/Welcome_to_the_USA_Toy_Library_Association.html.

2. The Oppenheim Toy Portfolio award winners are visible at www.toyportfolio.com/awards-1.

3. For an example, see First Chance for Children in Columbia, Missouri, at www.firstchanceforchildren.org.

# REFERENCES

Froebel, F. (1889). *The education of man.* (W. N. Hailmann, Trans.). New York: D. Appleton and Co.

Hall, G. S. (1911). *Educational problems.* New York: D. Appleton and Company.

Howes, C., & Smith, E. W. (1995). Relations among child care quality, teacher behavior, children's play activities, emotional security, and cognitive activity in child care. *Early Childhood Research Quarterly, 10*(4), 381–404.

Huang, T., & Plass, J. L. (2009). *History of play in education.* (White Paper # 06/2009). New York: Institute for Games for Learning. Retrieved from http://docplayer.net/11081640-History-of-play-in-education.html.

Kant, I. (1960). *Education.* (A. Churton, Trans.). Ann Arbor, MI: University of Michigan Press.

Moore, J. E. (1995). *A history of toy lending libraries in the United States since 1935* (master's thesis). Retrieved from ERIC database (ED No. 390414).

National Association for the Education of Young Children. (2009). *NAEYC standards for early childhood professional preparation programs.* Retrieved from the www.naeyc.org/files/naeyc/file/positions/ProfPrepStandards09.pdf.

Neuman, S. B., & Celano, D. (2010). *An evaluation of Every Child Ready to Read: A parent education initiative.* Retrieved from the Association of Library Service to Children website, www.ala.org/alsc/sites/ala.org.alsc/files/content/initiatives/evaluationreport.pdf.

# 7

# Create, Share, Play: Sacramento's Library of Things

*Michelle Coleman Alvarado, Justin Azevedo, and Amy Calhoun*

## SELECTION: CHOOSING THE THINGS

When the members of a given community are asked what they know about their local library and what they would like to improve, the answers vary wildly based on socioeconomic background, patterns of actual library usage, and the exact type of questions asked. However, many people can be relied upon to know (or quickly learn) at least one thing about their library: it is a place where you can check out a book and take it home. So if we assume users hold that basic expectation, how can it be used to surprise and delight them?

Sacramento Public Library serves the entirety of Sacramento County, with 28 locations that serve a diverse array of communities, from the urban neighborhoods around the state capitol building to the rural towns of the Sacramento-San Joaquin River Delta. Accordingly, library staff in Sacramento are skilled in designing and delivering services for a wide range of people who have very different needs and expectations. This is the environment in which Library Unexpected was born. Library Unexpected, a multifaceted project funded with a grant from the Institute of Museum and Library Sciences, was designed to engage both library staff and library patrons in rethinking and redesigning how the library serves its community.

Though Library Unexpected comprised a number of innovative purchases, workflow changes, and staff-training models, the showpiece of the project is the Library of Things, a circulating collection that moves beyond the "take home a book" expectation. The idea behind this collection is to broaden expectations of what a library collection is and what it can do for its users by offering something for checkout that they would not expect to find on a library shelf. However, the Sacramento Public Library system already makes available unusual items such as museum passes, art packs, and electricity-usage monitors, which people are continually surprised to find even though the items circulate well. Conversely, potentially we could venture far afield from the library's core mission and collection development policies to add all manner of items that would attract attention but might not necessarily resonate with library users or lend themselves to sustainability or a greater collection-management ethos. In the interest of addressing both promotion and relevance, we determined that the best way to move forward was to ask the Sacramento community what free-to-use items they, if given the chance, would add to their library's collection.

The library employed the UserVoice software platform to implement a series of polls that were heavily promoted on the library's website and social media platforms. The polls were organized into categories like Entertainment and Arts, and users were asked to suggest items they would like to see at the library and give a short explanation why. Most importantly, they were also given the opportunity to vote on others' suggestions. Library staff monitored the results and began the process of researching the suggested items to assess their suitability for circulation. The first round of community polling took place over the course of four months and resulted in thousands of votes from the public. Once that round was completed, the library used the most popular results as the basis for the first phase of items in the Library of Things, which began circulating in March 2015: sewing machines, board games, console video games, musical instruments, GoPro cameras, and a laminator. Additionally, an all-in-one bike repair station was purchased for the exterior of the library and has been heavily used since its installation.

Within three months of the collection's launch, it was clear that the public approved of the idea. Many items were immediately checked out and began accruing waiting lists, and patrons asked questions about the availability of more items, going so far as to attempt donating "things" of their own. Using a portion of the remaining Library Unexpected grant funding, the library gathered up the next most popular suggestions from each category in the original polls and offered them a second chance in a single poll to the community. The resulting four winners were acquired and made available as a second phase of Library of Things items: drawing tablets, digital projectors, fabric screening kits, and a button maker. During both selection rounds, a portion of the grant funds was used to purchase "reference" versions of the Library of Things items that would be stored and used exclusively inside the branch.

Library futurists often return to the idea of reinventing traditional services when envisioning how public libraries will evolve to meet the changing needs and desires of their communities. The library branch that hosts the community-driven Library of Things, the Arcade Library, also hosts a free-to-use Maker-space. This service requires the same innovative and proactive thinking to be truly relevant. Foote (2015) recently wrote: "Another trend we see both in restaurant offerings and YouTube is 'fusion'—or mashups—which is what the sharing economy is all about. How can we fuse . . . services together to make something new and different?" This idea of fusion has driven the integration of the collection into the library's existing services and plays a big part in measuring its success.

The sewing machines and musical instruments in the Library of Things were displayed with accompanying print materials, such as instructional pattern books and sheet music, packaged as complete do-it-yourself "kits" that allowed borrowers to practice what they learned. Then community experts were brought in to develop programming around the new items. Volunteers hosted sewing basics classes, and a local musician and guitar teacher provided soothing ambient music while advertising the guitars available for checkout. In this manner, the library addressed potential criticisms of the collection not being a central service by fusing it with the services that patrons know and love (in this case, traditional collections and library programming) to support the library's core mission: community building and lifelong learning.

## CIRCULATION: FROM IDEA TO WORKFLOW

To minimize patron confusion and remove barriers to access, the ideal Library of Things collection would have a circulation process identical to what has been used for other items in the library collection. However, due to the challenges inherent in acquiring, cataloging, and transporting some of the selected items, there were a number of special considerations. Specifically, library staff had to consider the potential problems of repairing or replacing expensive items, storing large items on an already-crowded library floor or in a workroom, and exposing items sent between branches to an increased risk of damage and theft. Finding solutions to these issues offered library staff opportunities to exercise creative, roundabout thinking. With these challenges in mind, the pilot collection is currently available at only one branch. Items must be picked up and returned only at that branch. Because most of them are too fragile or unwieldy for the book drop, they must be returned when the library is open. Though this can be inconvenient for users of the collection, the location presents some advantages.

The Library of Things is kept at a library located in a mostly commercial area that serves a large population of mixed socioeconomic means. Housing the initial collection at this branch gave priority to a community that could most benefit from new and exciting library services. In a recent study on community-based efforts to promote early literacy, Peifer and Perez (2010) observe that a visit to the library has a positive impact on disadvantaged families simply by making books, programs, and prereading behaviors visible. Prior to the advent of the Library of Things, this particular library branch had successfully hosted educational programs in a free, publicly accessible 3-D printing lab, which inspired students, inventors, and dabblers of all ages by removing barriers to the technology and making the makerspace ethos visible. The lab's success has since led to 3-D printing technology being implemented at other library branches, due to patron demand. The location has a track record of successfully offering both traditional and nontraditional library services to underserved communities, and was a logical testing ground for the latest idea of making the library more visible. It also created a "destination library" by attracting people from other areas who may have been unaware that individual library branches often offer customized programming and services. The Library of Things has indeed drawn repeat users from all over the Sacramento Public Library service area, which speaks not only to its success as a destination collection, but also to the need for expanding it to other locations.

A signed waiver and verification of photo identification and address (including making and holding a copy of documentation) is required upon checkout. The waiver asks the user to acknowledge a special fine structure to account for expensive repairs and replacements and absolves the library of liability for any injuries that may occur while patrons are using the items. This fulfills the library's legal obligations and fits the profile for some of the items, but it does not make much sense for others. Although an argument can be made for a board game being a choking hazard, it still does not seem like a good use of time and resources to demand photo identification each time somebody wants to take home Candy Land. This particular issue was resolved by allowing library staff to discover the solution through a trial-and-error process. Staff modified requirements by verifying patron addresses on the first checkout only, making descriptive notations indicating the date of the verification in patron records in lieu of physical copies, and setting up a readily accessible binder for the paperwork. These steps made the process as simple as possible for repeat checkouts, while still fulfilling the legal requirements in place. Library staff could immediately see if the patron's information had already been verified. Although patrons are required to sign a new waiver for each subsequent checkout, it is a relatively painless process that is usually completed in the time it takes for library staff to retrieve their item.

Indeed, much of the procedure for circulating the Library of Things items came from staff ingenuity in real time. The board games were numbered on both the box and the material bags. The boxes were then placed on the shelves, with the currently available games in a special display and the others available for browsing to facilitate viewing the entire board game collection. The material bags were placed in concealed bins at the circulation desk in numerical order, making them easy to find and retrieve for both checkout and holds.

Storage space is a pressing issue for large items like sewing machines and acoustic guitars, but staging areas near the front of the workroom both hide the items from the public and make them easy for staff to retrieve. Laminated cards serve as stand-ins for displaying the items in the library. Even the circulation policies are subject to fine-tuning to make the process easier for staff and patrons.

In addition to the modified waiver process, library staff incorporated user feedback and frontline experience with the collection to lift the waiver requirement and accompanying age restriction from the console video games. Patrons also were allowed to check out more than one board game at a time, in accordance with how the games were being requested and used. Although adjusting circulation policy on the fly presents a number of challenges and inefficiencies that eventually need to be studied and resolved, it also empowers staff to think and act outside the confines of their daily routines and directly acknowledges and incorporates the feedback of the community using the collection. These outcomes were explicitly encouraged by the Library Unexpected project.

# WHAT EXACTLY IS A THING? CATALOGING AND PROCESSING

All of the circulating items in the Library of Things are cataloged and processed. This serves two purposes: first, it increases visibility of the collection and, second, it allows the library to track the checkout of the items. The challenge of nontraditional objects is to adequately describe them using traditional rules, making them easily accessible via the catalog, and processing them to ensure the longest possible life span. Fortunately, almost anything can be cataloged using Anglo-American Cataloging Rules (AACR2) or Resource Description and Access (RDA) rules.

Each item has a bibliographic record in the catalog. Although almost all of the items required original cataloging, a simple template was used to fill in the information. Every item has a title, a publisher, a physical description, key words, and a summary. Everything was also given a basic call number, which was "THING" and the item's title (for example, THING Screenprint). Key words were relied upon heavily rather than subject headings, because the library's online public access catalog (OPAC) uses key word searches anyway.

For the purposes of cataloging and processing, the Library of Things can be thought of as having three parts: video games, board games, and physical objects. Video games were the easiest, both for cataloging and processing; most of them had existing records available, and the processing was the same as that used for DVDs. Board games were relatively easy to catalog but the most labor intensive to process. The physical objects, which included things like a sewing machine, a button maker, a guitar, a screen-printing kit, and a video projector, required the most creativity.

The board games that we chose were simple to catalog because each was well described by the publisher. We collected games such as Settlers of Catan, Dead of Winter, and Machi Koro, which are popular among serious board game fans. Every board game was clearly labeled not only with a title, publisher, and publication date, but also with a recommended age for players, playing time, and number of players, along with a detailed list of the contents. In processing, the games were taken out of the box and the pieces were placed in a resealable plastic bag that was labeled with the game's title, a contents list, and a bar code. The boxes are placed on display, and the bags are stored in the staff area. Using the plastic bags makes the games a uniform size, which makes storage easier. In the future, a sturdier bag or even a box may be considered. A patron checking out a board game gets one large plastic bag. Inside that bag are smaller bags of pieces (one bag for playing cards, one or more bags for little plastic pieces), the playing board, and laminated instruction sheets. Each of the smaller plastic bags is labeled with the name of the game and its contents, in case the smaller bag gets separated from the larger bag. The pieces were separated in the same way that the game manufacturer had, and, in retrospect, that was too granular. In the future, labeling may be more generic, using terms such as "game pieces," instead of separating player pieces, money tokens, trading pieces, and so on. When the board games are returned, staff do not count the pieces but visually check to see that all of the smaller bags are in the larger bag. Consequently, we are unable to charge for missing pieces because we cannot be sure when they went missing. However, because most of the game manufacturers are willing to provide replacement pieces, often at no cost, this compromise is well worth the savings in staff time.

The physical objects are easier to process but harder to catalog. We found guidance in archives and museum cataloging, where physical objects are routinely cataloged without titles. Catalogers supplied titles for most of these objects and provided several alternative titles to aid searchers. Things were given generic titles like "guitar" and also more specific titles such as "Fender FA 100." We used the summary field to give a more detailed description. Because our summaries are searchable in the OPAC, this field provides additional access points for patrons. Luckily, RDA provides a framework for catalogers to use their judgment and provide a description in a way that serves end users. Many patrons wanted to browse the collection, rather than search for something specific, so it was necessary to add the key word "Library of Things" to every record. In processing, the physical objects were simply labeled with a title and bar code. In most cases, staff were able to find an appropriate case or a hard-sided box for storage.

Library Unexpected has been an adventure for staff and patrons, a chance to try different approaches and see what worked. To that end, staff feedback was welcomed, and all involved were promised that there would be no permanent procedural changes until everyone understood how such changes would affect them. A special processing station was set up so that everyone could work together. Each step was discussed, and staff made great suggestions. Overall, technical services staff were very invested in the project and appreciated when public services staff shared patron feedback with the larger group.

## MARKETING: THE #LIBRARYBRAG CAMPAIGN

The Library of Things had several elements that made it both simple and inexpensive to promote. The rarity of libraries lending "things" meant that the concept felt novel on both a local and national level. Pitching to the media was extremely effective because the story was unusual, community-driven, and offered excellent visuals. Rather than issue a formal press release, staff put together a fact sheet on the program and made phone and e-mail pitches to the press, resulting in several local television, radio, and print spots that eventually led to an article in the *New York Times* (Garrison, 2015; Milne, 2015; Nakano, 2015). By focusing on the community-engagement, voting angle of the collection development, staff were able to make the story more about meeting the needs and desires of the Sacramento community than about simply providing this new collection.

The library also ran a marketing campaign themed "#librarybrag" concurrently with the launch of the Library of Things. The objective was to get the community thinking about Sacramento Public Library in different and unexpected ways. The campaign shared an interactive and community-driven aspect with the Library of Things in that patrons were encouraged to submit their own posts on social media, using the #librarybrags hashtag. The library's creative project coordinator then created magazine and bus shelter ads, vehicle wraps for book delivery trucks, magnets and pencils, and social media graphics featuring the

**FIGURE 7.1**   #librarybrag Advertisement.

various slogans. Examples of #librarybrags included: "Much more than books," "Travel all across time and space with endless authors and possibilities . . . for free" and "Anything you can do, my library can teach me to do better." Many of the #librarybrags highlighted "things" from the Library of Things, including the sewing machines and video games. Judging from the positive response by the community and the media, not to mention the popularity and high demand for the "things," the interactive and community-focused marketing campaign has proven to be hugely successful.

## PUBLIC PERCEPTION: DOES THE CONCEPT WORK?

The Library of Things collection has been incredibly popular since its debut in March 2015, with most of the items being checked out immediately, while still leaving a selection to display for browsing. After some items proved popular enough to accrue sizable holds lists, additional units were purchased during the second round of selection and spending. At the end of the initial grant period, the collection consisted of eight sewing machines, three GoPro cameras, nine musical instruments, two digital projectors, two digital drawing tablets, two fabric screening kits, a button maker, a laminator, and over a hundred video and board games. The hold ratio for these items is comparable to the more popular items in the library's circulating book and movie collection, though patron requests for more items continue to come in. After a year of circulation, a sizable wait still remains for the sewing machines, GoPro cameras, and button maker.

Staff successfully met the initial goal of using the collection to get the Sacramento community talking about the library and its services. Patrons continue to be surprised and intrigued by the options in the Library of Things, with a community of regular users from both the immediate area and all over Sacramento County now using the collection to support activities such as special sewing projects and weekly game nights.

However, not all of the community response has been unequivocally positive. A small amount of the community's feedback questioned the decision to spend public funds on items that could be considered fanciful or extraneous. This is a valid concern, but it is also a symptom of the basic, entrenched view of what libraries are and how communities are supposed to use them that the project was designed to challenge. The Library of Things is meant to help the library transcend the stereotype of a book warehouse and exemplify a deeper, more modern idea of a library: a community space for lifelong learning. In interviewing various public library decision makers about their efforts to position their libraries as centers of communication and civic engagement, Houghton (2014) found that those libraries were finding success by focusing on the specific interests of their immediate population as we have done and, notably, ensuring that the resulting new activities and services would "connect with the services that libraries already provide for their local population" (p. 49). This methodology underpins the Library of Things and allows the library to use the collection's novelty to educate its users on why, exactly, the items are more relevant and educational than they might appear, through connections with related books, programming, and services. This has created a number of outreach opportunities, with items from the collection traveling to places like comic conventions and sports arenas to grab potential users' attention and get them thinking about their library. Still, there remains a careful focus on aligning Library of Things items to core library services and collections to keep this approach in mind as the library starts considering how to expand its offerings.

A much larger amount of the criticism received has been from those who are enthusiastic about the collection but are inconvenienced by how checkouts are currently implemented (for example, the inability to pick up and return at their local branches). The library is taking this constructive feedback into account as it examines how to support and sustain the collection based on its steady usage and demand.

## NEXT STEPS: BIGGER, EASIER, MORE?

As of this writing, the Library of Things is still functionally a pilot project, and library staff is in the process of analyzing a year's worth of circulation statistics before deciding how to proceed. It is expected that this will give the library enough data to organize a system of metrics that can definitively gauge the collection's cost per use. As Dewland and See (2015) note in the conclusion of their recent study of metrics for patron-driven acquisitions, consistent metrics facilitate better maintenance of authority control; in our case, having solid data for analysis will allow staff to better address the unexpected cataloging issues that complicated the project in the beginning. The library will then focus on two aspects of the feedback gathered from the collection's users: increasing the variety of items offered and allowing circulation at more than one library branch.

To get around the problems that come with a floating Library of Things collection, the library will study how to create node collections that are specific to a particular branch. This could allow branches to offer unique selections of "things" that fit their respective workflows, storage-space limitations, and local community input, while bypassing the risks associated with transporting fragile items. A different set of logistical issues is inherent in creating a separate collection alongside the floating library collection, but the library has a precedent for this in its special collections of popular and best-selling books that are confined to single branches.

With regard to maintaining the items in the collection, replacing lost items, and most importantly, expanding the selection of offerings, funding remains the biggest sustainability challenge. The Friends of the Library are the most obvious source of help, especially in the case of branch-specific collections, but Friends' funds are already stretched thin to accommodate programming and other local branch needs. Instead, the library is working to integrate funding for the Library of Things into the system-wide collections budget. This is a challenge, considering how costly some of the items can be. However, this funding approach not only affords the collection a measure of stability, but also creates the necessity for explicit language in the library's collection development policy that will expedite future decisions on what to acquire, how to expand, and how to handle community input and donation.

Building on the current success of the Library of Things collection creates the possibility of reshaping the image of the library and the expectations of its users. The original Library Unexpected project was designed to surprise and delight library patrons, but ultimately, a successful Library of Things will eventually no longer be surprising. Ideally, nobody will think it strange that the library offers a guitar with its selection of songbooks, or a board game that teaches coding to go along with a third-grader's stack of chapter books. Accordingly, when it comes time to argue the library's value as a hub of discovery and lifelong, freely accessible learning to stakeholders and funders worried about the institution's relevancy, the argument will be that much easier to make.

## REFERENCES

Dewland, J. C., & See, A. (2015). Patron driven acquisitions. *Library Resources & Technical Services, 59*(1), 13–23.

Foote, C. (2015). Far beyond makerspaces. *Internet@Schools, 22*(5), 12–13.

Garrison, E. (2015, Feb. 1). Borrow a sewing machine? Sacramento Public Library to start loaning more than books. *The Sacramento Bee.* Retrieved from www.sacbee.com/news/local/education/article8920145.html.

Houghton, K. (2014). The local library across the digital and physical city: Opportunities for economic development. *Commonwealth Journal of Local Governance 15* (June 2014). Retrieved from www.austlii.edu.au/au/journals/ComJlLocGov/2014/3.pdf.

Milne, S. (2015, March 12). Library of things launches on Saturday. *Capital Public Radio.* Retrieved from www.capradio.org/articles/2015/03/12/library-of-things-launches-on-saturday.

Nakano, R. (2015, Feb. 2). Sacramento Public Library to expand check-out options. *FOX40 News.* Retrieved from fox40.com/2015/02/02/sacramento-public-library-to-expand-check-out-options.

Peifer, K., & Perez, L. (2011). Effectiveness of a coordinated effort to promote early literacy behaviors. *Maternal & Child Health Journal, 15*(6), 765–771.

# Part III

## Things Collections in Academic Libraries

# 8

# Technology and Small College Libraries: Trying to Be Everything to Everyone

*Brian Burns*

## INTRODUCTION

The mission of an academic library, generally speaking, is to support the academic mission of the college or university of which the library is an integral part, and by definition the library should work toward accomplishing said mission by building a diverse and accessible collection (Bangers, 2016). Books alone are obviously no longer sufficient, but neither is text, whether fixed in analog or digital form. Long ago, libraries began collecting works in other formats such as filmstrips, microfilm, and vinyl record albums. Whether textually based or audiovisually based, the commonality among all of these items is that they are all used for one of three reasons: education, recreation, or creation of new materials. Small (mostly liberal arts) academic libraries have been branching out into the realm of technology/equipment collection and circulation for exactly the same reasons, but with more of an emphasis on education and the creation of new materials, but not without keeping the recreation aspect in mind. At Hampden-Sydney College, a small, private, liberal arts college for men in rural Virginia, we at the Bortz Library do our best to provide the 1,000-plus students of this residential campus with as many different devices and tools as possible for their convenience, thus saving time by limiting unnecessary trips into town. By providing movies (both streaming and DVD), pleasure reading, bicycle pumps, tool kits, and more we can eliminate unnecessary student spending, increase convenience, and create a more comfortable and welcoming environment in general. By providing video cameras, microphones, specialized software, scanners, printers, presentation remotes, projectors, and more, we can keep student costs lower, make multimedia projects a more attractive option to faculty, and create a space where students can learn how to use these tools and skills.

Small colleges have a limited number of majors and minors to offer, sports on a smaller scale, and fewer amenities than larger universities, but even colleges with only a thousand students must provide a wide array of resources to their main constituent population. This, of course, includes the library. With over a hundred faculty members giving a wide array of assignments, from research papers to multimedia-based assignments, libraries must be prepared to handle the demand placed upon them. By viewing the big picture through the eyes of both faculty (assignments) and students (assignments, entertainment, and other needs), libraries can diversify their holdings in such a way that will make a real and tangible difference. Other chapters in this book focus more on specific collections or types of collections, while this chapter seeks to propose a variety of possible items that a small college library could circulate to keep its community satisfied. From electronic technology to accessories to simple tools, readers will discover ideas within this chapter that can bolster any small library collection.

It is necessary to preface this chapter with a brief discussion of purchasing decisions. In most cases, the two overwhelmingly most important factors in selecting any technology for circulating to patrons will be cost and need or purpose. Cost almost always factors into decision-making strategies. The author recommends temporarily suspending the consideration of monetary factors, in an attempt to make the best decisions based on need and/or purpose first. Initially determining the intended use(s) of a piece of equipment and why it is necessary will assist in locating workable options. Once the search is narrowed, then one can begin to seek the best pricing alternatives available. There are also methods of reducing direct cost to the library by exploring grant opportunities, departmental sharing options, or even donations or gifts. Without first discerning exactly what is needed, inadequate equipment choices may result simply from being unnecessarily cost conscious.

## PRESENTATION AND EVENT SUPPORT EQUIPMENT

Small colleges often have limited human resources to support the myriad cocurricular events and programs that student clubs and organizations host across campus, not to mention the many small, informal groups that gather for recreation and entertainment purposes. On the Hampden-Sydney College campus, circulating a projector kit consisting of projector, remote control, and appropriate connecting cables saves both the library and users time. A single bar code is sufficient to check out a projector, VGA cable, HDMI cable, Apple Lightning to HDMI cable, power cable, and presentation remote, as long as the library personnel are consistent and persistent in ensuring all pieces are present upon checkout and check-in. Some venues will require a screen as well. Several companies make a lightweight, portable screen with a pneumatic scissor mechanism that can be placed on the floor or on a tabletop and raised with relative ease. These make a nice alternative to the heavier tripod screens to which many have become accustomed.

PowerPoint presentation remotes are a helpful bonus item that your library can offer users. Although remaining close to the laptop and using the arrow keys to advance slides is always an option, presentation remotes, especially those with laser pointers built in, add a certain professional quality to a presentation that any lecturer, club, or organization will appreciate. Users now have everything they need for a presentation. Although PowerPoint seems to be ubiquitous at any campus speech or event, other types of visuals are occasionally necessary. Students will welcome circulation of smaller-sized DVD players or even Blu-ray players.

Providing alternatives to events that are dominated by the presence of alcohol is something most institutions are attempting to accomplish (Neighbors et al., 2007). Movies and marathon television seasons can sometimes fill the void. If the venue to which the students will be taking the DVD/Blu-ray player does not have adequate built-in audio equipment, the library can continue to assist. Both compact speaker systems (Bose Companion 2 Series) as well as boombox-sized speakers (TDK Life on Record 3-Speaker Boombox) can certainly do the job, as will sound bars that are typically made for televisions (Sony HTCT260H). One word of caution: it may or may not be the responsibility of the library, but checking with student organizations that wish to host movie events to make sure they have the proper public performance permissions could save the group, the library, and the institution headaches. Librarians are occasionally tabbed to be the campus "copyright police," but even if that does not hold true on your campus, someone will likely believe that the library staff should be at least somewhat knowledgeable on the subject. A final note on sound: a small, portable PA system could be very helpful in certain circumstances such as student groups attempting to draw attention to their fundraiser "on the quad" or even to assist an ill faculty member who has lost his voice.

Webcams and small tripods can also be beneficial when presenting via Skype or WebEx. Increasingly, students seeking jobs after graduation and faculty seeking jobs at our institution are expected to complete an initial interview online and in real time. A webcam that can be placed on the upper rim of a laptop or monitor can be helpful, but so can one with a standard tripod mounting slot. When purchasing equipment for circulating, multipurpose is often the most useful, thus seeking a webcam with both capabilities will suit users well. It is recommended that you spend enough to get a webcam with a frame rate of at least 30 frames per second. The choices between glass or plastic lenses, standard definition or HD, the resolution, and type of sensor can all add to the cost and clarity of the webcam.

Lastly, of great use in classrooms and in almost any lecture situation, audience response systems are a tremendous way to gauge an audience's comprehension of, or reaction to, the material presented. The tools available today easily allow for both well-planned questions and feedback as well as impromptu voting on the fly. Most sets utilize radio frequency (RF), which is superior to infrared (IR) technology. Typically, vendors (for example, Turning Technologies, Meridia, and i>clicker) will allow libraries to purchase custom sets of varying numbers of "clicker" remotes that come self-contained in handy carry pouches for convenience as well as protection for the devices. Data collected from the audience or group can be saved for future examination, and software can be installed on multiple machines, whether in classrooms or on laptops.

# ELECTRONICS—PHOTO/VIDEO

Why circulate video cameras in your library? Consider the professor of German who assigns his upper-level students to create a newscast consisting of a sports segment, weather segment, news, and a commercial—a creative way to assess students' language, syntactic, and pronunciation abilities. Or the mathematics professor who requires her students to create a short video explaining how to solve a complex equation. Students learn much from teaching their peers, and others in the course can view and review the video until full comprehension takes place. Video is a powerful tool, and making cameras available, along with the expertise to assist in post-production work, can be very helpful.

From personal experience, libraries that were early adopters of providing recording technology in a lending capacity started with analog SLR (single-lens reflex) cameras, reel-to-reel or cassette tape recorders, and the like, and followed a natural progression as the technology advanced on to VHS camcorders, then on to point-and-shoot digital cameras and flip-style video cameras, then to palmcorders. Equipment collections must continue to not only grow, but also adapt with the times, as the wants and needs of users do so necessarily. Digital SLR cameras can be expensive, but worth the investment if faculty are teaching upper-level digital photography classes. If a tight budget situation precludes the purchase of expensive items, one must be aware that there are compact point-and-shoot cameras and a variety of bridge cameras providing levels of affordability. Similar choices of quality and affordability exist within the realm of video cameras. Many types of accessories are available, some more necessary than others, to enhance the user experience with both still and video cameras, and nearly all budgets can afford something.

Although point-and-shoot cameras are sufficient for some applications, their necessity has been eroded by cameras now built into smartphones. Libraries may need to consider upgrading to something more robust if photography is taught on campus or if there is an established student interest in photography as a hobby through a club or organization or some other measure. As a side note, becoming knowledgeable of mobile apps and knowing how to assist students with photography and videography editing on their mobile devices may well become a valuable service. Bridge cameras are those that exist between the fully automatic nature of point-and-shoot and the high-quality, fully manual nature, and interchangeable lenses of digital SLR cameras. A less-expensive bridge camera may not be built for interchangeable lenses, but may have a built-in megazoom for higher quality at a distance, such as the Canon PowerShot SX60 with its 65x optical zoom. Other camera models may have greater sensitivity due to a larger image sensor for producing crisper, higher-definition images. Many bridge cameras today are constructed to have a similar shape and size to DSLR cameras, but this is mainly for marketability.

The current world of video cameras, like still photography cameras, has differing levels of quality and price based on specifications. Less-expensive hand-held camcorders are convenient due to both their size and the fact that they are fully automatic, some with digital image stabilization. Better-quality cameras include manual controls, higher-quality sensors for increased picture quality, and higher-quality microphones. Also, more expensive cameras will have an electronic viewfinder in addition to the LCD screen, which can prove to be invaluable during sunny, outdoor shoots involving sports coverage, environmental biology trips, visits to historic sites, or any variety of campus shots. Most video cameras have moved completely away from any type of traditional recording medium and have instead moved to storing video on internal hard drives or SD cards, both of which utilize flash memory. More expensive cameras will have a hard drive and an additional SD card slot that can be helpful when involved in a long shoot that may max out memory. Finally, although some camcorders record video in the MPEG-4 format, which is fairly ubiquitous, better video cameras will offer MPEG-2, which is a higher-quality video file format. AVCHD is a fairly high-quality video format that has been adopted by a few specific manufacturers and can be found in both less-expensive and pricier cameras. Finally, more expensive cameras will allow users to connect external microphones (both wireless and on-board shotgun), lights, lenses and filters, and more, thus offering much flexibility and allowing for greater creativity for users.

A short addendum to the discussion on cameras is necessary to discuss time-lapse, GoPro, and drone video cameras. Time-lapse cameras take a series of single-frame shots of video at preset times, then stitch those images together into a short video where the images can span hours, days, or weeks. With most, users can specify the file format, image quality, output resolution, and more. These are handy for biology/botany courses to see plants grow, weather formations, traffic patterns, people flow, and more.

GoPro cameras are solidly constructed cameras designed for much more rugged use; students will use GoPro cameras for recording activities that normal cameras would never sustain. Some GoPro models are made to withstand full submersion, and the accessories available allow users to attach the cameras to everything from skateboards, to helmets, to bicycles, and even dogs. These cameras can be beneficial for circulating to students for both fun and for pedagogical fieldwork where it would be less desirable for a normal camera to be used. The other pedagogical advantage is that some of the GoPro cameras can shoot 4K video, so that students and faculty can create customized 4K content on their own. This feature is a bonus considering that more 4K televisions are being installed in classrooms and labs, but content is not yet widely available. Because 4K televisions can display four separate HD videos simultaneously, students in an environmental biology course could be assigned to shoot a particular type of animal for study, and the instructor can place four versions on the same screen for direct comparison of behaviors. Imagine four videos of a particularly busy walkway on campus being recorded at intervals during which something unexpected occurs. Students in the class could study the sociological implications in comparison. As a tip, when adding a GoPro to a circulating collection, ensure the library has plenty of attachment accessories available to users.

Finally, drone cameras are coming to campuses. Drones are capable of recording fantastic campus shots never before possible, highlighting particular buildings and the general splendor of a campus, both of which are terrific for promotional use. As drone cameras are likely to continue to make a larger impact, visual journalism students would surely benefit, as would students studying the environment. As of the writing of this chapter, the Federal Aviation Administration (FAA) requires that most drones be registered (Federal Aviation Administration, 2016), but drone regulations continue to be debated and changed and will likely continue to change quickly. Campus personnel, particularly librarians, must be aware of relevant laws when considering purchasing drones for circulation.

Accessories for both still photo and video cameras are abundant. Most libraries that circulate cameras also circulate tripods (Sanchez, 2013). Often overlooked are monopods, which are lighter weight, less bulky, and can be set up faster than tripods. These are terrific for still photography and can be very useful for video as well. Smaller, tabletop tripods have specific uses with smaller video cameras (Flips, Bloggies, webcams, etc.) and point-and-shoot still cameras. Tripods can be found inexpensively at local big box retail stores or at online retailers, but often these do not last as long as sturdier, more well-built models. Two main purchasing options exist: buy inexpensive plastic tripods and replace when necessary and possibly upgrade slightly, or purchase expensive, mostly metal tripods and hope they are not abused. For professional photographers and videographers, a high-quality tripod is nearly as essential as a high-quality camera. However, for circulation to undergraduate students, the author prefers to keep costs down and purchase inexpensive tripods more often with the bonus of having newer inventory for the students. Libraries should also consider circulating storage, both USB for transferring files and SD cards for initial recording, for video and image files generated by these cameras. Camera lights and external flashes can be very helpful for users capturing images or video in lower-light situations. Light kits can also be desired for a more polished and professional quality video assignment. Because the higher-quality versions of both types of cameras have the ability to use different lenses, libraries can circulate extra lenses independently from the cameras. Another accessory that could be very beneficial to any student needing to do high-level work in photography or videography is a light meter. These are not inexpensive, but can be an invaluable tool and likely not something students will own. Ultimately, accessories can make all the difference in a project.

## MICROPHONES

Microphones can be used for a wide array of projects and tasks. Class homework sometimes includes creating podcasts, audio recordings for foreign language courses, voice-over recordings for videos, audio tracks for PowerPoint presentations, and other such assignments. Sometimes a simple digital voice recorder will suffice, as many current devices will save as MP3 files that can be utilized by most software. Olympus and Sony both make a variety of good-quality digital voice recorders in all price ranges. Inexpensive microphones, both USB-style as well as those utilizing the 3.5-mm jack on any computer, are available for purchase from online retailers that will fit the bill as well. If users prefer to use their smartphones, offering something like an iRig Mic Cast will afford them a higher-quality audio file than they could possibly get with the built-in microphone already present on their phone. High-quality USB microphones will plug into any computer if the user has audio recording and editing software; a good example is the Snowflake from Blue Microphones, which is a small yet effective microphone for one- or two-person recording. It comes with a helpful shell that can be used to hang the microphone on a monitor or the top of a laptop. If an assortment of uses and room configurations is anticipated, seek a microphone that offers pattern choices such as omnidirectional, cardioid, etc. Again, Blue Microphones makes a microphone that is priced within reason, especially for the quality of recording. The Yeti allows an increase or decrease in the gain during recording by turning a dial on the microphone. This microphone can clearly meet the needs of a full conference table recording or that of an amateur musician. If audio recording software is required, Audacity should be high on the list. It is absolutely one of the very best free pieces of software created. Audacity is powerful, reliable, and affordable. Students have come to the Bortz Library at Hampden-Sydney College with needs for video voice-overs, audio commenting, oral foreign language assignments, storytelling assignments, and more, and Audacity is our go-to audio recording and editing program.

## COMPUTING/GEEK ITEMS

Campuses contain any number of amateur computer programmers who may be seeking new ways to experiment and be creative, and these amateur programmers may come from a variety of majors. If the library were to offer a few microcontrollers such as Raspberry Pi devices for circulation, some of the needs of this more unique and specialized population may be met, and would certainly be available to all students instead of only those in a particular department or major (Johnson et al., 2015). Due to the experimentation that takes place with these types of devices, it is strongly recommended that the circulation period be set for a much longer period than most items, perhaps as long as a few months or even a semester. A Raspberry Pi can be purchased for only 35 dollars. The Bortz Library at Hampden-Sydney College is currently in the exploratory phase of creating a couple of Raspberry Pi stations consisting of monitor, keyboard, and mouse. Students would be able to check out a Raspberry Pi and micro SD card from the Fuqua Technology Commons and connect to the station. Once an operating system is downloaded (Raspbian is the official OS of Raspberry Pi), students can begin to experiment and code. Raspbian includes software such as Python and Java so that students with a desire to learn coding on their own (or for a class) can do so.

## OTHER/MISCELLANEOUS

Paying attention to the "chatter" of student assistants and other users in the library, one can begin to recognize needs in the circulating collection of technology and things. Providing students free access to an assortment of items from the library at no cost to them is certainly beneficial. The reputation of the library will be heightened when students see these additions. Students and student assistants at the Bortz Library initially encouraged the addition of some of the following items to our circulating collection, which have proven to be wise purchases. This is not to suggest a patron-driven model of acquisition, but rather to show how heightened awareness on the part of staff can lead to worthy purchasing decisions.

Students love to watch television and play video games. Providing HDMI cables that they can check out for several days at a time can get them over the hump from a broken or missing cable that prevents them from their favorite leisure activities to when they can purchase a new cable. Listening to music at nearly all times and all places is a part of many students' lives. Circulating headphones in the library keeps them happy and, for those students who need to escape from the distraction of their friends, can help them focus and center on the task at hand. Although sanitary concerns certainly exist, an inexpensive pair of over-the-ear headphones is much better quality and much cleaner than an inexpensive pair of earbuds.

Most people, never mind students, do not realize that Windows and iOSx have a scientific calculator built in—they are used to the basic calculator good only for addition, subtraction, multiplication, division, and possibly square root. Consider purchasing a few scientific calculators such as the TI-84 Plus and bar-coding them for circulation when students have homework and their calculator is in their dorm room, or for when they have an important exam and their calculator somehow ceased to function. Students somehow seem to find their way into too many adverse scenarios, and this is an easy way to earn your cape!

Whether watching documentaries or reserve movies for class assignments or purely for entertainment purposes, students will be viewing DVDs in your library. Providing a portable DVD player and a set of headphones offers students ultimate flexibility in whether they view their homework at a table for ease of note taking or on a comfortable sofa as they kick back for a break. These devices do one thing only, and they typically do it well without instructions or upgrade concerns. Consider trying out a couple at your library to see what happens.

In most cases, certain things are scarce for students on campus, and this is particularly true with pianos. If general music courses require students to learn to play a few basic tunes, students will need to practice. Consider circulating electronic keyboards or electronic pianos (same thing). One should consider consulting with music faculty in determining which of the many choices available will best fulfill needs, most importantly the number of keys on the device. Generally speaking, a 61-key portable piano will be sufficient, but if the faculty are picky or if the goal is to support upper-level music courses, a full 88-key portable piano may be necessary. It is possible to purchase a quality Yamaha or Casio 61-key device in the $150 price range, which should not break the bank. Experience dictates that more students on campus either want to keep up their piano skills or are making their own music for fun and enjoyment. It is recommended that a MIDI interface be one of the included features, which would help to support the latter category of users and their recording needs.

## CONCLUSION

If the library is well equipped and willing to circulate equipment, even a small college can have a much larger feel as far as students are concerned. This is especially true on rural campuses where access to other venues and opportunities is diminished by distance and travel time.

Worth noting is the necessity to include replacement costs due to damage or loss into the equation when considering any piece of equipment for purchase and subsequent circulation. Students are not always able to afford to replace or repair higher-end equipment. It is recommended that libraries purchase what is necessary to support needs first and, if possible, avoid overspending on individual items. For example, without any type of journalism major or television studio on the Hampden-Sydney College campus, we had no need for high-end video cameras. Thus, a $350 Canon VIXIA HF R30 sufficiently meets our needs at a reasonable cost, and a Canon XA25 would be overkill and quite expensive at $2,200.

We hope the ideas listed in this chapter are helpful, but these ideas are merely a guide. Each institution, indeed each library, is on its own educational and service-oriented journey. Readers are encouraged to further focus more specifically on their library's intended goals and mission. Speak openly and candidly with faculty and students to discover their distinctive wants and needs. Seek out ideas by reading available curricula and syllabi. One certainly does not want to promise the sun, the moon, and the stars, but one can undeniably take small steps to grow holdings molded by constituents' suggestions. Add data to small steps, and suddenly what was once nothing becomes something special. This may sound grandiose, but the author has experienced the wonder of an idea—spoken in a few brief words at a meeting, juxtaposed with brainstorming and work and research, and an idea becomes reality. You are encouraged to be creative in ideas, fiscal resources, and implementation. Go forth and build a diverse collection, and they will come, and they will appreciate.

## REFERENCES

Bangers, S. R. (n.d.). Thinking boldly!: College and university library mission statements as roadsigns to the future. Retrieved from www.ala.org/acrl/publications/whitepapers/nashville/bangert.

Federal Aviation Administration. (2016). Unmanned Aircraft Systems (UAS) registration. Retrieved May 27, 2016, from www.faa.gov/uas/registration.

Johnson, L., Adams Becker, S., Estrada, V., & Freeman, A. (2015). *NMC horizon report: 2015 library edition.* Austin, TX: The New Media Consortium.

Sanchez, J. (2013). *From content warehouse to content producer: Libraries at the crossroads.* Castle Rock, CO: Douglas County Libraries. Retrieved from www.thebookmyfriend.com/uploads/6/1/1/3/6113160/from_content_warehouse_to_content_producer_libraries_at_the_crossroads.pdf.

# 9

# Providing Hands-On Teacher Preparation: Collecting and Maintaining Curriculum Materials

*Jennifer Harvey and Rochelle Hunt Krueger*

## BACKGROUND

Curriculum materials centers (CMCs) are collections of materials that are maintained to support preservice teachers and the faculty members who prepare students for their role in the classroom. Curriculum collections have traditionally included textbooks, juvenile literature, practical lesson planning resources, and educational objects. For example, the collection might include magnets, hand drums, maps, and photographs to aid in teaching science, music, and social studies. The primary purpose of the Curriculum Materials Center is to support teacher preparation; however, nonbook materials collected to support higher education instruction are often included in the collections (for example, movies and music in various formats or vocabulary-enhancing games for students learning English). The objects in the CMC collection can also be of use for instruction of students not affiliated with an education department (for example, to teach mathematical or science concepts).

Curriculum materials centers partner with teacher preparation programs to increase student success by providing access to tools that they might use in the classroom. Often, faculty members bring their students to the CMC to have hands-on time with the resources. Students frequently incorporate CMC resources into their lesson plans. It is our experience that as students begin

113

to utilize the CMC holdings, they begin to see the practical applications of the various objects available, and they highly value the resources. In addition, feedback from teaching faculty leads us to conclude that the lesson plans prepared by students who utilize the "things" that the CMC collects result in better learning experiences in both the methods classroom and in the student teaching environment.

Curriculum collections have a long history in the United States. In writing about the history of CMCs, Clark (1982) suggests that the collections had their origin in the 1920s, with the establishment of the normal school system for teacher preparation. Kohrman (2012) writes that references can be found to the existence of curriculum collections in autobiographies and memoirs from as early as the 1700s. CMCs have long played an important role in supporting teacher education by identifying, maintaining, and lending curriculum "things."

The Curriculum Materials Committee of the Education and Behavioral Sciences Section (EBSS) of the Association of College and Research Libraries (ACRL) examines issues related to maintaining CMC collections. According to *Guidelines for Curriculum Materials Centers* published by the Curriculum Materials Committee (2008), CMCs should acquire materials of varied formats, including instructional games, posters, kits, models, video recordings, sound recordings, puppets, manipulatives, rock collections, educational tests and measures, to name just a few. Some of these types of objects, along with information about how they can be maintained in a curriculum collection, are addressed in the following sections. The advice that follows is drawn from our experiences at the University of Nebraska at Kearney (UNK) and Bowling Green State University (BGSU). This list is not exhaustive, and the information provided can be applied to other materials.

## HANDS-ON/INTERACTIVE MATERIALS

Interactive instruction materials are popular with our patrons. Math manipulatives, games, kits, puppets, realia, social studies reproductions, and tests are examples of these types of items. Math manipulatives are sets of three-dimensional objects that are used to illustrate abstract mathematical concepts. Cuisenaire rods, tangrams, and geoboards are examples of math manipulatives. Kennedy (1986) defines manipulatives as "objects that appeal to several senses and that can be touched, moved about, rearranged, and otherwise handled by children" (p. 6). Akkan (2012) writes that using manipulatives encourages problem solving and provides opportunities to learn decision-making skills (p. 168). ETA hand2mind[1] is a good source for math manipulatives and other educational resources. To find the best prices, we often consult multiple resources and, when making a large purchase, we have been known to contact the vendor to see if they will provide a discount. Vendors benefit from an inclusion of resources they sell in the curriculum collections because a preservice teacher's familiarity with the interactive materials may incline them to recommend the purchase of these materials in their schools. Math manipulatives (and other multiple-part materials) are often rehoused in clear plastic storage bins. Being able to see the contents of the box without opening it helps patrons to see if the contents may be what they desire.

Commercially successful games with educational value (Scrabble, Bananagrams, Twister, and so on) are useful in the classroom and can be popular with students looking for an icebreaker for their club or other social event. These games can be easily acquired at local retail stores or online retailers. Games produced to address specific educational needs, such as how to tell time or count money, are also part of the collection and are generally available through education resources–related companies. These are often acquired in response to patron requests for a specific educational game or when a particular instruction need is identified. Lakeshore Learning[2] is a great resource for games for younger children.

When the games are first added to the collection, the various parts are marked with ownership information. UNK writes "UNK Library" or "UNK Lib" on the items, in addition to the call number. BGSU writes both "BGSU CRC" and the accession number assigned to the set of materials to mark the various parts. Both UNK and BGSU use accession numbers for processing "things." UNK uses the accession number as a part of the call number (for example, Kit 826). BGSU assigns an accession number to the "things" added to the collection, but uses the Dewey decimal classification scheme for call numbers. Neither system is perfect. At UNK, similar items may not collocate because they were purchased at different times. The Dewey decimal system places materials for elementary school–aged students in the same classification number. BGSU refines this by using a Cutter number for the publisher name. This refinement also results in materials that teach the same concept not necessarily collocating. We have not identified an ideal solution to this problem.

Of course, some parts are so small that it is impractical to mark them. In addition to marking the individual items, contents labels are prepared to aid in auditing games to verify that all of the parts are returned when a game circulates. Any missing pieces are identified in the audit process and the patron is notified to request return of missing pieces. Often, the patron is able to locate and return the missing item(s). If the pieces are not returned in a timely manner, a replacement charge for the missing items, if they can be replaced, or the full cost of the game is charged. If the game can be used without the missing piece, the contents label is updated to reflect the new contents. Awkwardly shaped items (where shelving may be difficult) are placed in more uniformly shaped containers.

Kits are comprised of two or more types of media (they may include juvenile literature, DVDs, CDs, game boards, manipulatives, and so on) and are often subject based. As an example, UNK has a calendar math kit. It contains a teacher's manual, calendar pieces, play money, a clock, and more. At UNK, "things" are classified primarily by format type. The first portion of the call number identifies the format of the item (for example, the first line of the call number for a kit would say "Kit," followed by the accession number). At BGSU, all three-dimensional objects and multiple-part items, no matter the material type, are interfiled on the shelves (the first line of the call number is "CURR TA," where TA abbreviates Teaching Aid, followed by the Dewey classification number).

**FIGURE 9.1** Traditional Library Shelving Units Are Used to House the Majority of the Items Collected in Curriculum Materials Centers.

Reproductions of historical primary sources are great tools for teaching history. Jackdaw[3] and Teacher Created Materials[4] are two resources for kits that contain reproductions of photographs, letters, and documents. History can come alive for students through these sorts of resources. Hearing of the atrocities of World War II is one thing, but seeing the mountains of shoes left behind by victims who died in the gas chambers and death camps of Nazi Germany gives scope to the massiveness of human destruction. Images of Japanese American citizens interned on U.S. soil during the same period can enrich the educational experience. These reproductions come in boxes, folders, and bags. Materials in folders may be stored upright between other items or between bookends. Some Jackdaw photo sets are large format (17-by-22-inch) and are stored in clear bags with a hanger at the top. These items are stored on racks.

Hand puppets that represent various animals and humans are useful in classroom settings. Students who are reluctant to read aloud may enjoy having a puppet voice the words for them. BGSU has an extensive collection of puppets. Folkmanis Puppets, RBI Sound Puppets, and Silly Puppets[5] are good resources for selecting puppets. On this type of item, ownership information is marked on the puppet with permanent marker (on the label or inside the puppet). Puppets can be bagged or boxed, with the bar code and other label placed on the container. Alternatively, tags may be attached to the puppet with "plastic tagging barbs" (Lare, 2004) of the sort retailers use to tag merchandise or hold items together (p. 64). In this case, the tag would include the label and the bar code.

Realia are samples of items from everyday life. Some examples might include musical instruments, hats, masks, rulers/yardsticks, protractors, timers, scales, and stethoscopes. Duplicate realia may be housed in a single container and circulated as a set. At BGSU, hats are labeled to warn borrowers to consider the possibility of lice and to discourage wearing the item. Hats are sprayed with RID as a preventative measure when they are returned.

The test collection includes commercially available standardized tests that students can utilize to become more familiar with testing instruments. Some test materials are restricted to individuals with advanced credentials based on education, training, and/or experience in the field of assessment. For this reason, tests should be placed where access is limited. Borrowing privileges should be to preauthorized individuals. Students with a proxy from their instructor are considered authorized users. Because the collection is a reference tool, the contents are not to be used to administer the test, and forms are not to be photocopied or used. Students may use versions of the testing instruments owned by the school where their student teaching occurs or may acquire access to tests for the purpose of administration from another resource, if they administer tests with a student.

**FIGURE 9.2**  Magnets, Feathers, Pinecones, and Buttons Are Examples of Real-World Objects That Can Be Useful in Lesson Planning.

No matter the format of the item, bar codes are assigned to the "things" at UNK and BGSU so that they might circulate. Other institutions may use other methods to allow for automated circulation, but we use bar codes.

# TECHNOLOGY

Digital technologies have made many analog, educational technologies obsolete. We withdrew vinyl records and filmstrips years ago. Digital streaming, whether through a library or personal subscription, is more convenient than visiting a library to borrow digital technologies stored on physical media. Nevertheless, we still have CDs and DVDs in our collections. CDs may contain music, recorded books, or other content, while DVDs provide video content. Both CDs and DVDs are typically kept in the original containers or placed in jewel cases. Ownership markings and call numbers are written on the media with a black, fine-tip Sharpie marker or a silver marker, for dark labels. Printed materials included in the case are marked with ownership stamps/labels and the call number. The call number and a title label are affixed to the outside of the case. For many years, CDs and DVDs at UNK were cataloged by accession number. As the collection grew, it became increasingly difficult to browse the shelves. It was determined that using the Library of Congress system would make it easier for patrons to browse, and the collection was retroactively reclassified. Faculty members from the music department frequently request music content on CD at UNK when the materials are not available through the streaming, subscription resources. DVD content may be purchased in response to faculty member requests if streaming access is not available. Digital content in these formats is not actively sought without a request from a faculty member or patron.

# DISAPPEARING FORMATS

The Internet has resulted in the obsolescence of analog materials that once circulated well. An example of this is art prints. At UNK, art education majors used the art print posters in the classroom to illustrate famous artworks and styles. There are still a couple of lessons to be learned from the experience of maintaining the collection. When the art prints were first acquired, they were laminated. It was hoped that they would retain their condition better; however, it presented a different set of problems. With high usage, the laminate began to peel apart, making the posters less attractive and less usable. There is another lesson in housing the collection: At one time, the art prints were stacked on back-to-back library shelving units, taking up both sides of the shelves, in accession number order. Browsing, which required sifting through the stacks of prints, was difficult for patrons and made reshelving difficult. To address this issue, plywood cases were constructed. The cases were divided into small sections and the art prints placed vertically between the sections, in accession number order, with the range of accession numbers per division marked to aid in locating particular items. The prints curled as a result of this storage method. If large-format prints are part of a collection, map cases or some other horizontal storage method that keeps the prints flat but not stacked too deep, might prove to be a better solution for maintaining the integrity of the items.

Another example of a collecting strategy that has been made obsolete by new technologies is acquiring educational software on digital media. Online educational resources and interactive training tools are currently more likely to be accessed through apps or through the Web. Some items are useful in three-dimensional format but become less accurate as time passes, such as globes. The round format can help students understand the shape of the Earth, but the content can become outdated quickly as country boundaries and names change. New globes are rarely added to the collection, yet we do retain some globes to support the visualization of the world.

## THINGS THAT SEEM LIKE THEY SHOULD BE OBSOLETE

Some "things" in the collection seem like they should be obsolete but somehow have managed to persist. Picture cards are one of these items. BGSU has a large picture card collection. The collection is made up of published pictures (for example, images published in magazines and wall calendars) cut out of the publication and mounted on card stock. Patrons continue to borrow the pictures. Picture cards are useful in classroom instruction where a physical object is useful, particularly when three-dimensional objects are not available for the concept. Items are rarely added to the collection. The images are grouped by subject and stored in file cabinets, in hanging file folders. The classification system is local. The subject of the image is the first part of the classification system (for example, pets, flags, sports) and is shared by all similar images. Unique numbers are also assigned to each image within the subject. A descriptive label may be attached to provide a description of the contents of the image (for example, an image of a redheaded young girl with a shaggy dog may be described as "Little Orphan Annie and her pet dog named Sandy"). Each card has a bar code. The wide availability of pictures on the Internet may argue against the viability of such a collection. However, the value of the cards has to do with the tangibility of them. Students can interact through the images. A lesson on seasons, for example, can be made interactive by distributing picture cards to students and having them hold up the image that contains a winter scene. Even the youngest children can interact through images to discuss the main theme of the image.

## ASSESSMENT

Any collection of "things" needs to change and grow. When technology and information changes, a library of things needs to adapt. In the 1990s, formats still included vinyl records, film loops, filmstrips, slides, VHS tapes, and 8-mm/16-mm films. These formats have paved the way for DVDs and CDs, not to mention online streaming capabilities. Before making decisions regarding withdrawing or replacing items, an analysis of the things collection needs to occur to determine next steps. Make a list or a chart of criteria to be met (for example, the desired subject coverage and age levels). When considering withdrawing items, one of the first things to examine is circulation statistics. This would include the number of times the item circulated, was used within the library, and the last date it was circulated. Is the item's informational content up to date? If not, should something more recent replace the item? Would a new format enhance the usefulness of the resource? If so, is it available in the new format? There are times when the item might need to be retained in the old format due to its curricular value. If this is the case, how long should the old format remain in the collection? One might consider setting a time frame to revisit the question.

These types of changes invariably incur costs. Determine if the budget can accommodate the desired updates. If not, consider researching grant opportunities. When UNK withdrew vinyl records and replaced them with CDs, a grant was obtained to assist with the replacement costs. Grant opportunities change constantly, so monitoring funding resources should be ongoing. Keeping the collection current and usable will make it a valuable resource for students and faculty. For further information about collection development strategies, refer to the *Guidelines for Curriculum Materials Centers* on the American Library Association's website.[6]

## CONCLUSION

Curriculum collections can include a variety of things that can be integrated into existing library circulation processes. Reach out and develop working relationships with teaching faculty and learn about their curricular needs. By working with a variety of academic departments, as well as the cataloging and circulation departments within the library, the CMC director can help determine what practices will work best for the lending institution. On a final note, contact other CMC directors when you have questions about processing and collecting things.

## NOTES

1. See www.hand2mind.com.
2. See www.lakeshorelearning.com.
3. See www.jackdaw.com.
4. See www.teachercreatedmaterials.com.
5. For more about Folkmanis puppets, see www.folkmanis.com/17/home.htm; for RBI Sound Puppets, see rbitoyco.com/puppets.html; for Silly Puppets, visit shop.sillypuppets.com.
6. See www.ala.org/acrl/standards/guidelinescurriculum.

## REFERENCES

Akkan, Y. (2012). Virtual or physical: In-service and pre-service teacher's beliefs and preferences on manipulatives. *Turkish Online Journal of Distance Education (TOJDE), 13*(4), 167–192.

Clark, A. S. (1982). *Managing curriculum materials in the academic library.* Metuchen, NJ: Scarecrow Press.

Curriculum Materials Committee. (2008). *Guidelines for curriculum materials centers.* Retrieved from www.ala.org/acrl/standards/guidelinescurriculum.

Kennedy, L. M. (1986). A rationale. *Arithmetic Teacher, 33*(6), 6–7, 32.

Kohrman, R. (2012). From collections to laboratories to centers: Development of curriculum materials collections or centers to 1940. In R. Kohrman (Ed.), *Curriculum materials collections and centers: Legacies from the past, visions of the future* (pp. 3–21). Chicago, IL: Association of College and Research Libraries.

Lare, G. A. (2004). *Acquiring and organizing curriculum materials: A guide and directory of resources.* Lanham, MD: Scarecrow Press.

# 10

# Loaning Technology and Media Production Equipment

*Shelly McCoy*

## DEVELOPMENT OF AN IDEA: A SERVICE AND A PLACE

Academic libraries have offered limited circulation of audiovisual equipment for many years, mainly to allow access to film and video collections in many formats owned by the library. Published information on contemporary academic library media equipment–lending programs, however, is scarce (Jensen, 2007). Much of the circulation services described in the literature feature in-house use of equipment only, or have such serious restrictions on use of equipment that it is not possible to fairly compare those programs with ours. Most of the literature regarding circulation of devices has been about laptops, and most device circulation programs emulate those of laptops. Recently, articles in library literature have specifically described iPad lending programs (Shurtz et al., 2015). In some institutions the information technology (IT) department handles support of all "academic equipment." Loaning multimedia equipment directly ties into the mission of the library to meet research needs of the campus and support the University of Delaware (UD) strategic plan in research, creativity, innovation, entrepreneurship, global leadership, and more.

The idea for the Student Multimedia Design Center began as a proposal to provide the space, equipment, and software for students, faculty, and staff to create multimedia (defined as any combination of text, graphics, audio, or video). At the University of Delaware, there were pockets of these spaces, such as a closet in the Department of Communication, a video equipment cage in the Department of Art and Design, and an instructor-focused space staffed by campus IT. When many of these spaces closed for the day, access to this equipment or space also ended. Expertise to help in using the equipment and software was also limited, and there was no tie-in with multimedia literacy to show that these skills are needed for students to be successful. Because the University of Delaware Library is central to campus, is of an interdisciplinary nature, and is focused on service to students, faculty, and staff, the library was the right choice for this support.

The space and project culminating in the Student Multimedia Design Center were initially comanaged by the library and campus IT, continuing an existing relationship between the two campus units for the library computing site. The project itself morphed from 3,000 square feet in the proposal to 15,000 square feet on the lower level of the library. It merged the Microforms and Copy Services unit and Computing Site into one department with one service desk, using six existing staff and initially adding one new librarian (two additional librarians have since been added) to focus on coordinating services. Planning took place starting in 2005, with a steering committee of library and campus IT representatives, and also involved faculty focus groups.

In June 2006, construction began on renovating the lower level of the library where Microforms and Copy Services, the Computing Site, and the Map Room were located. Due to less of a need to provide public service to the map collection, this collection was downsized and moved to an open alcove on the same level. Microforms were then moved into the Map Room space, which was upgraded with a stand-alone HVAC system, opening a considerable amount of space on the lower level of the library. The library managed the space and staff and IT initially managed the computer hardware and software and training in the Student Multimedia Design Center. The Library Computing Site had 47 computers, and 33 computers were added with this project for a total of 80 computers between 2 computer lab spaces, 2 open computer workspaces, and 6 studios. This space is open to the rest of the library, although the computers are to be used only by the UD community, not the public who has access to the library. Based on years of networking with others who have multimedia spaces, I can confidently say that the Student Multimedia Design Center is one of the largest, if not the largest, such space focused on multimedia in an academic library in the nation.

Early in the planning for the Student Multimedia Design Center, I researched literacy programs related to media, sometimes called digital literacy, metaliteracies, or transliteracy. I knew that having such a program would contribute to the success of integrating multimedia into the curriculum at the University of Delaware and to the continued success of the Student Multimedia Design Center. I also knew that this was something that I did not have staffing to do initially and that staff had enough to learn about the technology needed to successfully operate the center.

## INITIAL PHILOSOPHY AND CONSIDERATIONS FOR EQUIPMENT TO LOAN

Before any equipment for loan was purchased for the Student Multimedia Design Center, discussions were held with the head of access services and the coordinator of circulation and reserve, who provided the steering committee with circulation policy options for the equipment, because it was to be loaned using the integrated library system (ILS). Questions considered included: Who should we allow to check out the equipment, and for how long? Would we allow renewals? What would the fines and fine schedule be? And what should the overdue e-mails say?

Determining the philosophy for loaning the equipment was an important step that came up at this time. Who is the audience for this service? Is the equipment only to be used if there is a class assignment? If so, how will users prove this? How does this process impact staff who work the service desk? What is the impact on library users who cannot check out the equipment? In researching the processes that other libraries followed to loan equipment, many different methods are available for making sure that the equipment is used correctly and for reasons that align with the philosophy: required orientations, training classes, class lists checked, or assignment information forms.

The philosophy for loaning equipment from the Student Multimedia Design Center became the basis of the center's mission statement, highlighting the importance of this service: "to meet the current and future needs of the increasing number of classes which involve creation of multimedia projects." Users were not to be asked whether or not they were checking out equipment for a class project. The thought was that, even if the students were not using the equipment for a class this time, supporting their learning of the equipment would empower them to use it for class next time, leading to new assignments and possibilities. In other words, the growth of the use of equipment would directly impact the growth of assignments to create multimedia. This hypothesis was found to be true.

## PURCHASING AND MAINTAINING EQUIPMENT: INITIALLY AND TODAY

Together with campus IT, who had experience informally loaning video equipment to faculty, a list of initial equipment to purchase was made. Initial equipment kits for loan included lighting kits (basic and advanced), memory card readers, digital still cameras, wireless microphones, various levels of video cameras, shotgun microphones, tripods, portable hard drives, high-end headphones, audio kits for computer-based recording, digital voice recorders, 8-mm/Hi8 digital transfer kit, Avid Media software dongles, and various cables and adapters. This list was based on what we thought provided a good core for multimedia creation. At other libraries, equipment was purchased based on demand by users and on the abilities of staff (Jensen, 2007). We read reviews of equipment and also considered the maintenance that would be needed to keep the cumulative of these kits up and running. The amount of equipment purchased for the center was informed by taking the number of studios: 4 video editing studios, a sound studio for recording and mixing audio, and a transfer studio for transferring VHS, digital, and DVD formats to other formats, and the 2 hands-on instruction rooms. We considered the size of the average class assigning multimedia, which was at that time 22 students. Dividing that amount into 4, for groups of 4 per video project, gave us 5 cameras needed per class. At least 4 video cameras and other related equipment kits were given "In Library Use

**FIGURE 10.1** Examples of the Types of Equipment Kits Available for Checkout in the Student Media Design Center.

Only" status to make sure that these items would be there for users when they needed them in a studio. There were 117 kits of 21 kit types beyond cables, adapters, and general-use headphones.

Since 2010, the library has managed all aspects of the Student Multimedia Design Center. Now equipment is purchased after a small group discussion among the department head, the coordinator of services, and a nonexempt technology support specialist regarding the needs of the users, needs of the center, training considerations, cost, reviews, functionality needs (for example, audio ports, threads on the lens for a protective filter, etc.). The same brand is bought for most of the video camera kits, Canon for the first five or six years, and now Sony, to make staff training a little easier. Three-year accidental damage warranties are purchased for all equipment kits, if possible. These warranties have been used to repair and replace damaged equipment kits over the years, often enough to have made them a worthwhile investment. Peripherals for the equipment are purchased at the same time to make it into a kit.

## THE BUILDING AND PROCESSING OF A KIT

A kit is composed of the main item, such as a video camera, and then items found to be essential in its use. The motivation behind loaning items as parts of kits rather than separately was to make sure that students—especially those who were not as experienced with making decisions about what they need at the time of checkout—got what they needed. These essential kit items have morphed over time based on use and new technology. Initially, video camera kits included the case/bag, camera, media card, UV filter, remote control, AC adapter, batteries, instruction booklet or sheet, and multiple cables to use to import the video footage. There are also optional items for some kits, such as extra batteries and adapters for microphone kits. Because of the number of pieces in the kit, it is important to have a process to check that the pieces are accounted for and that they are not damaged. Because the overdue fine that was decided upon was 15 dollars per day, staff knew that we needed to be accountable to the next user that everything is there and working as expected with a kit.

When new items are received, mostly from B&H Photo Video,[1] the kit is assembled and as many pieces as possible are labeled with an identifying bar code. The main kit item, such as a camera, and the kit bag are given a copy number and an identifying label: "Student Multimedia Design Center, Video Camera Kit basic #5." The rest of the items are given smaller "piece" bar codes. The exterior of the kit bag or case is labeled with a bright Sharpie marker with identifying label information. The inside of the kit may also have compartments labeled to show where certain pieces are stored, as it can be tricky to fit all of the pieces inside safely and securely. All of the kit pieces are listed on a laminated sheet that goes with the kit, often hanging from a key ring, so that users can check to make sure all the pieces are with the kit before returning it. This key ring also lists the loan policy, reminding borrowers that they are responsible for any damage and for making sure that all pieces are returned with the kit. The laminated sheet will also list items that could not be bar-coded, such as an SD card, the UV filter, or a wrist strap. This labeling process is used in part because library security tags were too large for the kit itself but were added to the kit bag.

Instruction manuals or tip sheets are printed from online manufacturer pages, copied, or created by staff. We found that the instructions are the most common kit piece to be lost, because many times they are placed on top of the main item in the equipment kit bag/case, meaning it was the first to fall out or be taken out. Date due slip holders were originally placed on these instruction booklets. We also tried to attach date due slip holders to tags attached to the outside of kits. Now, those who check out equipment are asked if they would like a date due slip at all, after staff verbally say the date due and the fine for late returns. Many decide they do not want one. Just this year we started sending a reminder e-mail to users before items are due. This has helped to get kits back on time and ready for the next user.

A request is sent to the library Metadata Services department to create a basic record or add a copy to a basic record for the library catalog. Each record lists the pieces that are with the kit. At that time, the item status is chosen to denote what kind of loan the equipment kit has. Most items in the Student Multimedia Design Center are three-day loans with no renewals. The item process status is listed as "temporarily unavailable" until staff are ready to loan the item.

In the meantime, staff spend time with the kit to go over the basics: how to turn it on, how to record, how to play back, how to delete footage, how to reset or check settings, how to connect other kits to this kit (microphone, tripods, etc.), and more. This information is the "script" of what staff cover with library users at the service desk during the checkout process. Upon check-in or check-out, staff take out every piece from the kit and then return each piece to the bag as it is scanned. This assures that other things that do not belong are not also in the kit, like a user's cable or a piece from another kit. This process also allowed us to have optional pieces for the kits, pieces that were offered to the user, but that were situation-dependent, such as certain cables, microphone adapters, and remote controls. Oftentimes, new types of kits are added in the slower times of the year for the center, summer sessions and January, so that staff have more time to become proficient in the use of new kits. Student group training happens at the beginning of the fall semester, and equipment kits are introduced at that time as well. Replacement of existing kits happens as needed throughout the year.

Once the kit is ready for use, staff change the item process status so that it shows as "available" in the catalog. The item is then added to the webpage list of equipment for loan, and promotional material is created for the webpage or for posters and displays in the center. Staff then show student staff the new kit. Because kits are seldom searched in the ILS, but users want to know what we have, an equipment kit page was created as part of the website. It lists the kits and links directly to the discovery system record for the item to easily see the availability.[2]

To make video cameras easier for users to request, we initially put them into three categories and cataloged them accordingly in the library's ILS as "basic," "intermediate," or "advanced" camera equipment, based largely on extras in terms of manual settings or options. When library users come to the service desk and ask for a video camera, they are asked, "Have you ever used a camera before?" If the answer is "No," the users are given a basic video camera. Users who ask for more specific needs for a camera are given an intermediate camera, and those who can use an advanced camera usually ask for a "broadcast-level" camera.

Because the determination of which camera to check out largely happens at the service desk, cameras are now cataloged and labeled only by their model name: "Video Camera Kit, Sony HXR-NX70U." It should be noted that all of the cameras purchased were consumer-level cameras and continue to be so today, although that line has become blurred due to the advancement of camera technology.

## SECONDARY CHECKOUT PROCESS

Specific to the Student Multimedia Design Center is a secondary check of equipment kit pieces. This part of the checkout process started as a paper form, modeled largely on the form that the Student Multimedia Studio at Kent State used. When a kit was checked out, a staff person pulled a matching folder for that particular kit. The folder contained a form that had a line for each item in the kit. Staff, at the beginning, had a corresponding place mat for each kit, which had all of the pieces life-size and labeled, so that the items could be pulled from the kit bag or case and placed on the place mat. The lines on the form that corresponded to the kit items were then checked off, the staff person initialed the form, and the user signed and dated the form, which also contained the policy that "the person who checks out this kit is responsible for damage to the kit or for loss of kit or kit pieces."

Within a few years of opening the Student Multimedia Design Center, this second part of the checkout process became electronic. Each of the pieces of the kits is given smaller bar codes. These bar codes are added to a departmentally maintained database, separate from the ILS, for the item. On checkout, staff start by scanning the main bar code of the kit, which pulls up the piece list, and then scanning each piece bar code to ensure that the items are there on checkout and check-in. The staff person inputs their initials to end this process and then the item is checked out from the library catalog. This process ensures that everything is in the kit and makes staff accountable for checking for damage.

## MAINTENANCE OF EQUIPMENT KITS

Equipment kits sustain normal wear and tear and require maintenance throughout the year. Some maintenance is done each time a kit is checked in and out, including cleaning the lens filter, swapping out batteries, and erasing internal memory. Other maintenance is done as needed, including replacement of bar codes and repair of kit bags.

After having equipment kits be checked out over spring break and not returned on time during the first year the center opened (and coming back with sand in the bags), it was decided to designate that week and the week right before the holidays as a maintenance week for the camera kits, video and still, in particular. Center staff go through each kit individually and assess for wear, cleaning as needed. A sign is put up in advance of these weeks so that users know about the maintenance period. Those students who are on campus and doing valid projects during these weeks can ask us to make exceptions to allow cameras to be checked out. Staff are also encouraged to check out equipment kits during the maintenance times so that they have time to continue to practice with them.

Kits are flagged in the secondary checkout system if maintenance needs to be done and to stop a kit from going out. Detailed notes are also added to this system if a user reports a problem with a piece of equipment, even if staff cannot replicate the problem. Continued failure rates and complaints are reasons to take the equipment out of circulation completely.

## IMPACT OF LOANING ON OTHER SERVICES

One bit of information that cannot be underrepresented is the impact of the service of loaning equipment on other services. Equipment loaning is just one of the services offered from the Student Multimedia Design Center service desk. Equipment kits and the checkout process of equipment kits take up a great deal of physical space themselves. You have to also consider convenience in grabbing a kit from its storage spot to check it out for a user, secure storage for the kit whenever the desk is closed but the library is open, and proximity to alternative kits (if a specific type of kit is checked out). Consider whether it is worth creating secure storage space at a service desk for a number of the equipment kits so that these kits are at an arm's length when they are requested for checkout. Convenience to kits mean less staff time away from the desk and the face-to-face contact with users.

The desk at the Student Multimedia Design Center was originally designed for style as opposed to function in terms of materials used. The matte Corian top was getting scratched from kits being slid across the desk, so we quickly ordered a glass protective surface to go on top. The weight of the kits in the drawers caused them to eventually sag and not close correctly; and there was so little space for the lock to bite into the frame for the drawers that it became like a secret handshake to lock and unlock the drawers. A new service desk was designed a few years ago that had solid wood drawers, industrial-grade drawer slides, and was bigger than the previous desk, using all possible space for equipment storage. Instead of semicircular in shape, it is hexagonal. The top was made from a Corian with a pattern that hides the scratches well.

As the number of kits grew, some lesser-requested equipment kits were stored in the office behind the service desk. This configuration meant that staff either had to run back to the office to grab some kits to refill the front spots, or had to go back there to get a kit. Drawers were labeled with card catalog drawer–type label holders, so that as equipment kits were moved around, labels were changed and staff had to get used to new locations again. Optional pieces for kits, cables, and adapters for loan offered their own storage challenges, in that we wanted to keep them separated to easily find them and to keep them neat. Staff ended up creating drawer organizers out of cardboard, which were then labeled and put in the deeper drawers of the service desk. This organization makes quick work of finding what you need while working at the desk; it also relies on users and staff to neatly wind cables and cords so that they do not become entangled.

Loaning equipment impacts other services at the desk and other staff. Staff cannot stop in the middle of the loaning process to help another library user, as it would be easy to overlook damage on a kit or miss putting all of the pieces in the equipment kit. During the busiest times of the semester, all four staff scheduled at the desk could be checking out equipment kits at once. To call other staff to help in times like this, a wireless doorbell that rings back in the staff office was installed.

When kits are returned, we ask that users stay at the desk while checking it back in so that they know it was returned correctly. If a piece of the kit is missing, the initial check-in process is stopped and the kit is returned to the user until he/she finds the missing piece or declares it missing so that we can bill the user. This means that staff cannot put equipment kits aside for check-in at a later, less busy time; everything must be checked in at the time of return. Because equipment kits were being returned right at the service desk closing time of midnight, the return time was changed to be 30 minutes before closing. If a user still has a habit of returning right at closing, the supervisor talks to that user about incurring late charges for not returning a kit on time.

# IMPACT OF SPACES ON LOANING

Other spaces also have an impact on equipment loaning. The studios are spaces that can be reserved a week in advance and are only for multimedia work or for practicing presentations. These six rooms are locked at all times, and staff let users who are vetted for their use into the rooms. Users sometimes need to come to check out hard drives or other equipment in the middle of their studio sessions.

The two hands-on instruction spaces (one with Mac computers and one with PCs) are available to reserve by instructors who need computers to teach a hands-on class session. These rooms are open for individual student use when they are not reserved, so a class cannot be scheduled there for the whole semester or be reserved during the last three weeks of the semester, when all available space in the library is at its highest demand. Classes using the labs and also needing to check out equipment can present a bit of challenge unless the instructor or class comes early to check out equipment or the instructor tells us in advance that equipment will be needed for the class.

Our reservation system features an online form for faculty to reserve the instruction rooms and a form to be filled out from the service desk by staff whenever students call or stop by to reserve a studio. This homemade system is not tied with our ILS. It is a calendar system that displays all information about the class gleaned from the instructor-submitted reservation form on a staff-only calendar, and strips this information so that only the class name displays on the public calendar.

The other result related to space is that, because the center is an open space, any library users could come and use the computers in the open areas and the hands-on instruction rooms for multiple purposes—not just for multimedia. This is one of the advantages of the Student Multimedia Design Center in comparison to other such spaces, in that the users rely on the computers to be able to multitask and to complete all of their work. All computers in the center have access to the black-and-white as well as the color printer; staff need to be away from the desk to provide support for that service as well.

# SERVICE DESK STAFFING

The Student Multimedia Design Center consists of over 70 computers, roughly half Mac and half PC in open spaces, 6 studios, and 2 hands-on instruction rooms. This space is open, so there are no doors to close the unit earlier than other parts of the library. This also means that it was necessary for the desk to be staffed many of the hours that the library was open, 110 hours a week, with exempt, nonexempt, and student staff.

All Student Multimedia Design Center staff have assigned hours at the service desk, which is in front of the staff office space. Those who work evening and weekend shifts spend more of their shifts on the service desk, approximately six hours as opposed to three and a half, and are primarily in charge of the space in the absence of the department head. Typically, two students are at the desk with at least one staff person, librarian or nonlibrarian, at all times. A staff backup is also scheduled, meaning that person will not sit at the desk, but will be available to call out to if the desk gets busy. At certain times of the day, four people are needed at the service desk and others are reached in the adjacent staff office by pushing a wireless doorbell.

Library users expect those at the service desk to be able to help them or refer them to someone else who can. These high expectations mean that student staff are hired who are already proficient in at least one video editing software and who have customer service skills; they are paid a dollar more per hour than other places in the library for these skills. Nonexempt and salaried staff are also hired for their mix of technology and customer service skills.

## BUDGET IMPACTS

The Student Multimedia Design Center has a budget of roughly $30,000 to $50,000 per year to spend on computer hardware, software, and equipment from the state of Delaware. This is not enough money to maintain 70 computers or to even purchase Adobe Creative Cloud yearly for the site. What is not spent on student wages can be used toward equipment, so there is a delicate balancing act of making sure we have enough staffing to provide excellent customer service and hoping there is money left to purchase cameras for the following semester. So far, it is working, but not without money from other library budgets.

Year-end money means making decisions to purchase items quickly, so there is always a wish list section of the ledger spreadsheet with items ready to purchase at any time. Information to make purchasing easier, such as where to buy equipment parts for tripods, is important when you want to replace damaged or missing parts and get the equipment ready again as soon as possible for the students who rely on it. Purchases of computer hardware and software add the additional layer of working with the library IT group to discuss and have them purchased.

Although some university libraries have expanded these lending programs to accommodate the demand, others have had to reduce and in some cases cancel these high-demand and well-positioned services due to lack of staffing and reduced budgets. Computer hardware has to last longer, it is harder to justify getting a new kind of computer software, and new types of equipment we would like to try may go by the wayside for well-reviewed equipment that we know works and will be used.

## WHAT WE LEARNED

Maintaining the Student Multimedia Design Center for several years has led to a range of insights about how this service can best meet students' needs. This section presents some of the key lessons we have learned and the resulting improvements we have made to the center's services.

## Need for Multimedia Literacy Program

In the center's early days, the coordinator of the Student Multimedia Design Center Services would work with classes to provide an orientation to the space and services, but staff saw a disconnect between students' excitement about what they could do and their knowledge of what to do next. We felt that there was also a lingering gap in the multimedia literacy competencies that instructors often expect students to already have and the knowledge and skills that students actually possess. Students would come to the service desk and say that they had an assignment to make a video, but they did not know where to start.

In January 2012, Renee Hobbs spoke about transforming higher education through digital and media literacy at the University of Delaware Winter Faculty Institute. There was a positive response to what she presented, but no plans were announced on how to move forward. In the meantime, I was already talking to a resident librarian about my wish to provide this type of instruction. We met with the coordinator of instruction in reference and a manager in IT-Academic Technology Services to propose the structure of this instruction program and the continued collaboration our departments would have. We defined multimedia literacy as "the set of abilities that enables an individual to effectively find, interpret, evaluate, use, and create multimedia." With this set of abilities, students are able to critically think about what they want to convey in their multimedia projects and understand how they can do this using the media and technology tools that are provided at the Student Multimedia Design Center.

Multimedia literacy embraces interdisciplinary connections across campus and community and allows students to make sense of and take part in the mediated messages around them. These are competencies that students need to critically engage in society today, and libraries need to equip students with the tools that they need to do so. Now, the multimedia literacy program reaches almost 1,000 students each semester, most recently from 12 different departments, and continues to grow.

The multimedia literacy program had two impacts on the loaning of equipment: we needed to ensure that a number of equipment kits were available for teaching these multimedia literacy sessions, and we also had to try to ensure that we had enough equipment kits to meet the demands of students working on assignments in those classes. As a first step, a number of equipment kits were purchased and then held back for teaching the sessions; then six to eight kits, including video cameras and tripods, were put in kit bags of a different color and held back specifically for student groups from those classes to request from the service desk. These class-only cameras became an incentive for those classes to use the multimedia literacy program.

This program has been working well so far, and the three librarians now involved in multimedia literacy instruction continually reassess their methods. Although students may use their own video equipment, such as cell phones, we find that most projects still involve the use of the Student Multimedia Design Center equipment. A cell phone accessory kit was created to give users ways to improve the quality of video and audio taken on their cell phones.

The expectation of librarian staff that provide the multimedia literacy instruction is to create lasting relationships with faculty and departments on campus and to showcase their value by the success of the projects created, whether by faculty or students. These librarians are still given desk hours to be seen by their students and to not lose sight of what happens daily at the service desk. The service desk also provides an informal method of assessment by allowing those instructors to see the impact of their instruction on the students who come to the desk and ask for help.

## Safety, Liability

Out of all of the equipment kits for loan, the light kits are the ones that can get hot enough to burn someone. In fact, despite warnings, those kits have been put away while they were still warm, causing plastic kit pieces to melt. Now users are required to watch a two-minute safety video that staff created semester before they can check out the three-point lighting kit.

The other liability issue may be surprising for some to hear, but in purchasing and trying various battery chargers for the kits for loan and power adapters for laptops, we have found that only the brand name chargers for these items work best and do not burn up, although they do get very warm! We put warning labels on these items, and it is up to users to make sure that they are using the appropriate chargers and adapters for their technology.

## Equipment Kit Reservation

Some student projects involve interviewing subjects for their projects, so they need to schedule the interviews in advance. Others involve recording a music practice or recital on a specific day. In the past, it was a toss-up whether or not the kit would be available, especially if a DSLR was being requested, because kits are first come, first served. This has led to some very unhappy users who had to reschedule interviews or use a type of equipment they were not familiar with due to all of the other kits being checked out. This has also led to interviews being scheduled to take place in the center just to ensure camera availability. Because of these types of projects, one kit was made available for reservation. This kit contains a camera, tripod, and wireless lavalier microphone. Users reserve it by completing and submitting a Google form, then by staff through the scheduling module of our OCLC discovery system. The policy is that the user must have a reason for needing the kit on a specific date and that reason must be "UD-related." There was much hesitation in going in this direction, the main concern being that users may not return the kit on time for the next person, but the thought is that the benefits outweighed the risks.

## Relationship Forming and Marketing

Word gets around with very little promotional effort that various equipment kits can be checked out for free from the library with a valid UD identification card. Students working for other offices and units on campus offer that they know where to find equipment that can be used, and in low-budget times, these offices turn to making their own promotional videos and photos. For example, faculty members who were taking a group to Ghana for a Study Abroad program wanted to borrow equipment kits for a month. This increase in use of the Student Multimedia Design Center by staff was an unanticipated effect of the success of the center and has led to some great relationship forming with units such as Residence Life, the English Language Institute, and others. The challenge has been gingerly telling these groups that the top-priority audience is for the students, and then faculty, and then staff. Although exceptions have been made in some circumstances, we are firm with sticking to the first-come, first-served, three-day loan policy and have recommended cameras for purchase by these groups, some of which are grant funded, so that cameras are not taken away from students for this period of time.

## Lessons Learned

Policies and procedures were adjusted several times over the years to accommodate lessons learned. In just two years from opening the center, the number of equipment kits swelled to 24 different types of kits of 245 items for loan. Equipment purchases were strongly influenced by what was used the most. The following are some examples of what we found worked and did not work.

### *Durability*

Durability is another consideration when exploring purchasing kits. Some of the first things to break because of a durability factor were headphones. Students like to use headphones throughout the library, and service desk staff saw how quickly cheap headphones broke. We invested in slightly higher-quality headphones that seemed to have a better connection between the wires and the headphones itself and nonfoam earpieces.

Kits that have pieces made of cheap plastic never last as long as those coated with rubber. For instance, for external hard drives, we purchase the LaCie Rugged hard drive that has a rubber protective sleeve on the outside to provide some more protection for the drive itself.

When looking at kit durability, we had never considered how one opens the battery compartment to be an important consideration. In the case of our first digital voice recorders, the tabs that hold the cover on the battery compartment got smashed when users would push down instead of sliding the compartment closed. Batteries were taken in and out so often that the tabs would quickly become broken. Battery covers would not stay closed, and staff had to MacGyver the equipment using Velcro wraps to keep these covers on.

In the same vein, stress on ports of the cameras and on the computers themselves became an issue. Damage was often not easily apparent visually, and staff could not test each port whenever kits were returned to the desk; we would just find out about the damage when a user would inform us of a problem getting footage off a camera. When most cameras used MiniDV tapes or memory cards, this was not as large of an issue. Now that internal memory is most common, staff have to gingerly prompt the ports to work at least one more time to get user footage off the cameras. Once the footage is retrieved, if we're lucky, the camera is sent to have the port repaired. On computers, which often have more than one port, we found that users would not tell us that a port was not working but would simply move on to the next port. Staff performed some testing during slower times to identify and tape over bad ports, if they could not be repaired right away.

## Technology Evolution

Evolution of video production technology happens quickly. In early 2011, the first GoPro video camera was purchased for loan. Since then, several other versions and peripheral equipment have been purchased. Sports cameras have opened up many options for video camera use for research and creativity.

We added a Blu-ray burner kit to the collection when computers started to come standard without DVD burners. This new kit helped to cover the evolution of computer hardware and also to meet the needs of those who wanted to produce Blu-ray discs.

In loaning iPads, we had to come up with an image to give a basic app tool set, but allow users to log in with their own Apple ID to download their own apps as well. This need for personal access to a multiuser device means resetting the iPad to the factory default and then loading the image we created with certain apps, the library wallpaper, etc., when the iPad is returned. This procedure takes a bit of time and could mean leaving an iPad connected at a service desk computer for this work to happen when the iPads are returned, but it has not been much of a problem. At first iPads were only four-hour loans, but since we changed the loan period to three days, the iPads have been consistently checked out.

Although technology continues to evolve, we decided to keep older cameras that are still in working order to have something for users when all of the new technology is checked out and for staff to use for longer-term projects of their own. There comes a certain point in the semester when every available piece of equipment is checked out.

## Circulation Policy Lessons

We knew in setting up the original circulation policies that some tweaking of the policies would be needed based on issues that would arise after real use and circulation of the equipment. For instance, we originally allowed renewal of cameras, but it caused too many problems with the same students renewing the same kits over and over. Currently, equipment kits have a 24-hour wait time between checking them in and back out. Students have found a way around this by having others in their group come to the service desk to request checkout of the same equipment soon after it is returned. Fortunately, this has not been a huge problem so far, and staff have been able to suggest alternative options to groups who come in to check out something and all equipment kits are out, such as recording using one of the in-studio cameras or the new one-button studio.

### *Batteries*

Batteries and the space and process needed for battery charging should not be underestimated. When a kit is returned, we replace the batteries with fresh ones from the drawer. When the "used" batteries section of the drawer gets full or there is a lull at the service desk, these batteries are taken into the office to the charging area. Any fully charged batteries on the chargers are then moved to the appropriate sections of the drawer. When checking out a kit, we do not need to do anything with the batteries because we will presume they are fresh ones that were installed at check-in.

### *Inventory*

Having a spreadsheet of the equipment as an inventory has been helpful. This spreadsheet tracks the date equipment was purchased, added to the collection, taken out of the collection, the serial number, and whether it was sent for maintenance or was damaged. It is amazing how many items can show up missing, even with a closed-stack collection, and how many items end up on staff desks.

## THE FUTURE

At the University of Delaware Student Multimedia Design Center, the future will continue to be shaped not only by the university community's needs, but also by an expansion to the broader community. Engagement with the community through classes, high school programs, summer camps, and research is a priority for the whole campus. Collaborations with others on campus will become more important, with the first formal collaboration happening a year ago with the College of Arts and Sciences to create a Multimedia Writing Center adjacent to the Student Multimedia Design Center. The philosophy of meeting the needs of the community—whether it is providing equipment that they would not be able to afford otherwise, or making the connection to multimedia literacy—is something we continue to strive for on campus.

As media evolve, users will still need multimedia literacy skills, just as they need information literacy skills, to guide them along. Like at the University of North Carolina-Pembroke, procedures at the Student Multimedia Design Center continue to evolve and be redefined as the technology changes and the needs of our users change (Power, 2007). The trickle-down effect will also mean other changes, as this loaning service does impact other services in the department and is impacted by space. Multimedia production equipment and technology can be an expensive investment and have a limited life span in terms of the physical wear, as well as their popularity (Shurtz et al., 2015). As technology continues to advance, staff will keep pace, but what will future staffing expertise and responsibilities be? Proactively reaching out to get feedback, whether through formal or informal assessment methods, will also go a long way toward helping to determine equipment needs (Anderson & Weatherbee, 2012).

When the University of Delaware Library Student Multimedia Design Center opened in February 2007, David E. Hollowell, the executive vice president at the time, remarked: "The faculty told us that there were needs that they could not fulfill, and that new things were starting to develop, with new types of laboratories, and the ideas started to bubble up. . . . I think this will be a great success and a great asset to our students now and for years to come."

# NOTES

1. See www.bhphotovideo.com.
2. See library.udel.edu/multimedia/equipment-kits.

# REFERENCES

Anderson, S., & Weatherbee, S. (2012). Growing a technology equipment service in an academic library. *Computers in Libraries, 32*(6), 6–8.

Jensen, K. (2007). Beyond "classroom" technology: The equipment circulation program at Rasmuson Library, University of Alaska Fairbanks. *Journal of Access Services, 5*(1–2), 221–231.

Power, J. L. (2007). Circulation on the go: Implementing wireless laptop circulation in a state university academic library. *Journal of Access Services, 5*(1–2), 197–209.

Shurtz, S., Sewell, R., Halling, T. D., McKay, B., & Pepper, C. (2015). Assessment of an iPad loan program in an academic medical library: A case study. *Medical Reference Services Quarterly, 34*(3): 265–281.

# 11

# Faculty/Librarian Collaboration in the Age of Media: Building a Collection of Media Services to Support the Integration of Video Production into the Curriculum

*Mitchell Shuldman*

Media Services is one of three divisions that make up the University of Massachusetts Lowell Library. We offer a wide range of services to all sectors of the university for anything and everything media, assisting faculty, students, staff, and the occasional Mr. or Ms. Public-at-Large. We accommodate all levels of walk-in service from equipment loans and on-the-spot media conversions, to general advice on how to create a media project including one-on-one hands-on editing instruction. However, when a faculty member commits to integrating a video production assignment into their course, we offer a deeper, more complete set of services. These services that further the library aims of information, media and technology literacy, reposition librarians back into the heart of the academic process, and most importantly, facilitate learning and enhance the academic experience through the educational use of multimedia technologies.

# BACKSTORY

Twelve years ago (2004), the library's Division of Media Services, more commonly known as the Media Center, was awarded a grant from the university provost's office that allowed us to recruit faculty interested in assigning their students a video production assignment. Three faculty members signed on at the time and were each offered a single course buyout in exchange for working closely with the library to design and implement a video production assignment on a topic that lies within the curriculum of their course. This collection of services, although perhaps not out of the ordinary today, was surely more so in 2004. Since that time, supporting student production projects has become a major focus of the Media Center. For the past 12 years, we have offered a coordinated collection of ICT (information and communication technology) instruction and services to faculty interested in adopting and integrating a video production assignment into their syllabi. In support of asking their students to produce a short three- to five-minute documentary-style video, the library brings a collection of media and related services to bear on the design, implementation, instruction, and support of the production assignment. This includes individual faculty consultations along with in-class, in-lab, and on-site student instruction and support. We loan all the equipment students will need to be successful, and we house, support, and maintain the lab where they do their work. We supply the computers and the software along with on-site hands-on application and technical support. We help students find, download, and cite media resources. And we help them to better understand media file formats and conversions while fostering an appreciation for the tricky legal and ethical issues surrounding copyright, plagiarism, and fair use. In short, we help students become more skillful users and creators of scholarly digital content.

The pilot project that led to the grant was a three-way, multidisciplinary collaboration that asked English majors enrolled in a newswriting course to create short video stories on a variety of topics related to concepts of sustainability and sustainable practices as championed by the UMass Lowell Toxic Use Reduction Institute. Topics from this first round of projects ranged from campus recycling efforts to the toxic materials used in beauty cosmetics. The grant also allowed us to expand our initial offering of media equipment to support what we knew would be a growing number of projects. At that time, we purchased 10 complete kits of consumer-level video production equipment that included Canon Elura MiniDV tape camcorders, Samsung wireless lavalier microphones, tripods, lights (Lowel light kits), external hard drives, and other peripheral devices and cables. This collection has grown over the years as the library continued to make modest investments in equipment and technology updates. Today, we have enough equipment to accommodate 20 simultaneous production projects. We offer Canon Vixia SD card cameras (HF M400 and 500) and a few other production tools and toys like portable green screens, LED light kits, a Tiffen Steadicam JR for iPhones and other small video cameras, and a never-ending supply of SD cards.

# FACILITIES AND STAFFING

The University of Massachusetts Lowell, one of five university campuses in the UMass system, is the result of a 1976 merger of two separate institutions a mile apart and separated by the mighty Merrimack River. The north side of the river was formerly the Lowell Technological Institute. And on the south side, Lowell State College. A consequence of this merger is two separate library buildings to staff and to maintain, one on each side of the river, with duplicate basic services, which is difficult in even the best of times. The Lowell campus has witnessed unprecedented growth in the past eight years. We currently have a student body (undergraduate, graduate, and online) of more than 17,000 students, up from a head count of 11,000 in 2007 and a stated goal of 21,000 by 2020. Although student and faculty ranks have exploded over the past several years, the same has not been true for the library.

The Division of Media Services (located on the South Campus) is a small operation with two professional librarians, two support staff, and one very skilled part-time evening support supervisor overseeing four work-study students. We are open 68 hours a week (Monday through Thursday, 7:30 a.m. to 10:00 p.m., and Friday until 5:00 p.m.), with no weekend service. We house a media lab with 22 public computers (iMacs), all of which are loaded with multimedia productivity software including the complete Adobe Creative Cloud (CC), Final Cut Pro X, and iMovie. Each machine also has video/audio conversion software (Wondershare), audio recording and production software (Audacity and GarageBand), and the full Microsoft Office suite. In addition, we have two small rooms (7-by-8 feet) set aside for audio recording. These former preview rooms are not soundproof but they do have a door, giving a relative sense of privacy. Each room is equipped with a Shure SM58 vocal microphone hooked up to a small Mackie mixer with a line-in connection to the computer. The South Campus Library Media Center is the only facility of its kind anywhere on either campus.

The South Campus Library recently converted its bibliographic instruction lab from 25 Virtual Desktop Interface (VDI) boxes to 25 iMacs, all loaded with media productivity software. The VDI boxes, which present a virtual Windows desktop interface, do not support video or other CPU-intensive media work very well. This new lab configuration now allows students to sign out their projects from the Media Center, many of which are stored on external hard drives, and continue to work after hours and on the weekend. At the same time, it offers the library an opportunity to repurpose the instructional lab into a bona fide creative teaching and learning space.

Offering the same level of media support on two campuses has not been possible. As a consequence, the North Campus media facility is staffed by only one support person and a small contingent of work-study students who are mostly responsible for supporting the group study rooms of the learning commons and lending a small complement of equipment, cables, and DVDs/VHS tapes that support the business, science, and engineering focus of the campus.

# THE INITIATIVE: VIDEO PRODUCTION ASSIGNMENTS

Integrating a video production project as a major course assignment may not be everyone's cup of tea. Interestingly however, in our experience, we have always found faculty members, even those without any of the requisite technology skills, who can see the advantages that learning to "write" with these new media technologies brings to their students. Over the past 13 years, we have formally collaborated more than 55 times in 20 courses across more than a dozen different disciplines. We have worked with 13 faculty members and nearly 2,000 students who, all combined, have produced more than 350 video projects. Looked at another way, this is nearly 24 hours of continuous student-created content.

We have successfully integrated this project assignment into health, history, education, English, business/management, and more recently science, specifically virology, ecology, and climate change. These collaborations place the Library Media Center on the frontlines of student success and squarely inside faculty syllabi offering library supports and services that facilitate learning and enhance the academic experience. One shining example of success was the university's recognition on the President's Honor Roll for Community Service, with distinction, in 2009 and 2010. A collaborative project integrating video production with the Department of Community Health and Sustainability's community service learning initiative was one of the three campus projects cited.[1] Other examples are the climate change videos and public service announcements[2] that students have produced working under a NASA grant that puts digital media tools into the hands of students, allowing them to engage directly with climate change science while learning the tools that will help empower their own voices (Rooney-Varga et al., 2015).

These production assignments, which account for anywhere between 10 to 40 percent of a student's final grade, have all been in nonmedia disciplines. Why nonmedia disciplines? In my view, if a university offers a degree in a media-based discipline like journalism or digital media and communication studies, then it is the department or the college that would ensure students have access to the tools and labs they need to do their work. My interest, and I would argue the library's broader interest, is in everyone else. That would be, for example, students who need to learn these technologies so they can better promote health messages in their communities. Or future scientists who need to learn to communicate more effectively to nonscientists. In this day and age, students need to be more than simply content consumers. They also need to be content creators and digital scholars in their fields, learning to write and express their ideas and disciplinary knowledge with digital media (Lippincott, 2007). And if, in the process, they become smarter, savvier consumers of media, better able to bring a critical perspective to the media they encounter every day, then all the better. It has been suggested that only those who can "read and write the multimedia language of the screen" will be considered truly literate (Daley, 2003, p. 34).

The library's role in this regard, as a central resource, is to support all disciplines and ensure that all students have an equal opportunity to learn to communicate with these multimedia tools. The interest here is not to teach media technology as a subject unto itself nor to teach students to be filmmakers, but rather, to give students in nonmedia disciplines opportunities to gain a better understanding of the tools and technologies, to develop production skills and their accompanying literacies, to learn to use these new tools to further their understanding of their discipline, and in the end, to be able to communicate in new ways with a new and different set of tools, in multiple formats, and on multiple platforms.

This story of integrating media production into the curriculum is just a modern-day version of the original role and function of a university media center. Nonprint information has always been the responsibility of the library. And it has always required a variety of technologies to both read and write the language of a particular medium. Those of us who have been in the media field for a time have witnessed a remarkable evolution from 16-mm film, through three-quarter-inch U-matic, and half-inch VHS to DVD and now digital streaming. We have seen the transformation from analog to digital audio as well the almost limitless capabilities of relatively inexpensive, easy-to-use graphic editing programs. Many media formats have come and gone over the past 40 years, including the 15 minutes of fame for the videodisc. In the 1980s, we taught students and faculty how to edit half-inch VHS video. We loaned "portable" video cameras and half-inch recording decks before lightweight camcorders were available. We had VHS control track tape-to-tape editing stations. Faculty and students borrowed 35-mm film cameras to create multicarousel slide shows with programmable and synced narrative audio. In the 1990s, we began to seriously dabble with digital video when stuttering small-form video (320 by 240) was the best one could do. And yet, it was amazing at the time and held great promise for the future.

However, once the world went digital, everything changed—except our underlying mission! The difference today is that it is now possible and affordable for anyone and everyone to make a video . . . and they do! Regardless of the technology du jour, our job was the same then as it is today, that is, to collect media content to support the curriculum and discipline strengths of the university, and to facilitate the use of media information and technologies for the purpose of teaching and learning. Alongside the many classes that adopt this more intensive project, we also work with other faculty and students interested in creating their own media-based digital scholarship. We assist multiple hundreds of students each year in producing video and other various multimedia coursework, and we continue to work with faculty to create instructional media materials.

## EDUCATIONAL VALUE

"What is the value of having students create documentary-style videos?" "Why should I do this?" "What will I have to change or do differently?" "How will this affect my teaching?" "What would I be giving up in terms of instructional time or content?" These are just a few of the many questions that are part of the mental cost-benefit analysis that every faculty member must go through as they consider adopting an assignment like this.

This assignment is a project-based, active, and experiential learning activity all rolled into one. It facilitates learning by engaging students with the course content throughout the process of creating the video. Video production is recognized as a versatile and effective learning strategy that instills not only creative and critical thinking, (Meeks & Ilyasova, 2003; New Media Consortium, 2008; Rooney-Varga et al., 2015; Shewbridge & Berge, 2004), but also seems to have no disciplinary boundaries. This is a time-intensive process where we see students develop a strong sense of ownership of the material. As a consequence, they learn science, or history, or concepts of health promotion. At the same time, they are learning new media tools, technologies, skills, and literacies, which are all part of a larger set of 21st-century skills (Rooney-Varga et al., 2014; Tajik, Shuldman, & Garlo, 2011). Students hone their collaboration skills and learn to work with others. They learn time management and are often pushed to step up to a leadership role to move their project forward.

This assignment essentially asks students to become experts, with a small "e," on a topic and then to turn right around and explain what they have just learned to someone else, only in the form of a video. They are being asked to synthesize this new knowledge into a limited number of words—and minutes. A three- to five-minute video script is only about two and a half pages of double-spaced text, not a lot of time or space to convey all one has learned. Anyone who has ever written an abstract for a research article can appreciate this challenge. To be brief, clear, and succinct, both in writing and in the marriage of images to words, students have to be fluent with the content and have a solid understanding of their topic. The final video is a reflection of this knowledge and learning, as is a written paper.

Video production is an iterative process of research, writing, editing, and rewriting. Scripts almost always go through multiple drafts, offering double duty as a writing assignment (Courtney, 2014). Faculty frequently require students to submit a draft of the narrative before they can begin to create their video. Students experience postproduction as an iterative process as well, changing images, testing different transitions, even rewriting and re-recording the narration as needed. All the while, they are continually in direct contact with the course content, which can only serve to deepen their learning.

The power of technology in this vision "is not simply its potential to replicate existing education practice, but its ability to encourage students to engage in deeper cognitive activity" (Hooper & Rieber, 1995, p. 163). These words get to the heart of using technology to facilitate learning. The relationship and level of engagement between the students, the content, the technology, and the production process contributes to their learning. Students are learning with technology, not from technology. Using technology in this way asks students to collaborate and problem solve with a common purpose. They are faced with having to think critically, ask questions, discuss and defend their ideas with their peers, and reflect on their learning. They have to learn how to listen, collaborate, compromise, lead, manage their time effectively, and exercise tact and social finesse while engaging in critical and creative discussions.

We have observed, and to some extent participated in, all of these activities and interactions in the Media Center. Students talk strategy and process. They discuss content and debate their written narrative and image choices, as well as aesthetic and technical considerations of pacing, transitions, music, and audio levels. To be successful, students must become functionally fluent with information in its many forms, develop a broad understanding of the ICT land-scape, and a working knowledge of basic library research. They must exercise critical thinking to evaluate information resources and become more comfort-able with the technologies required to access and make use of this information. They begin to understand the implications of changing notions of authority as it relates to the trustworthiness and reliability of information and develop a general familiarity with how to use media to communicate effectively. A more in-depth look at how ICT skills and literacies map to the video production pro-cess can be found in one of my earlier publications (Shuldman, 2013).

On top of all this, students actually get their "hands dirty," so to speak, as they learn to create a video. They are introduced to the equipment and its accom-panying skill set. They create and gather digital media resources and concep-tualize what their video will look like. They learn to manage their media assets, organize their files, and keep track of citations for both their media and text-based research. Some projects require students to videotape and transcribe interviews, and then weave select sound bites ("quotes") into their narrative. As they become more familiar with the media technologies, they can begin to see for themselves how this particular set of tools allows them to communicate differently than pen and paper. A colleague once suggested that one think of the video production process like an iceberg, where the final video product is just the tip above the water that is easily evident, while the vast majority of the work and the learning is down "below the surface," evident during its creation (Rooney-Varga et al., 2015, p. 5).

## ENGAGEMENT THEORY

Technology is also recognized as an effective tool to facilitate student engage-ment, and engagement leads to learning. Underlying much of the thinking behind this initiative has been a particular vision of engagement theory. In 1998, Kearsley and Shneiderman introduced a framework for student engagement that suggested technology as a perfect catalyst to facilitate deeper learning through an active, purposeful collaborative group project that has an external, outside-of-the-classroom, real-world focus. The authors characterize these core principles best as "relate, create, and donate," that is, students work together in teams (relate: engage with one another), create a project (create: hands-on engagement with the technology) that has meaning beyond the classroom (donate: civic engagement, service learning), and whose activities encourage and engage "active cognitive processes such as creating, problem solving, reason-ing, decision making, and evaluating" (Kearsley & Shneiderman, p. 20). All of the more than 350 projects completed to date have been grounded in this ideal of "relate, create, and donate."

## A COLLECTION OF SERVICES

When a faculty member agrees to adopt a multimedia assignment, a whole set of media and other related services are offered. This begins with any number of one-on-one conversations to help faculty members better understand what they are about to ask their students to do, how the students will go about doing it, and the supports they will receive. We talk about project design and assignment structure, benchmarks, outcomes, expectations, and assessment. The students themselves receive multiple levels of in-class and in-lab instruction and support ranging from basic equipment operation (both in-class and one-on-one as needed), to troubleshooting, production guidance and advice, script editing, and audio/video recording and editing instruction and support. We throw in a sympathetic ear, when necessary. And, inevitably, we cover issues of copyright and other complexities that arise with the use of online digital media particularly fair use, the repurposing of copyrighted materials, proper citation, and their rights as students to assert fair use for educational purposes.

## In-Class Instructional Services

We offer a series of in-class instructional sessions with students who are working on these projects. The number and focus of these sessions varies depending on the course, the assignment, and the faculty member. Typically, toward the beginning of the semester, we would have about 30 to 45 minutes of a class session to give students a conceptual overview of the project and walk them through the production process. We talk them through a visual image of an editing time line describing how various media resources are brought together and arranged to tell a story. In this way, they can see, conceptually, what a video looks like when laid out across a time line. One benefit of having collaborated on so many projects over the years is that we have many good examples to show.

We offer equipment demos and an introduction to video editing (both process overview and software) in class when, and if, requested. Although we have on occasion offered custom online instructional modules when in-class time has been difficult to carve out, a majority of faculty members actually prefer in-class instruction. This is good news for librarians because it gives us another opportunity to build strong relationships with faculty and students. In addition, the IT department has purchased a university-wide subscription to Atomic Learning, which we suggest students take a look at as well.[3] Atomic Learning offers online instructional video modules on a wide variety of software applications including all the audio, video, and multimedia applications faculty and students might need to successfully complete their projects. By the time students come to the Media Center to begin the postproduction editing phase of the project, they will have already done their research, written their narrative, started to research and accumulate media resources, and/or capture their interview and other supplementary footage (B-roll), and have had a very basic introduction to the software.

## In-Lab Services

The Media Center itself is physically self-contained. We are a circular space designed with offices on the periphery surrounding the lab. This layout makes it easy for us to always be within earshot and available to offer assistance. In this setting we offer one-on-one equipment demos on how to set up the tripod and camcorder, hook up the microphone, and, most importantly, capture good audio, if that is what students need. We sit down with them, talk about their project, and briefly walk them through the editing process. We help them create their project file, show them how to import their resources, work the time line, cut and trim their clips, and create transitions. Students are often working on their own within 10 to 15 minutes. When they have something to show, we sit with them, watch a draft of their video, discuss their work, and offer all manner of advice and suggestions from message clarity, design and layout to audience, pacing, transitions, and audio levels.

Although we support multiple audio and video editing applications, we want students to understand that it is not about a particular software package. All video editing applications, for the most part, offer the same tools and opportunities for creative expression. And no doubt they will all continue to change. The important thing is to conceptually understand how all the various media elements come together to tell a compelling story. In the early days we used iMovie HD. When the first new version of iMovie was released, we switched to Final Cut Express. We now use Final Cut Pro X. Although we occasionally use iMovie for walk-in projects, we have found that Final Cut Pro X is just fine, even for novice editors as long as help and support are readily available. The university recently added a campus-wide license to the full Adobe CC, so Premiere Pro is now loaded on all machines. We support this as well; however, for the time being, we continue to use Final Cut X for production projects.

We encourage faculty to bring their students to the Media Center during their regularly scheduled class time to work on their projects. Quite a few do. Some have scheduled one or two end-of-the-semester class sessions in the lab, offering students more time to put the final touches on their work. One class that we worked with for five years (Introduction to Health Promotion) designated every Wednesday as "video day." The class would meet in the Media Center on Wednesdays so students could focus on whatever stage of the process they were working on, whether preproduction planning or postproduction editing. Classes, in general, have about 20 to 25 students, but we have accommodated as many as 45 students in the Media Center at one time, working on as many as 10 to 13 different group projects. And all the while, people are walking up to the Media Center service desk to ask a question, to get assistance with their own media issues, to borrow equipment, or to request a video that was placed on reserve. We think of the Media Center as an innovative, forward-thinking, creative, active learning space: loud, bustling, busy, and exciting—just the way we like it.

## Equipment Loans

We loan all of the equipment students will need to successfully complete their project. This includes basic production equipment, from camcorders, SD cards, tripods, and a variety of microphones (lavalier, handheld, and shotgun), to digital audio recorders, lights, cables connectors, and the occasional laptop. For a while we were loaning 300 to 400 video kits each year in support of all projects, both academic and nonacademic. However, as cell phone cameras have improved, we have seen these numbers decline. It is evident that students prefer to use their own equipment whenever possible. They also tend not to want to use tripods when they shoot with their own phone cameras. We suggest that personal cameras may not be the best way to capture certain kinds of important footage, particularly interviews. Handheld camera work is wobbly even in the best of circumstances. Yet despite the trend toward personal cell phone cameras, we continue to circulate production equipment averaging 150 to 200 kits each year. One other possible reason for the decline in numbers has to do with the growing interest in mash-up videos. This is an assignment that asks students to research and write a narrative, and then combine multiple preexisting video and other media resources found online into a coherent, unified video. This form of the assignment does not require students to capture interviews or supplementary B-roll footage and so there is no need to borrow any video equipment. It is often confounding to students that something as simple and easy as downloading images or video clips from the Internet for their video or PowerPoint presentation might be illegal. This mash-up assignment gives us another opportunity to expand on the fair use doctrine and help students to better understand the nature of derivative works and how their use of copyrighted materials in this way is a repurposing of the work of others and as such is protected under fair use.

Over time, as the number of assignments grew, we began to buy and loan external hard drives for student projects. In the early days of this initiative, projects were saved on individual machines and students would reserve time on a particular computer. As more students began to create content, it became clear that projects needed to be mobile. Because every computer already had the necessary software, the data itself (that is, media and edit files) could travel. We have been through multiple iterations of external drives from the big, heavy, clunky, silver LaCie drives (100, 250, and 500 GB), to our current crop of 500 GB orange LaCie Rugged drives and, more recently, 500 GB USB 3.0 My Passport drives. We assign 25 to 30 external hard drives every semester for group projects in addition to 20 small (tiny, actually) 32 GB flash drives that allow for easy file transfer from one machine to another. In some cases, these flash drives actually house a whole project. We try to assign a hard drive to every group that is working on a video project. We tend to see external hard drives as more of a consumable commodity than a piece of hardware. Walk-in projects that can be completed within a few days, however, continue to be stored on individual machines.

As a department, we have opted not to use Deep Freeze[4] or any other type of software that would automatically erase files saved to the hard drive and restore the computer to its original configuration at every restart. We allow students to save and keep projects directly on the computer hard drive. In this way, perhaps, we may be unlike most computer labs. Although it does contribute to desktop clutter, it allows us to be as user-friendly as possible. Deep Freeze can be an obstacle for students, especially if they do not understand its purpose and in the end lose their work. We choose to delete files and projects along the way during the semester, if and when space becomes an issue. Administrative functions are password protected. We will typically save a project in a separate folder for a week or more after its due date, sometimes even longer depending upon space, just in case. Students do come back for fine-tune reedits even after the semester is over. We generally wipe the computers clean at the end of every semester, but we have, on occasion, seen both faculty and students extremely happy to learn that we had not deleted their project.

Students are, of course, welcome to do their work at home and to use their own hard drives for these class projects, but we do encourage them to consider using one of ours and leaving it with us when not in use. Faculty and students alike need to feel confident that their work will be protected and available whenever needed. Although we do not have a file storage policy and our promise is not rock solid, we have not lost one project in the 12 years students have been producing videos. This is not to say that students have not lost large chunks of time back in the days when computers unexpectedly quit, and students had not been saving their projects as they went along.

This issue has also given us a little more perspective on the question of technology literacy. It is evident to us that students, and faculty for that matter, do not have much experience with audio and video file management and formats. And why would they? For the most part, this is new territory and something one learns in the process of creating a video. They learn that different applications handle files differently. Some require that audio and video files literally accompany the edit file. Others offer the option of copying the media files into the application file itself, making the whole project more self-contained and portable. When students opt to work at home or on their own, their lack of technology literacy and knowledge is a little more evident. It is not uncommon for students who opt to work on their own to bring their projects to class often without the accompanying audio and video media files. When they open their project to show their work, they are surprised that nothing is there to show, only placeholders. They did not know they had to bring the files with them or they were not aware they could/should export their video draft an as independent MP4 or MOV file. In these situations, we are at a loss to offer full support to students who choose not to work in the Media Center. We do the best we can, given the circumstances, and encourage faculty to strongly suggest that students do their work in the Media Center.

## Faculty and Student Comments and Concerns

When all is said and done, do faculty and students think this is a worthwhile assignment? To begin with, let me just reiterate that this is not an assignment faculty members would ordinarily decide to do on their own. More often than not, they simply do not have the requisite knowledge or skills. Also, one cannot assume that a similar collection of services and supports is available on every campus, although it is more likely today than it was 12 years ago. Nevertheless, the onus is on the librarian to be proactive; to reach out to the faculty and suggest, propose, cajole, and convince them that not only is this a project worth doing but also that it can be successfully supported. As you solicit participation, it is worth remembering that there are many factors working against a faculty member adopting a project like this. Prime among all else is time: instructional class time, faculty time, and student time. For one, it can take time away from direct content instruction. Although this is often true, it does not always have to be so. But it is a concern. On the flip side, this assignment could be viewed as a huge opportunity for faculty members wishing to redesign a course and possibly rethink their instructional style.

This type of project also takes an individual faculty member's personal time—time that is precious and already in short supply. Because faculty do not typically have a mental image of what the production process and final product look like, it takes time to engage in conversations and to inform their understanding as to what they are actually asking their students to do, along with the how and the why. It takes time for them to plan and customize assignments, readjust their syllabi, and think a little differently about assessment. It is important not to forget that this is also a lot of work and a very time-intensive activity for students. They not only have to go through the process of researching and writing a paper to become that small "e" expert on their topic, but they also have to go one step further, and that is to make the film.

The most telling data point on the question of value is that faculty members become repeat customers. In spite of all the potential obstacles inherent in this assignment, faculty by and large believe this is a worthwhile assignment that enhances the academic experience and brings value to student learning. One former colleague in the Department of Community Health and Sustainability (College of Health Sciences) did not, in fact, believe that it was a question of giving up instructional teaching time, but rather simply a different way of achieving the same goal. In her view, it was not a question of "if," but a question of "how" to redesign the course to accommodate a production project, one deemed important to the field moving forward, without sacrificing any course learning objectives. Another colleague in the Graduate School of Education thinks visual communication is a part of basic literacy and suggests that one is not truly literate if they do not have facility with these media tools.

A colleague in the Biology Department (College of Sciences) observed that the process of creating videos had substantially improved students' understanding of the science content in her course. Another science colleague quietly remarked that he continues to assign the project because he believes the project requires more work from his students than a traditional term paper. And lastly, a colleague in the English Department (College of Fine Arts, Humanities, and Social Sciences) sees video and other media production projects as an excellent service learning opportunity. It engages students with "real-life" partners in the community, asking them to use media for rhetorical purposes by crafting and producing videos that their partners need and will use. At the same time, the process deepens the students' understanding and appreciation of technology and media literacies.

In a qualitative study of UMass Lowell health majors who participated in this video production assignment, the students commented on how this experience challenged them to hone their communication skills, to be more succinct in their writing, to manage their time better, to listen to others' ideas, to compromise, to find ways to motivate their team members, and to step up to a leadership role when necessary all in the name of completing the project (Tajik, Shuldman, & Garlo, 2011). Students described their experience of producing the videos and how this impacted their media literacy and critical thinking. The experience changed how they perceive what they see in the media and opened their critical eye to be more attuned to the subtle ways images, music, and narrative can inform or sway. In this way, they may begin to "develop a critical understanding of media and perhaps gain some degree of power over its intrusive nature" (Shewbridge & Berge, 2004, p. 33).

## CONCLUSION

This is, first and foremost, a story about faculty/librarian collaboration built around a collection of services offered to facilitate learning and to enhance the academic experience. The strength of this collaboration is the combination of faculty disciplinary knowledge with the library's expertise in media information and its surrounding technologies. The role of librarians is to enable and support this process. In our case, we created the active learning environment in the form of a lab that supports media-based projects and scholarship. We support the research process and both instruct and support students in all aspects of understanding and using media information and technologies. And we bring a solid collection of services and skills that contribute to and facilitate student learning in a purposeful, meaningful way.

Since we crossed the threshold into the digital age, librarians have been slowly disintermediated from the educational process. Although we were once the critical link between students and information, this is no longer the case. This trend needs to be reversed, and collaborations are an essential way forward, whether it is "infiltrating" college writing courses with effective information literacy instruction and assignments or integrating media production into the curriculum. We must be proactive, socially and academically engaged with our community, and transformative in our approach. Lankes (2011) suggests that the role of a librarian is to create communities around information and ideas to facilitate the creation of knowledge. This is about librarians as people and not libraries as only technology. To be able to do this, librarians need opportunities to create and build these collaborative relationships, along with space and entrepreneurial encouragement to create library-centric active learning environments and activities. We must be civically engaged in the greater academic community, attend meetings, participate in campus committees, and network with faculty, always looking for ways to open new conversations. We must find our own way back into the educational process by fostering these collaborative relationships with faculty, bringing unique value into the equation, and focusing on innovative and creative ideas and services that enhance the academic experience and facilitate student learning.

## NOTES

1. See www.youtube.com/watch?v=ScCAaLXjks4
2. See https://vimeo.com/camprojectvideos/videos
3. See www.atomiclearning.com/
4. See www.faronics.com/products/deep-freeze/

# REFERENCES

Courtney, A. (2014, June 16). Using video documentary creation in the science classroom. (weblog comment). *Education Electrons: An educational technology blog.* Retrieved from www.wou.edu/wp/courtna/2014/06/16/using-video-documentary-creation-in-the-science-classroom.

Daley, E. (2003). Expanding the concept of literacy. *EDUCAUSE Review, 38,* 33–40.

Hooper, S., & Rieber, L. P. (1995). Teaching with technology. In A. C. Ornstein (Ed.), *Teaching: Theory into practice* (pp. 154–170). Needham Heights, MA: Allyn and Bacon.

Kearsley, G., & Shneiderman, B. (1998). Engagement theory: A framework for technology-based teaching and learning. *Educational Technology, 38*(5), 20–23.

Lankes, R. D. (2011). *The atlas of new librarianship.* Cambridge, MA: MIT Press.

Lippincott, J. K. (2007). Student content creators: Convergence of literacies. *EDUCAUSE Review, 42*(6), 16–17.

Meeks, M., & Ilyasova, M. (2003). A review of digital video production in post-secondary English classrooms at three universities. *KAIROS, 8*(2).

New Media Consortium. (2008). The 2008 horizon report. Austin, TX: The New Media Consortium and Boulder, CO: EDUCAUSE Learning Initiative. Retrieved from library.educause.edu/resources/2008/1/2008-horizon-report.

Rooney-Varga, J. N., Brisk, A. A., Adams, E., Shuldman, M., & Rath, K. (2014). Student media production to meet challenges in climate change science education. *Journal of Geoscience Education, 62*(4), 598–608.

Rooney-Varga, J. N., Brisk, A. A., Shuldman, M., & Rath, K. (2015). The CAM Project: Tools for bringing student media production into climate change education. *In the trenches: The news magazine of the National Association of Geoscience Teachers, 5*(1), 4–7.

Shewbridge, W., & Berge, Z. L. (2004). The role of theory and technology in learning video production: The challenge of change. *International Journal on E-Learning, 3*(1), 31–39.

Shuldman, M. (2013). Video production as an academic learning tool in non-media courses. Mapping ICT literacies and skills to the video production process and engagement theory. In L. Gómez Chova, A. López Martínez, I. Candel Torres (Eds.), *INTED2013 Proceedings.* Paper presented at the 7th International Technology, Education and Development Conference, Valencia, Spain (pp. 1630–1637). International Association of Technology, Education and Development.

Tajik, M., Shuldman, M., & Garlo, E. (2011). Engaged education through integrated service learning video production. In L. Gómez Chova, I. Candel Torres, A. López Martínez (Eds.), *INTED2011 Proceedings.* Paper presented at the 5th International Technology, Education and Development Conference, Valencia, Spain (pp. 3971–3980). International Association of Technology, Education and Development.

# 12

# Going Beyond Books: Lendable Technology, Interdisciplinary Innovation, and the Revitalization of an Academic Library

*Tara Radniecki and Patrick "Tod" Colegrove*

In early 2010, the DeLaMare Library, on the campus of the University of Nevada, Reno, had become known on campus as the "quiet library." The primary campus library in support of the physical sciences and engineering had a problem: Although the print collections of the library saw regular use, the library as place remained severely underutilized by its membership. At any given time only a handful of individuals could be found within its walls; faculty paused only long enough to drop off course reserves, and students hurried through checking out or returning materials. The library seemed to be growing less relevant to its community by the day. Rather than a dynamic hub of collaboration, learning, and discovery, it had become a beautiful, but largely unused warehouse of print materials. The vibrant hub of knowledge creation and discovery it would become seemed inconceivable.

Library faculty and staff began an open and frank dialogue across the communities of practice that otherwise should have been using the library. What was missing? Were there gaps that could be bridged by the library to better enable meeting institutional learning, discovery, and outreach objectives? What could the library do to recover centrality in the day-to-day learning and research lives of its membership? In modest response to initial feedback, the library began its experimentation with the integration of technologies into its lending collection in the spring of 2010. A pattern of repeated requests at the service desk drove the decision to purchase and make available for checkout three handheld graphing calculators. Over the years since, both the use and the diversity of items in the lending technology collection has expanded dramatically, the result of active communication and responsive development informing curation of the collection. Even better, the library has continued to grow more central to the heart of the engineering and science communities served. The community influenced collection curation, and the resulting collections influenced the community in a reinforcing loop; even physical spaces of the library were transformed as a result. The library was becoming a vibrant hub, integral to the lives of the communities served.

From experimenting with lending technology collections to their integration with more traditional services and support, the library has seen adoption, growth, and use of both collections and physical library space increase at near-exponential rates. This chapter tells the story of the development and use of the library's expanding collection of "things," and how the open communication and dialogue fostered relationships that led directly to the revitalization of the library. Over the span of a small number of years, the lending technology collection of the library has grown from nonexistent to one of its most heavily utilized collections; the following pages explore the origins and development of the collection, its impact on the library spaces and services and vice versa, practical insights, and the future of libraries as seen in the context of the historical roots of librarianship.

## LENDABLE TECHNOLOGY: SOMETHING NEW OR MORE OF WHAT LIBRARIES HAVE ALWAYS DONE?

Libraries have a long history of provisioning technology in direct support of learning and knowledge creation. Consider that the word *technology* itself derives from the Greek words *techne*, meaning "art," "craft," or "skill," and *logos* meaning "word" or "consciousness," first joined by Aristotle (Mitcham, 1994). Uniting *techne* with *logos* refers to both the means by which the learning is acquired and the words about and by which the associated knowledge is created or transferred. In the library, familiar examples of such technology might include not only the print book, or codex, itself, but the active conversation derived from engagement with the book—potentially including discussion, collaboration, and learning. Earlier examples would have included papyrus scrolls and clay tablets on which the raw building blocks of knowledge were recorded, and the dialogue and discovery associated with their use. Libraries have long been in the technology business.

Over the past decades, lendable library technology has grown increasingly diverse: the print book alongside the e-book, and even e-reader; calculator to notepad or laptop computer; collaboration and meeting areas where learning and knowledge creation occurs not only in the interaction of participants with library resources, but in the interaction with one another. Across higher education the landscape continues to shift, as experimentation with new models of curriculum and instruction yields potential opportunities for the academic library. Seen in light of the greater organizational mission, services and resources become part of an ongoing effort in terms of meeting expectations and needs not only of incoming students, teachers, and research faculty, but also of students' future employers.

Long considered the heart of the academic community, libraries are places to find information and assistance, collaborate, and be inspired. How to reconcile these enduring values with relentlessly increasing rates of change? The ubiquitous spread of Wi-Fi and caffeine is enabling knowledge creation of all kinds far beyond the walls of the library as technology grows ever smaller and more portable. Just as being able to check out a book can enable the user time to read, understand, put down, come back to, and ultimately synthesize information into knowledge creation, other technologies can benefit from similar treatment. Users who have the opportunity to check out and play with an Inventor's Kit for Arduino may well be able to learn much more, at their own pace, than in any hour-long workshop. Similarly, checking out a recently released Google Glass can enable exploration by users of innovative apps and development that could make it an integral technology for daily life—indeed, enable contribution to their development. Deliberately expanding the lendable collections of the library beyond the book gives users the opportunity to acquire knowledge and innovate, overcoming both physical and financial boundaries.

Some fear the library is losing itself as technology and makerspaces become more common. Yet across the literature and in daily practice, we see that the

**FIGURE 12.1**  Students Utilizing Audiovisual Editing Resources (Photo by Nick Crowl).

importance of libraries is not what they provide but rather how and why. In a compilation from Young and Belanger (1983), Martin (2003), and Marcum (2003), *The Librarian's Book of Lists* offers this definition of a library:

> A library is a collection of resources in a variety of formats that is (1) organized by information professionals or other experts who (2) provide convenient physical, digital, bibliographic, or intellectual access and (3) offer targeted services and programs (4) with the mission of educating, informing, or entertaining a variety of audiences (5) and the goal of stimulating individual learning and advancing society as a whole. (Eberhart, 2010, p.1)

A lending technology collection fits easily within this definition. An effective lending technology collection is created with input from experts and information professionals, teaching faculty, students, and other stakeholders who often have a highly developed sense of particular technology they need to enable what they want to be able to accomplish. It is then up to the information professionals to find a suitable match, organizing and provisioning access as appropriate. Lending technology collections help us live up to our missions in offering services and resources created specifically for our targeted user groups, targeting learning and informational needs with a laser-sharp focus, moving past just lending laptops to provide a range of curated resources that can truly drive individual learning and innovative advancement.

## A REVIEW OF THE LITERATURE

Although an increasing number of academic libraries are exploring lending technology collections containing a wide variety of devices, the literature focuses heavily on laptop lending programs and seems largely lacking in coverage of more diverse collections. Numerous articles discuss the planning, policies, troubleshooting, marketing, and hardware selection of laptop lending programs, including Vaughan and Burnes (2002), Allmang (2003), Kwon and Soules (2003), Williams (2003), Power (2007), Dodd and Drennan (2007), Sharpe (2009), and Buzzard and Teetor (2011). Assessment of laptop lending programs and changes made afterward are addressed by Holden and Deng (2005), Atlas, Garza, and Hinshaw (2007), Feldmann, Wess, and Moothart (2008), and Hsieh and Holden (2008). These studies proved that lending technology could be successfully administered, assessed, and ultimately a tremendously convenient resource for patrons needing a mobile computer for any number of reasons.

Although fewer in numbers, some articles in the literature deal with lendable items other than laptops. Hahn (2011) outlines the process through which the University of Illinois Urbana-Champaign's (UIUC) University Library developed and curated its lending technology collection that extended beyond laptops to include audio and visual recording equipment, gaming platforms and accessories, and digital storage items. UIUC's University Library conducted focus groups, surveys, and informal interviews to determine which equipment to purchase; assessment efforts showed the program to be successful. Pointing out that one can infer the library is also helping students engage with technology outside of the traditional curricula, about 50 percent of the time items were checked out for uses other than directly related to a class. Anderson and Weatherbee (2012) present a case study of their lending technology collection, offering three important questions to ask when starting such a project: What technology should you purchase? How will you maintain the device and keep it functioning? How will you circulate the devices? The paper goes on to detail how their collection has grown and how the collection has inspired the creation of new multimedia spaces. Chapman and Woodbury (2012) of North Carolina State University (NCSU) Libraries discuss assessment of their growing lending technology collection using quantitative data to make informed decisions. Their collection includes laptops, but also contains audio and visual recorders, GPS units, tablets, projectors, and MP3 devices. By analyzing quantitative data, including circulation and wait list numbers, they were able to make adjustments to their collection and policies to better meet the needs of their community.

In an attempt to fill the void in the literature, a recently published book by Sander, Mestre, and Kurt (2015), *Going Beyond Loaning Books to Loaning Technologies: A Practical Guide for Librarians,* offers a wealth of detailed information for libraries looking to expand their lending collection into technology. Chapters focus on practical tactics for identifying needs, budgeting, and assessment, and offer insight on many topics often overlooked by libraries just establishing lending technology collections. This piece offers particular insights associated with a range of technologies such as might be provisioned in support of prototyping, including robotics, virtual reality, gaming, programming, and 3-D modeling and scanning.

Although our contribution to the literature will cover some less frequently discussed implications of lending technology collections, such as legal and privacy considerations, we ultimately aim to provide a wider context in which these collections can play an important role in creating and maintaining an open dialogue with patrons and even revitalizing the library.

## ORIGINS AND DEVELOPMENT

Although DeLaMare Library had for some time maintained a collection of wired headsets that were regularly checked out by users of the computer workstations in the library, their availability was considered more of a work-around for the lack of speakers than an active collection. With the decision to make calculators available for checkout, as part of the "gadgets" collection in the library catalog, that perception began to change. Questions beyond simply cost and marginal functionality began to enter the picture. Should items from the collection be allowed out of the library? In what ways would they see use? Were there particular features of interest and use, and would that vary by discipline? After a relatively brief period of dialogue with students and faculty as to functional needs, a model of graphing calculator was selected. Three were purchased, cataloged, and made available mid-semester in the spring of 2010. Despite high hopes, the calculators only saw occasional use in the first year—a lukewarm reception at best.

**FIGURE 12.2** Student Working on a Drone Quadricopter in the Library (Photo by Nick Crowl).

Undeterred, with the addition of two wireless drone quadricopters to the collection in time for the start of the next term, the library was able to further demonstrate just how far it was willing to go in support of the learning, discovery, and outreach missions of the greater university. Selected for the availability of an applications programming interface (API) to enable programmatic control of the drones, a relatively low cost of the drones further enabled the choice. Although not in and of themselves robots, the existence of the API for the drones offered a potentially interesting development platform for aspiring programmers, and when presented to the computer science and engineering (CSE) department's capstone senior projects course, the drones began to see immediate and active use. With the ready availability of the drones for development, testing, and use, by the end of the course sequence two completely distinct working robotic systems had been developed using the flying platform (Dascalus, 2011) and leveraging the open source Robot Operating System (ROS).[1] The finalized systems, essentially a flying platform driven by the automation programming developed in ROS, were in principle ready for potential use and even commercialization. As further evidence of the developing relationship between the supported communities and the library, unprompted, the CSE department offered to purchase a third drone to be added to the library's collection. Success!

The next targeted addition to the lending technology collections was suggested by the library's liaison to the separate departments of computer science and mathematics. On our campus, all first-year engineering students were tasked with building robotic hovercraft based on LEGO Mindstorms NXT.[2] Reasoning that there might be interest and advantage to students and faculty from outside the engineering disciplines having access, two LEGO Mindstorms NXT 2.0 robotics kits were purchased and made available for checkout. With a reported 619 separate pieces comprising the kit, including sensors and the programmable "brick" computer, the kits presented an interesting packaging challenge to enable accountability at check-in and checkout. Suitably compartmented carrying cases were identified, purchased, and appropriately labeled, while explanatory checklists were noted in the catalog record before the kits were made available. Supporting how-to books in the library's print and electronic collections were identified, and users were enabled to leverage a campus site license for the Mindstorms programming environment, ROBOLAB, allowing for immediate exploration of the platform and development of their creations. Leveraging the power of play, individuals that would otherwise likely never have been exposed to the concepts of programming, much less developing a robot and acquiring associated literacies, were soon expanding their horizons.

Building on the growing success of the collection, microcontrollers and other programmables were targeted and added: six SparkFun Inventor's Kits for Arduino,[3] along with six Raspberry Pi single-board computers[4] and associated peripherals such as displays, wireless daughterboards, and other development modules. Used primarily by individuals interested in prototyping or learning about electronics and programming, these microcontrollers have seen regular use since they were first made available in the collection. In addition to use in group events, such as kids' camps and science, technology, engineering, and math education (STEM) outreach to local K–12 schools and museums, these resources see occasional use in high-level prototypes in potential product development. Anecdotal evidence of adoption might include the particularly enthusiastic student who went so far as to recruit the library as the site for an all-day celebration outreach event in honor of Arduino Day, hosting a variety of hands-on projects utilizing the programmable device. Alternatively, consider

**FIGURE 12.3**  Student Playing with a Makey Makey Kit at Arduino Day 2014 Event (Photo by Nick Crowl).

the example of a journalism professor interested in studying problems associated with the relative lack of touch-related haptic feedback options for individuals with vision impairment attempting to use much of today's handheld electronics. Leveraging the ability to check out a SparkFun Inventor's Kit for Arduino from the library for an extended period, the professor was able to prototype and program a haptic version of the familiar childhood game of Simon on a wristband wearable device, rendering the game playable by those unable to see by producing patterns of long and short vibrations. Proof of concept in hand, the research project was immediately upgraded to utilize the Apple Watch, working with human subjects to probe the potential of the concept. To facilitate similar prototyping projects, the library immediately ordered an Apple Watch for the lending collection.

A pattern of collection development and use began to emerge. Informed by active dialogue with the communities of practice returning to the library in ever-increasing numbers, targeted acquisitions were informed by individual suggestions and vetted in conversation with other members of the library. Each successive addition amplified the message that the library genuinely shared the community's interest. The library became a partner in helping them bridge critical path learning and discovery gaps, and providing new opportunities across disciplinary boundaries.

## A POSITIVE FEEDBACK LOOP

By introducing the communities potentially served into the conversation, a feedback loop between the community and the library developed. Compound interest, such as might be earned on funds in a bank account, is a common example of a positive feedback loop: to the extent the interest earned is not withdrawn, the fund compounds and the asset grows exponentially. Similarly, a relatively small investment on the part of the library, such as might be involved in the dialogue with potential members of the library in an attempt to identify and potentially bridge gaps, can result in progressively greater impact. Open dialogue can be enhanced by similarly open-ended conversation within and across communities of practice supported by the library; followed through in appropriate cases with timely acquisition and notification of individuals involved, behaviors are reinforced and relationships strengthened. Small actions, consistently and timely applied, lead to big results.

In our case, the initial conversations and decision to make graphing calculators available as part of the lending technology collection required a relatively small investment. With no more than an hour of conversation overall, spread across multiple students and faculty, and a modest cost of entry on the order of a print book, the library was able to send a message to the potential membership of the library. Sharing the news that the suggestion had been acted upon, both in person with each of the individuals making the original suggestion, and across media channels, kick-started the cycle. Soon members of the community began to open up to library faculty and staff as to other possibilities. Library membership began to wonder aloud why no whiteboards large enough for collaborative work were available in the library. Again, a relatively minimal conversation across multiple individuals revealed that a minimal effective size would be on the order of four feet high and six feet wide. To paraphrase community input, "Anything less, and it's too small to even get started. Why bother?"

In short order, two double-sided rolling whiteboards had been purchased and made available in the library. Staff immediately began to report that the whiteboards were seeing active use and being moved all over the four floors of the library. In response, another four whiteboards were purchased and deployed. Members of the community potentially served by the library began to rediscover its spaces, working individually as well as in collaboration with others. The library began to come alive, and even the calculators of the original lending technology collection began to see use.

## IMPACTS ON SPACE

Challenges related to the physical space in the library were an unanticipated impact of the engagement fed by the responsive development of the lending collection. Over the years, the print collections of the library had grown to the point that precious little space remained for use, and the recently added rolling whiteboards were already being fully utilized, with the increasingly engaged and invested users of the library calling for even more. Colegrove (2012) details the perhaps most dramatic impact on the spaces with the relocation of nearly 54 percent of the library's print collection. The decision was reached in partnership with the communities served by the library. The printed and bound journals held in the library's collections were relocated to the automated retrieval system of the main library on campus, enabling the library to open up floor space and more than tripling available space across the four floors of the library. As spaces opened up by shifting remaining print collections, entire walls throughout the library were turned into whiteboards by applying whiteboard paint, creating ad hoc collaboration areas while simultaneously meeting the requests for more and bigger whiteboards throughout the library.

The positive feedback loop between the community of the library and its collections had expanded to explicitly include the spaces of the library. Driven by active dialogue with the community of users, the lending technologies collection had grown beyond microprogrammables and robotics to include an apparently eclectic mix, from handheld device and laptop charging cables to portable projectors, soldering iron kits, and virtual reality headsets. Items from the collection were regularly seen in use across the floors of the library, yielding opportunity for library faculty and staff to engage and explore with individual members, strengthening community ties. A common thread between the items was the library's ability to actively identify a shared need and the opportunity for the library to effectively bridge gaps, enabling knowledge creation aligned with the learning, discovery, and engagement missions of the university.

By mid-2015, the lending technology collection comprised fully 18 different categories of items in active use. Excluding wired headsets, in the 2014–15 academic year, the top five most heavily utilized categories by total number of checkouts were as follows:

| | |
|---|---|
| Google Glass and Charger | 192 |
| TI-89 Graphing Calculators | 101 |
| Oculus Rift Development Kit & DK2 | 121 |
| SparkFun Inventor's Kit | 103 |
| Epson PowerLite Projector | 64 |

Over the same time frame, a total of 889 checkouts from the lending technology pool were made, an average of just over 49 checkouts per category. Note that although the top five categories listed accounted for the bulk of the activity, the balance of 308 checkouts, 34.6 percent of the total, were spread across the remaining categories. These include soldering irons and tools, Arduino Nanos and Raspberry Pis, 3-D scanners, a Leap Motion dongle, a VR ONE headset, and more.[5] Excluding the top five, the remaining items/categories, ranging from programmables to Dremels, saw an average of 24 checkouts each, suggesting that the method of selection and curation relative to community interest and needs is effective overall. Cost-per-use metrics for items in the collection range from on the order of pennies to tens of dollars, certainly on par with what one might expect from an actively used academic monograph or journal.

## IMPACTS ON SERVICES AND THE RISE OF THE MAKERSPACE

Beyond collaborative spaces and use, the feedback loop fed by the development of the collection began to bear fruit in the form of potential service suggestions. Students and faculty, recognizing the library's demonstrated willingness to change and adopt potentially unorthodox approaches, began asking for services in support of active learning. Starting with the relatively traditional offering of large-format poster printing and scanning services, by late 2011 the library was approached with a request that it consider provisioning 3-D printing and scanning services. Recognizing the adjunct role the services could play in bridging the gap between idea and reality, the case for the purchase was made and the services implemented in early 2012 (Colegrove, 2014). The service saw immediate use and has seen both expansion and continued heavy use in direct support of not only active learning, but also rapid prototyping and outreach.

As adoption of the library's novel services and collections ramped up among users of the space, the need for access to additional resources quickly escalated, requiring additions to both the lending technology pool and traditional collections. Examples include soldering irons and electronics kits, screwdriver sets and other manual tools, along with related books, periodical and academic journal subscriptions, and online learning guides. Whether working on a hovercraft based around LEGO Mindstorms as part of an Engineering 100 team, prototyping a design as part of a research endeavor, or dabbling to satisfy personal curiosity and learning, the library was becoming a vibrant center of the communities served. Lendable collections contributed significantly to adoption and use of both the collections and the library spaces, even as that use surfaced needs for additional services and collections. Informed by those needs, resources and associated services added to date include several varieties of 3-D printers, handheld 3-D scanners, a laser cutter, a printed circuit board printer/mill, a vinyl cutter and heat press, and most recently, soldering and sewing stations within the library.

A new word began to be used around the library: *makerspace*. By 2015 use of the revitalized library as place had grown from a peak of a few tens of individuals to several hundred at any given time; the library was regularly operating at or near capacity. Similarly, the lending technology collection had been realizing near-exponential growth, both in use and diversity over the five years of its existence. The library now wrestles with problems of a different kind: competing needs for physical space to provide needed resources and services, and for the library faculty and staff

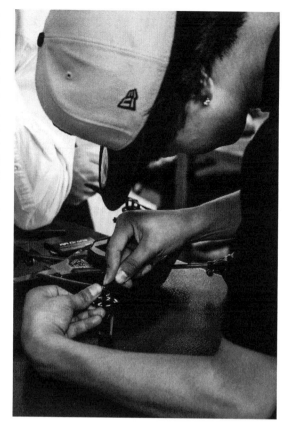

**FIGURE 12.4** Student Disassembling a Drone in the Library in Order to Access and Repair Embedded Electronics (Photo by Nick Crowl).

who can complete the bridge. Significant progress has been made by aggressively weeding the library print collections and relocating print materials such as archived and bound print journals, no longer in demand within the physical footprint of the library, to the automated retrieval system of the main library. The relocation of nearly 54 percent of the library print materials enabled removal of nearly all of the open bookshelves, opening nearly 80 percent of the floor space overall. A similar thought process guided library faculty and staff. In addition to realignment of existing positions to meet changing needs of the increasingly active membership of the library, efforts to remove barriers throughout the library resulted in faculty and staff exchanging their formerly private office space for the open floors of the library. The former office space was converted to student collaborative study space, while faculty and staff became immediately more accessible and embedded within the community of the library. In addition to efficiently enabling substantially deeper engagement with the communities served, the university administration has responded with nominal increases in staffing levels to the increased activity and improved alignment of the library with the greater missions of learning, discovery, and engagement.

## SIMPLE MARKETING AND OUTREACH

Although lessons have been learned and adjustments made throughout the course of the development and use of the lending technology collection, the program overall has proven successful in providing users with access to necessary equipment to further drive the university's learning, discovery, and outreach missions. With the deliberate inclusion of stakeholders from early on in the selection process, the library has been able to provide access to resources that see consistently high circulation numbers, with cost-per-use analysis demonstrating efficient use of limited fiscal resources.

Simple marketing efforts have repeatedly proven effective in generating interest and use for items in the lendable collection, in addition to new services. Leveraging the availability of the LibGuides product by Springshare, online content was created and can easily be updated with new information as the collection continues to grow. Information about lendable technologies is also linked directly from the library's home page.[6] Social media channels, including Facebook and Twitter, are used to advertise new acquisitions. Nevertheless, the most effective form of social networking for the library has been by means of face-to-face interactions, and by far, our greatest marketing asset has proven repeatedly to be word of mouth. Given the direct engagement and corresponding investment of individuals across library membership in development and curation of the collection, once users are advised that the resource has been acquired and is available, word spreads quickly among their networks.

Further amplifying the grassroots development, marketing, and awareness efforts, DeLaMare staff and librarians regularly take equipment from the collection "on the road" and do outreach at university, community, and school events. Whether a classroom "one-shot" instruction session, student organization meeting or event, faculty meeting, or community event such as the local Mini Maker Faire or a Startup Weekend event, the lending technology collection provides an excellent opportunity for participants to quickly go hands-on with a range of cutting-edge technology. Staff answer questions, walk users through the different ways to use the equipment, and encourage users to check out the equipment at a future date. It should be noted that rather than being exclusive to the university community, items from the lending technology collection are available for checkout across the library's membership. Specifically including library members from the general public regularly yields opportunities to strengthen and create new relationships with local individuals, groups, and businesses, in service to the land grant mission of the university.

## POLICY AND PROCEDURE

The popularity of our lending collection, although ultimately a positive result, did require the creation and adjustment of policies and procedures as the collection grew. As part of a land grant institution, DeLaMare Library is committed to serving the greater northern Nevada community. Yet, lending out expensive equipment to users outside the university required the library to collect more information about borrowers and communicate due dates and fee policies clearly. Oftentimes, a borrower record in the Library Management System (LMS) does not contain their most current contact information. Technology agreement forms were created and require current e-mails and phone numbers for all borrowers regardless of their affiliation. These forms have been critical in creating a system of personal responsibility. To date, none of the lendable technology in the collection has been lost.

Initially, we implemented too short and otherwise restrictive lending periods. For example, some items could only be checked out for a single day, while others were in-house use only. We realized that even though an item's popularity might require shorter loan periods to enable as many people as possible to use it, there was a real need for users to be able to take the borrowed equipment out of the library for an extended period of time. To allow adequate time to fully utilize the equipment, whether in support of personal exploration or in support of learning and research, the library now operates with a minimum functional loan period of three days. Programmables and robotic kits come with learning materials that allow users to learn coding through a series of projects, taking time; it is not uncommon for users to renew items two or more times, even with the longer lending periods.

Notable complications include the library's first-come, first-served policy for the lending technology collection; items cannot be reserved ahead of time. Although this offers some simplicity on the library's end, it can cause inconvenience and frustration for users who would like to plan on having items at a particular time, including library staff members who find they need to plan outreach activities farther in advance to allow time for checked-out items to either come in and be pulled. On more than one occasion, a late return has caused last-minute work-arounds. Further, the compromise of utilizing the library's LMS to account for items only containing brief, uncataloged bibliographic records has required the suppression of the catalog records associated with items in the lending technology collection. These records generally only contain MARC 245 and 246 fields to facilitate easy lookup by staff but are undiscoverable by patrons via our Sierra catalog.

Unfortunately, our current cataloging method means potential users cannot see when the items are due and will be back on the shelves. The library is currently investigating online reservation systems for our equipment that would better serve the customers of the library. Other libraries interested in creating this type of collection might be well advised to consider the potential impact related to cataloging and item representation and findability.

## PRIVACY AND PRESERVATION CONCERNS

Issues also arose in dealing with the physical items themselves. Many of the items in DeLaMare's lending technology collection were designed and made explicitly for personalized use. Items such as Google Glass and Apple Watch are designed to be connected to a user's individual Google or Apple accounts. As a work-around, the library provides such equipment connected to dummy accounts created for the purpose. Nevertheless, end users can and often do connect their own personal account to these devices to fully experience and utilize them as they were designed. The potential for the library to be unintentionally complicit in a resultant loss of personal privacy in such a case is all too real. When items that can be connected to a personal account are returned, library operating procedure requires a full reset and reconfiguration of the equipment to connect back to the appropriate dummy account. Even if users do not connect their personal account, libraries need to be mindful of privacy concerns. For example, the Google Glass can take pictures and video that are then saved on the library's dummy account—potentially available to the next user of the equipment if there is no intervention on the part of the library. With no option for automation, upon return of the item, library staff must take time to go into the account and manually delete any videos or pictures taken.

Although other programmables like the Lego Mindstorms, Arduinos, and Raspberry Pis do not require personal accounts, they are unlike traditional lendable materials in that the physical item is necessary for the final knowledge creation. When users borrow a book, they can acquire all the information they need for their knowledge creation, whatever that may be, and retain that information after they return the physical book. Similarly, when users borrow a SparkFun Inventor's Kit, they acquire information by using the learning aids and creating different projects, and through that process, they create personal knowledge that remains after the return of the item. However, in the process users often build potentially useful prototypes that will be disassembled upon return of the item, with no further benefit to either the user or society at large. In such cases, further prototyping services and support may be indicated to enable users to continue the process of innovation, including library support in terms of copyright, patent law, and digital preservation. Without such support the library risks losing much of value on behalf of both users and society.

## LEGAL CONCERNS

Depending on the type of equipment a library is lending, there may also be legal considerations to consider beyond licensing concerns. The library adopted the same stance with its technology as it does with its monograph collection: the library provides access to the resource, and what users do with that resource is the responsibility of the users. However, we cannot simply ignore laws, either. One particularly useful example is the wireless drone quadricopters that the library made available through the collection from 2010 to 2014. Although commercial and consumer drones were still in their infancy, few laws or policies regulated their use. However, following the development and adoption by the Federal Aviation Administration of regulations restricting drone use, particularly in light of the state of Nevada's designation as an Unmanned Aircraft System (UAS) research and test site in mid-2014, making the technology available for checkout became a potential violation of the law and placed the library in a tenuous position. In consulting with the university's legal counsel, University Libraries decided to remove the quadricopters from the collection. As we work across the profession to preserve our enduring values, it is good to be mindful that consulting with legal counsel can best enable the library to ensure users will have access to exciting new technology while protecting the library and any parent organizations.

## OPERATIONAL CONCERNS

Just like print books, wear and tear associated with use of items from the collection has proven to be a real concern, in particular because many of the lendable technologies are somewhat fragile in nature. Each item in the collection sees heavy use, and can require at best periodic maintenance and, at worst, repair or complete replacement due to broken parts rendering an item unusable. With library staff at the front lines, ongoing training is a requirement, along with that of an increased tolerance for the inevitable trial by fire associated with working on equipment outside our expertise. As an example, supporting the lendable drones required significantly more time than could be afforded to repair and replace parts in the ongoing attempt to keep them functional. Although at the time of purchase there were no options for more robust models, today we would recommend drones made for heavy, professional use rather than basic consumer models. This recommendation applies to all types of technologies considered for lending. We also learned to keep a stock of easily lost or broken pieces, especially power cords. Having them on hand greatly reduced the time an item was not available for use.

In all practicality, recognize that if lendable technology items can become germ-covered, sticky messes, they will. As with books, these items go into people's homes and workplaces, where they become integrated into their daily lives. The loaned items will be potentially used around food, in the bathroom, and in the case of the university, anywhere from a wide variety of laboratory environments to the dorm room and gym. Particularly with the addition of wearable technologies such as headsets, issues associated with personal cleanliness and sanitation of the items will inevitably need attention. Removal of oils, perspiration, and other grime have become an unglamorous aspect of making such technology available. In our experience, however, the benefit far outweighs the cost; we learned to be okay with a certain level of griminess, incorporating disinfectant wipes and appropriate personal protection into the equipment return and cleaning process.

## THE FUTURE OF LIBRARIES

Despite a crash course in the realities of supporting a lending collection of significant technological diversity, over the course of a few short years the collection has gone from a speculative exploration to one of the most heavily used collections of the library. Further, the adoption and use of the collection, along with the dialogue fostered among the library membership, contributed directly to a revitalization of the physical space, a success that bodes well for the future of libraries. At the same time, it bears mention that the very mechanism the library leveraged to increase the use of the collections and build relationships and engagement with its membership can have a darker side. Those considering doing similarly would do well to keep in mind that the feedback loop by its very nature can be either positive or negative; engaging the membership can prove equally damaging if not coupled with authentic dialogue and meaningful follow-through on the part of the library.

A particularly interesting side effect of the vibrant hub of collaborative learning and discovery fostered by the availability and use of the collection has been an apparent explosion of creativity and innovation across disciplines. One thrills to consider the prospect of renaissance driven by libraries around the world, as librarians grapple with larger issues of local preservation and dissemination, even as we endeavor to support our communities in resolving issues of copyright and patent law associated with the resulting innovation. What are best practices associated with broaching questions of digital preservation of an augmented reality walk-through created by a user of lendable library technology, and is unsolicited library involvement even appropriate? Where are the lines associated with potential infringement of 3-D scans and remixing of real-world items? How do we balance the perils of such brave new vistas against the potential and significant benefits of the support to innovation? These questions and more face practitioners in libraries today—indeed, a thrilling time to be in the library business.

## ACKNOWLEDGMENTS

The authors gratefully acknowledge the substantial support of faculty and staff across the greater organization of University Libraries, including Kevin MacDonald of DeLaMare Library; without their support, much of what has been accomplished here would not have been possible. Further, the Office of the Vice President of Research and Innovation at the university is explicitly acknowledged for its generous and unflagging support of the library in the form of grants for equipment acquisitions along the critical path that not only support but actively trigger the raw stuff of innovation: learning, discovery, and outreach.

## NOTES

1. See www.ros.org.
2. See mindstorms.lego.com.
3. See www.sparkfun.com/products/retired/10173.
4. See www.raspberrypi.org.
5. See www.delamare.unr.edu for the most current list of lendable technology.
6. See www.delamare.unr.edu.

## REFERENCES

Allmang, N. (2003). Our plan for a wireless loan service. *Computers in Libraries, 23*(3), 20–25.

Anderson, S., & Weatherbee, S. (2012). Growing a technology equipment service in an academic library. *Computers in Libraries, 32*(6), 6–8.

Atlas, M. C., Garza, F., & Hinshaw, R. (2007). Use of laptop computers in an academic medical library. *Medical Reference Services Quarterly, 26*(2), 27–36.

Buzzard, P. C, & Teetor, T. S. (2011). Best practices for a university laptop lending program. *Code4Lib Journal* (15). Retrieved from journal.code4lib.org/articles/5876.

Chapman, J., & Woodbury, D. (2012). Leveraging quantitative data to improve a device-lending program. *Library Hi Tech, 30*(2), 210–234.

Colegrove, P. (2014). Making it real: 3D printing as a library service. *EDUCAUSE Review, 49*(5). Retrieved from er.educause.edu/articles/2014/10/making-it-real-3d-printing-as-a-library-service.

Colegrove, P. T. (2012). Rediscovering relevance for the science & engineering library. In F. Baudino & C. Johnson (Eds.), *Brick and Click Libraries: An Academic Library Symposium Proceedings*. Paper presented at Brick and Click Libraries Symposium (pp. 57–65). Maryville, MO: Northwest Missouri State University. Retrieved from eric.ed.gov/?id=ED537605.

Dascalus, S. (2011). *Computer science and engineering senior projects*. Retrieved from www.cse.unr.edu/~dascalus/SP2011_WKS_schedule.pdf.

Dodd, L., & Drennan, S. (2007). Laptop loans in UCD Library. *SCONUL Focus, 42,* 53–56.

Eberhart, G. M. (2010). *The librarian's book of lists*. Chicago, IL: American Library Association Editions.

Feldmann, L., Wess, L., & Moothart, T. (2008). An assessment of student satisfaction with a circulating laptop service. *Information Technology & Libraries, 27*(2), 20–25.

Hahn, J., Mestre, L., Ward, D., & Avery, S. (2011). Technology on demand: Implementing loanable technology services at the University of Illinois at Urbana-Champaign. *Library Hi Tech, 29*(1), 34–50.

Holden, H. A., & Deng, M. (2005). Taking pro-action: A survey of potential users before the availability of wireless access and the implementation of a wireless notebook computer lending program in an academic library. *Library Hi Tech, 23*(4), 561–575.

Hsieh, M. L., & Holden, H. (2008). A university library laptop lending service: An analysis using two student surveys. *Library Hi Tech, 26*(3), 424–439.

Kwon, M. L., & Soules, A. (2003). *SPEC kit 275: Laptop computer services*. Washington, DC: Association of Research Libraries.

Marcum, D. B. (2003). Research questions for the digital era library. *Library Trends, 51*(4), 636–651.

Martin, R. S. (2003). Libraries and learners in the twenty-first century. Lecture presented at Cora Paul Bomar Lecture, University of North Carolina at Greensboro, Greensboro, NC.

Mitcham, C. (1994). *Thinking through technology: The path between engineering and philosophy*. Chicago: University of Chicago Press.

Power, J. L. (2007). Circulation on the go: Implementing wireless laptop circulation in a state university academic library. *Journal of Access Services, 5*(1–2), 197–209.

Sander, J., Mestre, L., & Kurt, E. (2015). *Going beyond loaning books to loaning technologies: A practical guide for librarians*. Lanham, MD: Rowman & Littlefield.

Sharpe, P. A. (2009). Circulating laptops: Lessons learned in an academic library. *Journal of Access Services, 6*(3), 337–345.

Vaughan, J., & Burnes, B. (2002). Bringing them in and checking them out: Laptop use in the modern academic library. *Information Technology and Libraries, 21*(2), 55–58.

Williams, J. (2003). Taming the wireless frontier: PDAs, tablets, and laptops at home on the range. *Computers in Libraries, 23*(3), 10–12, 63–64.

Young, H., & Belanger, T. (1983). *The ALA glossary of library and information science*. Chicago: American Library Association.

# 13

# Building Game Collections in Academic Libraries: A Case Study at the University of North Texas

*Diane Robson, Sue Parks, and Erin DeWitt Miller*

## INTRODUCTION

The University of North Texas (UNT) began offering courses in game programming and design in 1993. In the years following, the university expanded these course offerings beyond the Computer Science Department and into a variety of other disciplines. Classes offered cover all aspects and issues of gaming, including gender, race, communication, virtual environments, learning and educational value, and new media. Recognizing that game-related curricula and research was at a pivotal moment nationally, and that courses offered at UNT needed support from the library, Media Library personnel first created a project plan to develop game collections in 2006. The convergence of the new course offerings, technology, and student initiatives led to the financial support of this project by library administration in 2009. At that time the UNT Media Library began to collect both video and tabletop games, while continuing to maintain and build a collection focused on film and audiovisual media.

With 37,000 students, the University of North Texas is one of the largest public universities in Texas. Its main campus is located in Denton on the northern edge of the Dallas-Fort Worth metroplex. North Texas has a thriving game design industry that is growing yearly (Entertainment Software Association, 2014). This local industry includes both video and tabletop game design companies such as Gearbox Software, id Software, KingsIsle Entertainment,

Reaper Miniatures, Plaid Hat Games, and Tuesday Knight Games. The university recognizes the value of this industry and is well situated to provide graduates that support and enhance its growth.

The libraries at the University of North Texas support students, faculty, and the community with a variety of specialized on-campus branches. The UNT Media Library contains the libraries' nonprint, audiovisual collections. As of 2016, the game collection includes 473 tabletop games, 918 videogames, 61 PC games on CD-ROM, 49 consoles (regular and handheld), and 170 accessories. Items circulate from 3 to 7 days. The Media Library hosts 12 gaming events and leads 18 workshops related to game design each year. Additionally, the Media Library participates in both regional and international game-related organizations and events and has developed innovative and successful strategies for the planning and day-to-day management involved in curating and circulating game collections in libraries.

## GAME COLLECTIONS

Tabletop games, such as chess and other board games, have existed in libraries since the 1930s (Levine, 2008), but the advent and impact of digital games on American culture make it necessary for libraries to consider collecting these types of materials as well. At the time that the UNT Media Library game collection was first developed, very little professional literature identifying successful strategies or models for collecting either tabletop or video games in an academic environment existed. As the movement to establish game collections on university campuses gained steady momentum in the last decade, the literature on the management and uses of games in academic settings grew to outline this momentum.

In 2008, Smith wrote that "[a]lthough videogames have become ubiquitous in our culture over the last 30 years, we are just now seeing the emergence of computer game studies as an academic discipline, and it is growing fast." Additionally, Smith stated that "librarians need to recognize the challenges, opportunities and the potential impact [of games] on library collections and services" (2008, pp. 205–206). Noting the value of practical and research skills learned in gaming environments, Squire and Steinkuehler found that "game cultures promote various types of information literacy, develop information seeking habits and production practices (like writing), and require good, old-fashioned research skills, albeit using a wide spectrum of content. In short, librarians can't afford to ignore gamers" (2005, p. 38).

Levine (2008) addresses a case study that used gaming examples in developing and advancing information literacy skills by applying the Information Literacy Competency Standards from the Association of College and Research Libraries.[1] Her findings suggest that video games "model many of the stages students experience during the research process: search, evaluation, application, failure, frustration, revision, success. Even though games have not been considered tools for this, they help develop basic information literacy" (pp. 31–32). Although Smith (2008) notes that there will be additional challenges in transferring those skills to scholarly research, the message is clear that games support the mission of libraries in a variety of ways.

This chapter discusses some of the specific ways that games support the mission of the University of North Texas Libraries. It also provides an informal, but very practical case study of library game collections. By describing the practices, and including both what worked for us, as well as what did not, we hope to contribute to the existing literature by offering ideas and inspiration for other libraries and a chance to share our understanding of the value of games in libraries. The UNT Media Library was fortunate in that we had staff interested in starting a game collection, faculty that needed access to games for their coursework, local industry to support us, and a student population eager to participate in gaming and game design. These preliminary factors made it possible for us to begin formally planning and seeking support for game collections.

## PLANNING AND ADMINISTRATIVE SUPPORT

Development of the Media Library game collection officially began in the summer of 2009. At that time a group of representatives from various departments and work groups within the libraries met to discuss how to better coordinate outreach activities to support First Flight, a weeklong student services initiative that welcomes all new students to campus before each fall semester. Colleges and departments develop activities and programs for First Flight that encourage student participation and engage them in campus life. Traditionally, each library department sponsored its own program or event, but in 2009 it was decided that it would be more effective to coordinate and host one event with participation from all library work groups and departments.

To accomplish that goal, a proposal from the Media Library to develop a new collection of video games, consoles, and accessories was revisited. Initially developed in 2006, the proposal was amended to reflect a broader focus to expand and diversify the collection. The First Flight event would promote the launch of this new collection and would introduce students to the various services and collections of the other five campus libraries. For the proposal to be accepted and funded by library administration, it needed to reflect not only the recreational and social benefits of gaming, but also the educational value of gaming as a tool to develop critical thinking and problem-solving skills. Perhaps most importantly, it needed to include support for university curriculum in multiple departments.

Gaming courses were being taught in the Department of Computer Science, the College of Visual Arts and Design, the Laboratory for Recreational Computing, and the Department of Radio, Television, and Film. Gaming courses in these departments included Computer Game Programming, Advanced Game Programming, Art and Design of the Computer Game, Computers in Art: 3-Dimensional Modeling and Animation, and Video Game Theory, Design, and Culture. Demonstrating collaborative support for the curriculum, as well as support from a wide range of representatives across the libraries, led to administration's willingness to fund the proposal.

The initial Media Library proposal included funding for a Wii console, an Xbox console, a PlayStation 3 console, controllers, and five games for each system. To better support First Flight, the proposal was expanded to include funding for equipment rental for screens and portable projectors, food, and library promotional materials. During First Flight, students had the opportunity to play console games and watch a film screening of the documentary *King of Kong: A Fistful of Quarters,* an award-winning film about gamers competing to break world records on classic arcade games. Attendance was highest in the main library, with 400 attendees, while the smaller Media Library hosted 150 attendees.

The success of this event led to participation in the American Library Association's International Games Day event in November 2010 and the start of a monthly "Game On!" gaming event. Student, staff, and faculty responses were positive. This initial positivity moved the Media Library toward expanded program goals: to become a leader in innovative collection development for nontraditional media among the broader community of university libraries, to increase visibility of the libraries' collections and services, to support the curriculum, to investigate the long-term viability of establishing a game collection, to reach new users, and to provide opportunities to expand outreach.

## COLLECTION DEVELOPMENT

A game collection requires a flexible development plan that can be adapted to new findings as research on the impact of gaming on education and society develops. It must also be responsive to changing technology, especially for video games. The paper "New Directions for Academic Video Collections" notes that video game collections are always on the verge of a new generation as technology advances. This ever-changing landscape creates issues with platforms and equipment, as well as digital rights management (Durkee & Robson, 2012, p. 80). In many ways, developing a tabletop game collection is easier for libraries than managing a digital or video game collection, but determining the overall collection's goals and developing a sound collection development plan are still challenges.

The Media Library recognized that support of this new collection was a bit tenuous, and a formal proposal with set goals was needed for its continued growth. In 2011, Media Library staff created a more formal proposal that cited campus classes and their needs as well as challenges and actions needed to meet them. This formal plan continues to be valuable and is updated as the collection grows and changes each year to meet specific goals. The Media Library's policy includes the idea that the game collection be focused on the use, creation, and impact of gaming. Board games, video games (PC and console), and equipment will be collected to support students and faculty interested in games and gaming as a recreational and research area. The collection's primary purpose is to support academic research on the technical aspects of video game development, the study of mass media and popular culture, creative and educational game development, and the vitality of student life.

Initial collection development plans focused exclusively on video and digital gaming to support existing courses and the teaching and learning needs of faculty. These course support needs originated from the UNT Radio, Television, and Film Department from various faculty, including Dr. Derek Johnson who taught a class on video game theory, design, and culture, and Professor James

Martin who uses video games to teach students about storytelling. Building on the original interest, the Media Library began accepting donated consoles and console games into the collection. The collection continued to grow to include role-playing games (RPGs) and tabletop games.

The UNT Media Library collection is not intended to be a historical or archival collection. This may change as the collection ages, but as of 2016 the policy is to collect new items and equipment as they are released. Criteria for purchase include games that support curriculum and collection goals, are top rated or of high popular interest, are historically relevant to game history, or push design and technology boundaries. Collection goals are set each year with the current year's budget and programs in mind, but also include future goals in case funds become available to meet those needs as well. These goals include program, outreach, game, space, and equipment needs; plans for soliciting donations; and ideas for new programs or projects to promote use of this collection.

As the collection grew in influence and resource use, the opinions of more stakeholders were solicited. In 2015, an advisory group was convened to review the collection goals each spring. This group includes members from library

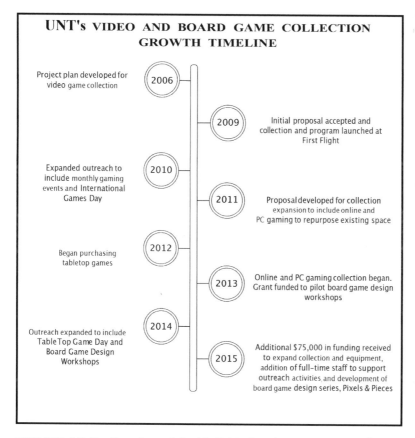

**FIGURE 13.1**   Time Line of the UNT Media Library's Game Collection Development.

technology services, library learning services, and public services. Each spring the collection goals are reviewed and revised to maintain currency with not only campus and program needs, but also new technology being developed in the games and gaming industry.

## Funding and Budget

The Media Library game collections have grown significantly over the last six years. Funding is allocated from the libraries' materials budget, but this amount can be inconsistent from year to year. Spending and growth are managed with both an equipment budget and a materials budget. Curating a game collection requires an awareness of trends in video games and tabletop gaming. Material costs are generally steady with a slight increase when new video games are released each November. Equipment costs can fluctuate as new consoles are released. New consoles are not released annually, and often multiple new consoles are released in the same year or even quarter. Planning for these releases involves not only budgetary concerns, but also consideration of user needs. It is common for one newly released console to be in higher demand than others. Quality and quantity of new video games vary by console, and this fact is taken into consideration as well.

The UNT Media Library rarely purchases consoles immediately upon release. Waiting one year to purchase can save up to $100 per console and up to $30 on games. It also provides time to gauge user demand and determine which games will add the most value to the collection. Additional costs associated with processing must also be considered. New equipment and materials always come with an added cost for processing. Tabletop games require sleeves for cards, fabric for reinforcing boxes, and often other specific materials. Circulating game consoles need bags; in-house consoles need cable locks. Video games need hub protectors, and every item must be labeled and bar-coded. Adequate processing to increase longevity requires budgetary consideration.

Because funding for the Media Library has not always been consistent, it is beneficial to be ready for any type of funding scenario. During years when funding is inadequate to support collection growth, the Media Library plans for future funding while actively seeking donations of new materials. The tabletop game industry, especially, is receptive to donation requests and encourages play and play testing. Donations keep the collection moving forward even in times of budget shortfalls. Good practices have led to more consistent funding for the Media Library budget over time. This is based on successfully planning for growth, good management of both space and collections, and ongoing collection assessment.

## Collection Contents

In 2016, the collection includes digital, console, video, and tabletop games. The collection's games are curated by one of the media librarians with input from faculty, staff, and students. The tabletop collection began with donations for participating in the American Library Association's International Games Day in 2010. The library began to actively purchase tabletop games in 2012. Our tabletop collection includes board games, card games, role-playing games, and giant games to use for outreach and events. The accessories for role-playing games, such as dice, figurines, and battle mats, are also available to our patrons.

The video game collection has continued to grow since 2009. Currently held consoles are from the sixth through eighth generations. They include PlayStation 2 (PS2), PlayStation 3 (PS3), PlayStation 4 (PS4), Nintendo Wii, Nintendo Wii U, Microsoft Xbox 360, Microsoft Xbox One, PlayStation Portable 3000, PlayStation Vita, Nintendo DS Lite, and Nintendo 3DS. Accessories are purchased to support game play on all of these systems. At this time the Media Library exclusively collects games on a physical format for play on these consoles, primarily because born-digital games are not yet available to license for multiple users.

The Media Library also provides in-house access to six personal computers (PCs) and four gaming laptops loaded with game platforms and game creation software. The PCs host the Steam client, Good Old Games client, League of Legends, Star Wars: The Old Republic, and the Blizzard Battlenet client. Available game creation software includes Plotbot, Inkscape, GIMP, Audacity, Stencyl, GameMaker: Studio, Unreal Engine 4, Unreal Development Kit, and Unity. All of the end user agreements and licenses for these programs and platforms are reviewed and approved by UNT's Office of General Counsel. The PC station software is reviewed each semester for updates and relevancy. New software is added when needed.

Patrons and faculty can request that a system or game be assessed for addition to the collection at any time. The Media Library accepts donations of tabletop, console, and video games. Donated tabletop games must be currently relevant and in good condition to be considered for permanent addition to the collection. Donations of PC games are accepted but only circulated if they play in modern operating systems (Windows 8 or greater) because 64-bit Windows no longer offers backward compatibility. An in-house PC Station that uses DOS-Box and Windows XP Emulator for older software is available. Patrons can set up a computer to run as an emulator or virtual machine.

## CATALOGING AND ORGANIZATION

The University of North Texas Media Library has closed stacks, providing access through the online catalog. Patrons request item(s) at the circulation desk, and staff retrieve them. This type of collection access prevents loss and also drives decisions regarding cataloging, processing, and circulation. Cataloging is done to the fullest extent because users rely on the catalog records to discover items in the collection. Each title is cataloged according to current cataloging standards with a local general accession number as its call number. A title available for multiple platforms, such as Wii, PS2, or Xbox 360, has the same general accession number and the appropriate platform information (for example, Game 444 Wii U). This simplifies our ability to provide access to these titles, of which many are available for four or more platforms. Assigning the same accession number regardless of platform eases confusion and allows for faster service.

Tabletop titles include the edition or version in its call number (for example, Boardgame 25 1965). Card games with multiple expansions share the same bibliographic record. A formatted title note lists each specific expansion to make them discoverable in the catalog. Notes in the record and messages in the item screen inform patrons and staff if an item needs another title to be playable. Equipment is cataloged as well. Each type of equipment receives its own bibliographic record that includes any necessary specifications needed for users to make an informed decision for checkout. At this time, game equipment records do not receive call numbers.

Current Library of Congress (LC) genre and subject terms for video and tabletop games are not robust, making this the LC search option limited to format and platform. Research into developing local subject and genre headings to support the discoverability of this collection is in progress. Improving subject and genre headings will support general searches for subjects and genres, searching for number of players, duration of play, and player age suggestions. As the collection is cataloged, the library is considering not only current needs, but also future needs as the collection grows to support coursework related to games. This consideration of future needs includes adding information to help educators using games as they design curriculum, game literacy, and game research. The needs of the users continue to determine the granularity of the information and subject headings in each record.

# PROCESSING

Methods used to process the collection have evolved over time. There was initially a focus in discovering ways to improve the longevity of items and prevent loss. In the beginning the biggest concern was loss of materials. Although closed stacks provide a certain amount of control over access, they do not negate the need to keep track of what is being checked out and by whom. Techniques involved in processing games are not much different from those involved in processing any audiovisual material, but processing equipment requires more time and consideration. Video games are given a single item record and a bar code affixed on the cover. Hub protectors marked "UNT Media Library" are used on game discs to minimize breakage and show ownership. Each case is labeled with a call number and UNT sticker on the spine and front of the case. Each console circulates in its own bag with a single controller. This bag is labeled with a luggage tag that includes a bar code. The luggage tag bar code is the only item record visible in the public catalog for this item.

Inside the console bag, each piece of equipment related to the console has a bar code and an item record. These item records are suppressed so are not visible in public catalog searches. This simplification of public-facing data allows for a streamlined interface, making it easier for patrons to see what is available, yet still keeps track of what is in each bag. Controllers that are checked out separately (and thus are not contained in a console bag) are given their own item record, then bar-coded and placed in a small bag. These bags are labeled with the type of controller inside. The cataloger includes notes in records to denote circulation requirements, such as "needs AA battery," "clear drive when returned," or "place on charger." These notes display when circulation staff scan the bar code to provide guidance for managing diverse items with varying specifications and requirements.

Tabletop games are also processed to prevent loss and increase longevity. In the interest of preventing loss, game pieces are bagged, and a corner band is added to prevent the box from falling open. Some physical components of each game are strategically enhanced to increase longevity: box corners are reinforced with cloth corners, and cards are sleeved in plastic. Each game gets a single bar code on the box lid or bag, as well as a call number. Tabletop games are weighed after cataloging and processing. The weight is noted in a message in the item record.

**FIGURE 13.2** Typical Contents of a Bag that Is Ready to Circulate (one console and its power cord, one controller and its charger, and one HDMI cable for connecting the console to a monitor).

## CIRCULATION

Critical to the success of implementing a new collection is the development of clear circulation and use policies. Circulation of any new type of collection introduces unique challenges. There are issues related to educating staff and patrons, providing efficient service, and being effective in circulating the collection with minimal loss or damage. During the beginning stages of the gaming collection in 2009, many staff members were not familiar with the equipment, what each item was, or how games worked, so additional time was needed for training. Additional time was also needed during the beginning stages for careful communication with users and for carefully managing checkouts.

Media Library circulation policies are posted on the library website, and patrons are reminded of due dates at each checkout. Additional steps were added for the game collection in its early years when patrons were required to read and initial a contract to check out equipment. The contract listed the equipment, and contained a privacy statement and an acknowledgment statement of the fine amounts for late returns or damage. A card containing an image and the name of each item was included in the equipment bag. Only full-time staff and student supervisors were allowed to perform checkouts. Over time, it was decided that some of these policies were excessive. As of 2016, the service desk verbally informs patrons about fines and privacy issues, but no longer requires extra documentation. All staff, both full-time and students, are allowed to perform checkouts. Streamlining these checkout procedures to align with our other resources has not increased issues with fines or overdue items.

Circulating tabletop games were introduced in the Media Library in late 2015. Although these games require more initial processing to prepare them for circulation, once they are fully processed, the amount of maintenance they require is similar to other audiovisual items. Each tabletop game has one bar code and is checked out with one scan. No additional paperwork is required from the patrons. Each game circulates with a bag to protect the game from outside elements or accidents and to prevent loss. At check-in, each tabletop game is weighed. If the weight is significantly different (more or less than 0.3 grams) from the weight listed in the item record, the front desk staff manually evaluates the game. Tabletop games that circulate will be inventoried yearly to evaluate the accuracy of this loss prevention process. As with video games, all staff are trained to perform checkouts of this collection.

# SPACE

How the 2,000 square feet of public space in the Media Library was transformed is one of the most visible and dynamic effects of incorporating games to the collection. In 2009, public space was used primarily by students watching reserve materials for their courses in dedicated film-viewing carrels equipped with various types of video playback equipment. This type of use began to decline as more reserve items were purchased in streaming format for ease of use and accessibility for online courses. This shift gave us an opportunity to evaluate needs and reallocate space to support new programs, services, and collections.

The physical transformation began with the removal of 12 viewing carrels. This freed up 600 square feet of space and allowed the addition of two in-house console game stations, each with access to a Wii, an Xbox 360, and a PS3 console. Students check out or reserve these stations in two-hour increments and check out accompanying controllers and games at the service desk. The success of the console stations was the impetus for adding additional in-house equipment for game play and design. In 2013, three PCs were purchased to support game design and gaming. These PCs took over three additional viewing carrel spots. These three new stations were also made available for checkout at the service desk for two-hour increments. Gaming continued to increase, and space was often crowded, particularly during gaming events. After a particularly crowded "Game On! @ First Flight" in 2014 (with a total of 125 participants in the Media Library each of the three nights), it became evident that additional viewing carrels needed to be removed to expand the space. Their removal opened up an additional 300 square feet of floor space, which made it possible to add moveable tables for individual study or tabletop play, and an additional console game station.

Additional funding received in 2015 allowed the addition of three more gaming PCs, including our first retro gaming PC running DOSBox and Windows XP Emulator that would make it possible for patrons to play older "retro" PC games like the original versions of Oregon Trail (1974), Warcraft (1994), and Doom (1993). In addition to the retro gaming PC, two more console game stations and three older TVs for use with personal consoles were added. This addition brought the total to six PC gaming stations, one retro PC station, one retro console station with access to PS2 and RetroN 5 consoles for playing older games, five console stations, and three TVs for personal console play. This space also includes six tables for tabletop play and individual study. Not only was the physical space transformed, but use of the space also changed drastically. The UNT Media Library is no longer a quiet area. It is vibrant and often noisy, with students interacting around all types of games while studying, socializing, and sharing experiences.

This collection also impacted shelf space, which in the Media Library is not open for public browsing. Until 2015, shelf space was adequate for what was then a slowly growing collection. However, following the dramatic collection expansion that occurred in the summer of 2015, shelving had to be reconfigured to include 12 new consoles, their accessories, and a rapidly increasing tabletop game collection. This was accomplished by sending some of the older audiovisual formats, such as CD-ROM, LaserDisc, and VHS cassettes to storage and rearranging remaining materials. This shift gained about 162 linear feet for the video game collection and 87 linear feet for the tabletop collection.

## OUTREACH

Although games and gaming are a great way to get students into the library to learn about other services, it still takes effective outreach and planning to develop a successful program around this type of collection. Initial outreach goals included attracting new users, introducing the libraries as a safe, comfortable place, and altering the perceptions of what libraries do and collect. Games are fun and engaging, but they also benefit outreach, community building, retention, and educational enhancement.

Felker (2014) notes the shift libraries have made to reinvent themselves as "places for communal discovery, conversation, and exploration" (p. 19). He states that gaming is a "strategy for engagement and a framework for immersive learning and play" that fosters positive user interactions and experiences with the library and helps create partnerships within communities (p. 20). Going beyond collection development and using a collection to engage users and educators requires learning how to communicate with others about the benefits of gaming in an academic environment. The UNT Media Library collection supports coursework, but it maintains focus on the value of games as an avenue for students to learn new skills through play, to engage with their peers, and to develop a supportive community.

The UNT Media Library began with a single event to bring students into the library using games and play in 2009. This effort grew into a robust program of regular monthly gaming, guided learning around tabletop games, and focused efforts on developing collaboration using design thinking around games and gaming on campus and in the community. Early connections were made with existing student groups, such as UNT Game Developers, Chess Club, and Tespa, an e-sports group. Students began new groups, such as the D20 Dungeons and Dragons group and a Magic the Gathering group. Not only do these programs engage students, but they also encourage input and involvement from campus residence life staff, student services departments, and interested faculty.

Early connections have led to increased programming, including a monthly "Game On!" open gaming event, participation in International Games Day,[2] cosponsorship of UNT's Tabletop Game Day, and other events. The Media Library also provides outreach and guided play for library staff each month, Tabletop Lunch and Learn, to familiarize them with games that support curricular needs. This hands-on experience helps staff relay the value of this collection to the faculty that they advise and support.

The success of early events and enthusiasm of the student population led the Media Library to apply for a Texas State Library and Archives Commission (TSLAC) grant to develop a Board Game Design workshop using the Stanford Design Thinking process[3] as a basis for collaborative game design. The grant was awarded in 2014 and funded two workshops for participants aged 12 to 45. Participation was enthusiastic and created several viable tabletop prototypes. It was determined that the designers would benefit from ongoing guidance in a casual environment as they developed their game prototypes. This need for interactive feedback led to the creation of a weekly game design workshop called "Pixels & Pieces: Level Up @ the Library," which provides guidance and encouragement for hopeful game designers and often includes speakers from the game industry. Instructors from both the English and Visual Arts and Design departments have taken advantage of this workshop. Both groups worked collaboratively to create a game; English students focused mostly on narrative in a different format, and Art Design 1 students focused on game design.

Considerable work goes into creating a social media presence, developing promotional designs and marketing, and building a community of gamers on the UNT campus. Outreach happens not only through events, but also through marketing programs on campus and communicating actively through various avenues of social media. This hard work led to considerable success. Building partnerships in and around the UNT and Denton communities elevated the profile of the Media Library, brought attention to growing collections and services, and, most importantly, provided creative and valuable support for students and their educational objectives. Future goals are to align the collection to the educational goals in Common Core and the Texas Essential Knowledge and Skills (TEKS) to encourage education students and faculty to include games in their curriculum.

# ASSESSMENT

A survey of the professional literature shows an increasing number of articles that address building video game collections and programs in academic libraries, but few organizations establishing program goals and assessing the success of those programs. Several case studies showed careful assessment of participation at events, programming, marketing efforts, and collections and equipment (Bishoff, Farrell, & Neeser, 2015; Durkee & Robson, 2012; Smith, 2008; Vanden Elzen & Roush, 2013), but most libraries are assessing short-term goals and not the long-term impact. Little has been written about assessment beyond general observations and recording of circulation, equipment usage, and attendance numbers.

More effective methodologies of assessment are needed to help determine the value and the level of continued support. In an article on video game assessment, Brown (2014) says, "implementation must be accompanied with equal attention devoted to assessment and measurement in order to understand the impact games are having on library spaces" and suggests that four broad perspectives be considered: program-centric, event-centric, game-centric, and player-centric (pp. 447–448). At UNT, an effort is under way to collect detailed data about program attendees over a period of several years to begin to correlate that data to other measures of student success, such as retention, academic performance, and campus involvement. Although there are clear indicators that short-term goals have been met, a need to analyze data more closely to determine the extent of the impact of collection building and programming remains a priority and long-term goal.

## CHALLENGES

Building and maintaining game collections presents challenges that are familiar to many libraries; a few being adequate funding, processing holdings, sufficient staff training, and maximizing available space. Being relatively new to the library world, game collections require creative planning and additional tasks to overcome these challenges. Tabletop games have a multitude of cards, dice, and small pieces that can be lost or damaged and need additional processing to minimize these risks. Video game consoles also have multiple components that circulate along with the consoles and must be checked separately upon return.

Controllers are often in a patron's hands for hours before being returned and require additional deep cleaning. Bar codes and labels on controllers, regardless of material, wear off quickly due to the constant cycle of use and cleaning, which includes the use of isopropyl alcohol. Users unconsciously peel off tape, so corners need to be rounded to discourage this behavior. Each of these issues results in additional time for managing the physical components of the collection and often results in the need for additional or repeated staff training as well. It has also become necessary to identify innovative ways to adapt existing space in the Media Library to balance the needs of gamers with patrons wishing to use the space to view films (the original focus of the Media Library). Providing noise cancellation headphones for patrons and offering a single-user viewing space outside the gaming area is part of this solution.

Educating staff and student employees on the use of equipment remains a challenge. The Media Library was fortunate to have recently been afforded a position for a dedicated staff member with expertise in games and gaming to help manage the collection exclusively. This staff person is able to provide more complicated troubleshooting and answer questions during regular business hours. Each semester, student employees and service desk staff are trained on how to use each console and perform basic functions and maintenance, such as syncing controllers for the various types of consoles.

The nature of online games introduces other challenges. University information technology requirements involve a high level of security that can make it difficult, if not impossible, for patrons to access online game content. At UNT, computers are protected by Deep Freeze technology that prevents users from altering the settings of a workstation. This technology enhances security, but makes it difficult to provide access to any games on the Steam platform that use Custom Executable Generation (CEG) to encrypt each person's game uniquely (Demerjian, 2009). Each user log-in necessitated a staff override to change the executable files; upon log-out all changes were deleted. Removing Deep Freeze so that Steam games could be accessed was eventually permitted in the UNT Media Library, but this required the cooperation of IT and other decision makers. Libraries that are considering adding access to PC games need to consider the barriers that might exist locally. Having a plan and working well with the IT department are necessary for keeping a digital collection running well. If technology barriers cannot be overcome, it will have a fairly large negative effect on collection growth and access.

Licensing online games is another issue. Many PC games can only be accessed through a platform like Steam, and these platforms do not offer multiuser licenses. This challenge limits a library's ability to purchase born-digital content for patrons. Born-digital content for consoles suffers a similar problem; Play-Station Network, Nintendo, and Xbox Live only include single-user licenses for online games. Currently most games are still distributed in a physical format, but if more distributors adopt online-only access models, libraries will face negotiating multiuser licenses. Library licensing and multiuser access to digital game content is in its early stages. A few vendors have models that allow multiusers, but the games available are not robust enough to fit our needs at this time. There is hope that larger vendors will see the need to support this type of collection and begin to offer licenses for libraries in the near future.

Those libraries building and managing game collections face broad challenges, such as predicting and securing the future of game collections in libraries. Libraries also face the challenge of interacting with gamer culture, which can be insular and esoteric. The Media Library continues to work to better understand and integrate gaming culture within the library. Work needs to be done to educate gamers and nongamers on appropriate use of language in public spaces and on developing a greater understanding of gender issues as they relate to gaming cultures. One challenge specific to an academic or school library is in demonstrating the educational and institutional value of game collections. Regularly educating library staff, university faculty, students, and the public about the value of game collections to both students and educators is an ongoing challenge. Connecting the world of gaming with the mission of the UNT libraries requires assessment, outreach, and communication, making it possible for librarians to "develop a deeper understanding of emergent digital literacies and find ways to put library cultures into conversation with gaming cultures" (Squire & Steinkuehler, 2005, p. 41).

## CONCLUSION AND FUTURE GOALS

The Media Library at the University of North Texas started with a small pilot project and went on to build a strong collection of both tabletop and video games, as well as to develop successful programs. Despite remaining issues and challenges, the future of this collection is bright. In the coming years, we hope to develop a campus-wide group around gaming, improve and expand our game design workshop, include curriculum information in our catalog records, expand our technology and space, and continue to encourage students, staff, and faculty to learn through play. Additionally, we continue to explore ways to use gaming principles in library instruction and orientation activities and plan to continue working collaboratively with other departments and organizations to further these goals.

## NOTES

1. See www.ala.org/acrl/standards/informationliteracycompetency.
2. See http://igd.ala.org.
3. See https://dschool.stanford.edu/resources-collections/a-virtual-crash-course -in-design-thinking.

## REFERENCES

Bishoff, C., Farrell, S. L., & Neeser, A. E. (2015). Outreach, collaboration, collegiality: Evolving approaches to library video game services. *Journal of Library Innovation, 6*(1), 92–109.

Brown, R. T. (2014). A literature review of how videogames are assessed in library and information science and beyond. *Journal of Academic Librarianship, 40*(5), 447–451.

Demerjian, C. (2009, Mar. 26). A closer look at Valve's CEG. *The Inquirer.* Retrieved from www.theinquirer.net/inquirer/news/1051534/a-closer-look-valve-ceg.

Durkee, P., & Robson, D. (2012). New directions for academic video game collections: Strategies for acquiring, supporting, and managing online materials. *The Journal of Academic Librarianship, 38*(2), 79–84.

Entertainment Software Association. (2014). Video games in the 21st century: The 2014 report: Economic contributions of the US video game industry, Texas. Retrieved from www.theesa.com/wp-content/uploads/2014/11/Texas.pdf.

Felker, K. (2014). Gamification in libraries: The state of the art. *Reference & User Services Quarterly, 54*(2), 19–23.

Levine, J. (2008). Gaming and libraries update: Broadening the intersections (special issue). *Library Technology Reports, 44*(3).

Smith, B. (2008). Twenty-first century game studies in the academy: Libraries and an emerging discipline. *Reference Services Review, 36*(2), 205–220.

Squire, K., & Steinkuehler, C. (2005). Meet the gamers. *Library Journal, 130*(7), 38–41.

Vanden Elzen, A. M., & Roush, J. (2013). Brawling in the library: Gaming programs for impactful outreach and instruction at an academic library. *Library Trends, 61*(4), 802–813.

# 14

# Seeing and Hearing the World in New Ways: VCU's Collection of Scopes and Other Instruments

*Eric D. M. Johnson*

## INTRODUCTION

In the summer of 2013, the Innovative Media department was created in the Virginia Commonwealth University (VCU) Libraries. Born from the division of the Media and Reserves Services department into three separate services, Innovative Media inherited and expands on the media production support provided by that department and adds to it an emphasis on "making" and emerging technologies.

In November 2015, the department moved into its new space, part of a long-planned expansion of James Branch Cabell Library, which had not received any major improvement since 1975. The Workshop in Cabell Library, as Innovative Media's new studio space is called, is a 4,000-square-foot, glass-enclosed facility whose offerings include an extensive collection of audio and video equipment for loan; computer workstations for capture and editing of audio, video, and still images; 3-D scanning and modeling; a 98-inch multitouch ultra-HD video display; a video gaming suite; and a makerspace with 3-D printers, laser cutter, handicraft supplies, programmable microcontrollers, and much more. In summer 2016, the space also added a video studio with green and blue screens and 4K cameras and an audio studio with professional-grade equipment and Pro Tools software.

Overall, the mission of the department within the scope of the library is twofold. The first is to help people communicate ideas in ways other than text. That is to say, in addition to the pillars of preserving and providing access to content, libraries have always supported the creation and communication of content as well. The second mission-critical focus is on emerging technologies, which certainly overlaps with the first. The Workshop is a place for people to come explore technologies that may soon become part of a more common technical vocabulary, such as video game creation, virtual and augmented reality, 3-D printing and scanning, wearable computing, and computer-aided tabletop fabrication. We do not yet know which of these technologies may become ubiquitous, but it is a powerful service for a library to offer people the opportunity to explore these technologies while they are still forming, and thereby give them a chance to be a part of the conversation that shapes those tools and their use.

## EYES AND EARS: OUR LIBRARY OF THINGS

Although the Workshop offers a lot of the same kinds of collections and services outlined in several other chapters in this book, one things collection that we have really enjoyed developing is what might loosely be called our "perception collection." Specifically, this refers to a collection of audio and video instruments that help people see and hear the world in new ways: a telescope, a microscope, an endoscopic camera, GoPro cameras with a waterproof case, a handheld audio field recorder with a parabolic dish, and other items.

Earman and Salmon (1991) describe the role of instruments as extenders of human sensory capacity this way:

> Human beings are medium-sized objects; we are much larger than atoms and much smaller than galaxies. Our environment is full of other medium-sized things—for example, insects, Frisbees, automobiles, and skyscrapers. These can be observed with normal unaided human senses. Other things, such as microbes, are too small to be seen directly; in these cases, we can use instruments of observation—microscopes—to extend our powers of observation. Similarly, telescopes are extensions of our senses that enable us to see things that are too far away to be observed directly. Our senses of hearing and touch can also be enhanced by various kinds of instruments. (p. 43)

It is just these sorts of "sensory enhancers" that we wanted to make available to the VCU community.

## ACQUISITION AND DEVELOPMENT OF ITEMS FOR THE COLLECTION

The best way to choose items for the collection is to ensure that they are meeting community needs. The first couple of instruments we acquired—really, the origin of the collection—were purchased as a result of direct requests from people at VCU. The endoscopic camera, a tiny camera on a long USB cable for seeing into small spaces (not for surgery!), was bought after a conversation with one of our staff archivists about unusual ways to look at our extensive pop-up book collection. We imagined creating a video by threading the endoscope through the book, letting the pop-up images loom and turn overhead as it passed by.

The telescope was obtained after an open forum we held months before our new space opened in which we discussed plans for the makerspace. Two student attendees, who were members of the university's space advocacy club, wondered out loud whether we would ever consider having a telescope available for circulation. They suggested it would be very popular among their members and would offer a lot of opportunities for outreach. It felt to us like just the sort of resource a library could offer.

From there, choosing items for the collection has really been a question of understanding the nature of the collection on the one hand, and then an analysis of likely community needs—based on university curricula, extracurricular organizations, and expressed interest by library users—on the other. This needs analysis is performed through several means: a regular review of descriptions in the university's course catalog, conversations with faculty about their courses, examination of student organizations on the university website, and a general attitude of "keeping an ear to the ground."

## Current Collection

Here are some specifications of instruments in our current collection:

**Endoscope/borescope wire camera**
*Purpose:* For video of tiny spaces and small objects
*Model:* The First 5 Meters HD 720p 6 LED USB Endoscope Borescope Snake Scope Wire Camera
*Features:* 720p camera, 9mm wide, ring of six LED lights, 5m USB cable
*Cost at purchase:* $23.90

**Telescope**
*Purpose:* For viewing celestial objects
*Model:* Orion 27191 StarBlast 6i IntelliScope Reflector Telescope
*Features:* 6-inch aperture, tabletop reflector telescope, computerized object locator, 23.5 lbs.
*Cost at purchase:* $499.99

**Microscope**
*Purpose:* For viewing tiny objects
*Model:* DBPOWER 5MP 20–300X USB Digital Microscope
*Features:* 5MP image, 300x optical magnification, 8 LED lights, USB connection
*Cost at purchase:* $109.99

### GoPro video cameras with waterproof housing
*Purpose:* For recording video in action and underwater
*Model:* HERO3+, HERO4
*Features:* HERO3+: 1080p recording at 60 frames per second (fps), 720p recording at 120 fps, 10MP photos at 10 fps, ultrawide angle glass lens; HERO4: supports 4K30, 2.7K60, and 1080p video, 12MP photos at 30 fps, ultra-wide angle glass lens + SuperView; time lapse; various action/sports mounts
*Cost at purchase:* $320–430

### Parabolic dish recording setup
*Purpose:* For capturing audio, such as birdsongs, at a distance
*Model:* Telinga Universal MK2 parabolic dish kit + Sennheiser ME62/K6 omnidirectional condenser microphone + Tascam HD-P2 Portable Stereo CF Recorder
*Features:* Telinga: 22-inch dish, pointing handle, Zeppelin mic holder, takes omni or cardioid microphones; Tascam recorder: 2-channel stereo, records to compact flash, BWF files, LCD display, phantom power
*Cost at purchase:* parabolic dish: $888 + microphone: $349 + field recorder: $596.99

## Future Additions

The Workshop's "perception collection" of instruments continues to grow. Expected additions include binoculars; additional lenses for our DSLR cameras, such as fish-eye, wide-angle, and macro lenses; and ultraviolet and infrared photography gear. We would also like to make available to the wider community our camera-mounted unmanned aerial vehicles (UAVs or drones), but this awaits policy guidance at the university level.

We are also exploring other areas for future investment, such as a high-speed camera capable of image exposures in excess of 1/1,000 of a second or frame rates in excess of 250 frames per second, for slowing high-speed objects; light-field (plenoptic) cameras, which take pictures that permit users to select which part of an image is in focus; 360-degree cameras to capture entire environments in a single shot; a remote-controlled submarine with camera, to give us the option of underwater photography to balance the aerial photography permitted by the UAVs; a photogrammetry rig, which is a circle of cameras on all sides of a subject or object that fire simultaneously, permitting 3-D reconstructions and *Matrix*-like "bullet time" effects. In addition to all of this, we are starting to explore development platforms related to augmented and virtual reality, such as the Oculus Rift and Microsoft HoloLens systems.

## Choosing Specific Models

Once a broad need for an item is identified (for example, we know we want a telescope), the next question is one of identifying the best specific model to purchase. For us, this generally involves addressing a series of questions:

- If there are options in this regard, are we seeking an entry-level instrument, something for more advanced users, or something that would work for both?
- Do any of our users, if they have a specific interest or expertise in this area, have recommendations from their experience or knowledge?
- What is our budget?
- Do we have other constraints to consider, such as storage or staff expertise (or lack thereof)?
- Can we maintain the instrument ourselves?

One way to get a good read on specific options, descriptions of an instrument's ease of use, and other important evaluative information is to look to reviews. There is no shortage of opinion on the Internet and in popular and professional literature, and instruments like the ones under consideration here have an especially rich and well-informed user base. This makes it easy to find arguments for and against particular features and models, which help in making a purchase decision.

I also look to user reviews on vendor sites such as Amazon.com and B&H, because those reviews can give the perspective of average users who might raise red flags in areas that professional users look right past. At the same time, I would never base my purchase decision solely on these quick-hitting "average user" reviews, because we to need to have something more like a "prosumer" level of knowledge of our instrument collection.

## Where to Buy

An extensive array of sellers carry the kinds of instruments that make up our collection, including manufacturers, small specialty boutiques, large theme retailers, chain stores, and massive online retailers (for example, Amazon.com).

In the end, for purchasing a specific model, the best choice may simply be to conduct a price comparison and buy from the most cost-effective vendor. However, if it seems likely that many purchases will be made over time, it might be helpful to establish a relationship with a store that offers expert support or discounts for educational institutions, which may include libraries. Two specialist vendors we often use for our equipment—B&H (photo, video, and pro audio) and Sweetwater (music technology)—offer advice on a whole range of manufacturers' products, discounts for educational institutions, and the ability to establish standing accounts. Some vendors also provide additional or extended warranties or repair plans for the instruments they sell, which can often prove very useful, as will be discussed later.

One thing to consider is that your institution may be bound by vendor relationships that have been negotiated by local or state purchasing departments. It is important to understand whether you need to turn first to those vendors when seeking to purchase particular items or kinds of items.

## Paying for the Collection

We were lucky in developing the initial collection at the Workshop as our funds came to us as part of the equipment budget related to the construction of the new library expansion. Sources that we will certainly explore in the future as we develop the collection further include student library and student technology fees (not unusual in a university setting) and grants.

Many libraries have pursued sponsorships, partnering with manufacturers and receiving donated or reduced-price equipment in exchange for unique exposure to the manufacturer's goods; these are often done in conjunction with specific outreach programs such as media production camps or other events. Creating a whole collection with an identified purpose (for example, "Helping our community see the world") is a wonderful opportunity for corporate sponsorship or community grants.

Other libraries include such purchases as part of their operating expenses, especially when it demonstrably meets the user community's needs, just as they do with any other library resource. Another route to the development of an initial collection is to solicit donations of instruments from the communities of interest in the area.

# HOUSING AND CIRCULATION

The collection presents unique logistical considerations in terms of circulating, storing, and maintaining the instruments. This section outlines some of these challenges and the approaches we have taken to meet them.

## The Challenge of Carrying Cases

Optical and audio instruments offer a particular challenge that I had not considered before diving deep into the world of these collections: that of carrying cases. One might think that it is easy enough to either keep the thing in the box in which it was shipped or pull it from the box and just put it on a shelf. Neither of those approaches always works.

Often, an instrument is shipped in a disassembled fashion, with pieces wrapped in plastic bags and tucked lovingly into purpose-shaped cavities cut into the Styrofoam packaging. The problem there is that users do not want to (nor should they be expected to) assemble the entire instrument each time it gets used. Instead, the library staff should assemble the instrument after receiving it and then make the whole thing available to users in a ready-to-use fashion, if possible.

This in turn introduces the issue of simply keeping the instrument on the shelf and handing it across the desk when a user wants to check it out. The problems there: How do you keep the instrument safe from damage? What if it has multiple pieces or accompanying accessories (for example, extra lenses, connectors, or user manuals) that need to circulate at the same time? How is all that kept together?

The solution, we have found, is to find some kind of carrying case for the assembled instrument. Some manufacturers have anticipated this need and provide (or sell for additional cost) cases in which to store their assembled instruments. Another approach is to find a stand-alone case, sometimes adapting cases intended for other instruments or devices and sometimes looking well outside the "instrument" category altogether.

As an example of the latter approach, the tabletop telescope in our collection is now stored in a rolling 50-gallon Stanley tool chest, which was less expensive than the manufacturer's case and has the advantage of being hard-sided (though the disadvantage of being more awkward to handle). We had to cut foam padding ourselves, but now the entire telescope and its peripherals are all stored together.

It is important to consider whether hard-sided cases are needed or if soft-sided or padded cases are sufficient (we often use Neoprene sleeves for smaller instruments); whether the manufacturer provides a purpose-built case or bag, and if so at what cost; what kinds of modifications (additional padding, adding carrying straps, etc.) might be required if a case must be adapted; and the overall cost of each approach in terms of money, time, and effort. It is also important to decide whether the various peripherals should always accompany the instrument as might be the case with a user manual, or if they could be circulated separately as items themselves because they do not always need to go with the main instrument, as might be the case with specialized lenses for a DSLR camera.

The same vendors that provide instruments (for example, optical, video, audio vendors) often also sell cases and bags for those and many other instruments, and some of the latter might be adapted to instruments in your collection. Other sources include hardware suppliers and online case manufacturers. An easy first step is to simply do a Web search for the particular item and the word *case* (for example, "GoPro camera case"). These searches will often turn up third-party manufacturers who provide cases for particular instruments. We often find ourselves turning to Amazon and B&H for our cases.

## Storage

Another challenge we faced is one of storage. Keeping the instruments near at hand for our circulation staff can be tricky, because they compete for space with other needs at the information desk and some of the instruments are large or otherwise require some unusually shaped storage. We have hunted around for storage cabinets with adjustable shelving and in one instance a more vertical storage space (like a high school locker) that can keep tall equipment safe. Even then, the telescope—our constant if wonderful challenge—has to be kept in a nearby storeroom and retrieved by a staff member when a user wants it.

One last key to any storage solution: we strongly recommend that storage cabinets or other spaces be lockable. The library staff may choose to unlock the storage at the beginning of the day and lock it up again at the end of the day or to unlock/lock at each transaction, but there is no substitute for an additional layer of security for what is often relatively expensive equipment.

## Replacement and Backup Parts

Experience has taught us that some instruments simply have parts that are easy to lose and break; for example, the GoPro cameras come with small thumb-screws that are regularly lost. We maintain a collection of replacement and backup parts like these that we dip into as needed, minimizing the time that an instrument might need to be out of circulation. Keep an eye on the stock of the replacement parts and replenish as needed.

## Extended Warranties/Repair Plans

As mentioned previously, a number of vendors and manufacturers of these kinds of instruments offer extended warranties and/or repair plans (such as SquareTrade) that, for a relatively small fee, can provide real peace of mind by providing protection in the case of the worst kinds of manufacturing defects, breaks, drops, and spills. If a knob is broken, for instance, the plan will cover its repair or replacement, or in extreme cases could cover the replacement of the entire instrument. In our experience, with equipment that circulates often to many different users, the rate of wear and tear is high enough to justify the investment.

## Considerations for Cataloging and Circulation

Our library management system (Ex Libris Alma) provides us with the ability to create records for equipment, as well as for the usual book and media formats, and we do this carefully as we get new items so that users can check on the availability of equipment or renew instruments the same way they could for other materials. We bar-code the instrument in some slightly hard-to-reach place (for instance, the inside of a battery cover) and scan the bar code to circulate it.

Fulfillment Notes:

Contents: Case, GoPro Hero3+ Camera, Waterproof Housing w/ Latch, SD Card Cover, 32GB Micro SD Card, Battery Cover, Li-ion Battery (1), Battery Charger, Lighter Charger Cord (MISSING), USB Cord, WiFi Controller, WiFi Controller Lock, WiFi Controller Charging Cord, Micro SD Adapter, Head Strap, Pivot Arm, 2 Screws (1 SCREW IS MISSING), Manual ***Please Delete Used Memory on the SD Card***

**FIGURE 14.1** Sample Fulfillment Note with Details for Staff; Patron Does Not See This Note.

One very useful feature of the library management system is the ability to add a notes field that pops up in front of the staff member as a particular item is circulated. We make extensive use of this field to record a list of all accompanying accessories, including the manual, the various pieces of the instrument, additional cables, or literally anything that can be separated from the main instrument.

The circulating staff member has to examine the instrument and ensure that all the pieces are present (or note when a piece is not present) before it goes out so that we and the patrons know they are getting the full instrument, or at least that we are aware of a missing piece. If a piece is missing, the notes field is modified to reflect that the piece is known to be gone, and the proper staff members are informed so a replacement can be ordered.

Similarly, when checking the item back in, the notes field (plus modifications) again pops up, this time to ensure that the user has returned the instrument and all its peripherals in their entirety. Users are responsible for replacement costs of any lost items, so this circulation process ensures that they know what they are receiving and what they are expected to return. We typically do not charge for broken items, because wear and tear is not unusual with these kinds of loans; your library may have its own policies to follow in this regard.

## TRAINING OF STAFF AND USERS

An instrument collection is not as complete as it could be if the library staff member simply slides one of its instruments across the desk without understanding its use and care. The staff should be able to answer questions about the instrument, how and why to use it, the specifics of its operation, and best practices in use and care by the user. This means that before it goes into circulation, appropriate staff members should be given an opportunity to read through the manual, assemble and disassemble the instrument, and ideally take it out for a spin in field conditions to make sure they can anticipate the user experience. Not all staff will become expert users, naturally, but ideally those that most interact with the instrument collection should be comfortable with the instruments, understand how to maintain them, and know where to turn for more advanced assistance (which may be a community of users found online).

Personal familiarity with the instruments will also make it easier for staff members to assist users. We often find that users benefit from a brief orientation to the item during checkout, including a recap of the major features, an explanation of the peripherals, and a recommendation that they turn to the user manual (which always accompanies the device) for in-depth questions. For some instruments, we have created a kind of "cheat sheet" or "quick guide" that covers its major operational aspects. Some libraries scan the user manuals in case the physical copy is lost; many manufacturers also make their manuals available online.

## DATA AND ASSESSMENT

For an instruments collection as well as any other library of things, data can be key to assessing its impact. Ideally, statistics would be kept of the number of times each item circulates and other circulation patterns, along with a sense of the demographics of the user base. Most library management systems (LMS) permit at least the transaction statistics reporting of this sort. If the collection is not integrated into the wider LMS, the system that is used—even if it's only a paper tally—should provide statistics about its use.

Despite whether usage information can be integrated into user demographics (whether to protect privacy, because the system does not provide this sort of functionality, or for some other reason), a periodic survey of users might be a good way to get a sense of who is using the collection. This is an important point of data when it comes to marketing the collection: knowing what kinds of users are targeting what kinds of items will help the library understand new audiences to whom they might reach out to expand the user base.

More qualitative information can also be gleaned about the use of the collection, formally through surveys, but even informally by way of conversation with users. There are clear ethical considerations to make when dealing with the question of why a user needs a particular instrument, as is the case with any other library item (American Library Association, 2008). However, the practical reality is that in conversation with library staff, many users reveal the origin of their need, and libraries can benefit from using that voluntary information to better understand the use of their collection.

## Assessment of the Collection

The aforementioned user data can be used in a wider analysis and assessment of the particular collection. As Johnson (2004) points out, "Although librarians tend to think of collection analysis as measuring the collection's quality (an amorphous concept, at best), the real intent is to measure the collection's utility or how well it is satisfying its purpose" (p. 268). Though Johnson is speaking of library collections generally, the advice and approach certainly applies to specialized things collections as well.

Johnson goes on to describe assessment approaches that can be either collection-based or use- or user-based, and quantitative or qualitative (pp. 270–72). The goals of these assessments include increasing knowledge about the collection and its use, marking progress toward performance goals, ensuring effective investments, assisting in creation and management of collection development policies, helping explain decisions and expenditures, and analyzing the potential to support new programs or partnerships (pp. 272–73).

# THE FUTURE OF AN INSTRUMENTS COLLECTION

Undergirding the information provided in this chapter is the expectation that a collection of optical, audio, and other instruments is no static thing, but an organic collection that will grow and change in response to changing user needs and technological developments. The approaches described previously should help carry a collection forward into the future, but it is critical that libraries continue to talk to their users and regularly assess the context in which an instruments collection is developed. Do we see the same needs now that we saw one, three, or five years ago? Do we see the same users that we saw one, three,

> Said the poet Yeats: "The world is full of magic things, patiently waiting for our senses to grow sharper."

or five years ago? What has changed, and have we altered the collection, the policies, or the procedures to match those changes?

In particular, the instrument collection of the sort described here comprises a number of technologies that are changing at a rapid clip: manufacturing improvements mean that quality goes up while prices come down, entrepreneurs seek to solve technical problems in novel ways, new products are regularly coming on the market. This means that the library responsible for these collections needs to stay abreast of these changes.

Easy and enjoyable ways to do that are to keep tabs on the popular press in various fields. For instance, if you have a telescope-using constituency, flip though *Astronomy* magazine on a regular basis (or better yet, consider subscribing to *Astronomy* magazine so that all your users may benefit). If you want to see developments in a number of fields, keep tabs on *Wired* or *MIT Technology Review* or other generalist publications and websites. Find blogs or Pinterest boards or podcasts in the fields of interest that your collection supports. Watch for new offerings from vendors. Listen to your users as they talk about new developments that interest them.

There can be no doubt that creating and maintaining a "perception collection" of optical and audio instruments is a relatively complex undertaking, given the sometimes elaborate nature of the items themselves and the attendant effort it takes to make the systems work smoothly for users and library alike. But it is not so complex as to warn anybody away from creating this kind of collection.

The excitement with which this collection is met—the delight among users that somebody would make these instruments available for them to use—is a deeply satisfying thing, on personal, professional, and community-building levels. Add to this the fact that such a collection lets people experience and perceive their world in new ways that they themselves get to control, and the satisfaction for the thoughtful library collection builder resonates all the deeper.

# REFERENCES

American Library Association. (2008). Code of ethics of the American Library Association. Retrieved from www.ala.org/advocacy/proethics/codeofethics/codeethics.

Earman, J., & Salmon, W. C. (1999). The confirmation of scientific hypotheses. In M. H. Salmon et al. (Eds.), *Introduction to the philosophy of science* (pp. 42–103). Indianapolis, IN: Hackett. (Original work published 1992.)

Johnson, P. (2004). *Fundamentals of collection development & management.* Chicago: American Library Association.

# Part IV

## Special Libraries

# 15

# Things Collections, Alaska-Style: Furs, Skulls, Mounts

*Celia Rozen, Helen Woods, and Ed Kazzimir*
*Photographs by Ed Kazzimir*

As the old saying goes, sometimes timing is everything. Alaska Resources Library and Information Services (ARLIS) was the right idea, formed at the right time, in the right place, and had the right people to become entrusted with a world-class collection of "things" (ARLIS tends to use the term *realia*). This chapter chronicles the story of how and why ARLIS now has an enviable collection of furs, skulls, bird mounts, fish mounts, and education curriculum kits (referred to hereafter as the "FMS" collection—that is, Furs-Mounts-Skulls, see Figure 15.1), and how its extremely successful public circulation program also serves ARLIS's overall larger mission as one of the foremost northern region's library collections. It is also the story of a library that intentionally stepped outside its traditional role as a "special library" to broaden its base of support.

## BACKGROUND

ARLIS was formed by the unification of many small resource agency libraries, most of which had been managed by a single librarian, into one entity, under one roof. Alaska branches of eight federal, state, and university agencies pooled their staffs, collections, and budgets to form ARLIS in 1997. The collection is largely technical reports and professional scientific materials, with the notable exception of the FMS collection. The agencies involved include two state agencies (Alaska Department of Fish and Game and the *Exxon*

**FIGURE 15.1**   This Photo Captures about One-Fourth of the Bird Mounts Available at ARLIS. In addition, a 500-square-foot room is filled to the brim with furs, skulls, and education kits.

*Valdez* Oil Spill Trustee Council), five federal agencies (Bureau of Land Management, Bureau of Ocean Energy Management, National Park Service, U.S. Fish and Wildlife Service, and U.S. Geological Survey), and one university agency (University of Alaska Anchorage, Environment and Natural Resources Institute).

In the pioneering spirit of the Last Frontier, this state, federal, and university merger was remarkable at the time, as was ARLIS's team-based management structure. It was one of the few existing multiagency libraries that included both a simultaneous federal and state presence.[1] The emphasis on the new consolidated library's uniqueness was underscored by ARLIS being awarded a National Partnership for Reinventing Government "Hammer" award from Vice President Al Gore in 1997 and in winning the Institute of Museum and Library Services' (IMLS) National Medal for Museum and Library Services in 2001. This consolidation not only saved several libraries from getting completely cut from agency budgets, but also preserved those precious Alaska materials that had been carefully collected for many years and were threatened with shipment to far-off libraries or even more remote inaccessible storage. The FMS collection was no insignificant part of the IMLS award, and was expressly mentioned to distinguish ARLIS as a unique library.

With its diverse agency management and staffing, ARLIS has to grapple with three overlapping fiscal years, an array of varying holidays and leave policies, agency cultures that see things a bit differently, even the capricious issuance of snow days (longed for by Alaskan students and workers alike), and a list of further differences. Yet, the economies and advantages realized by the partnerships far outweigh any potential difficulties, and as the Institute of Museum and Library Services expressed in its award booklet: "ARLIS has proven to be greater than the sum of its parts."

ARLIS is a serious research library that public-sector agency and private-sector consultants rely on to get their jobs and projects done. ARLIS is often the unique source for technical and consultant reports, development project output, and pre-statehood publications. Often the "old stuff" in ARLIS's comprehensive collection is vital to biologists, geologists, and other professionals to gain the best understanding of baseline environmental factors to determine how changes have occurred over time. Its collections on Alaska, the Arctic, and northern regions are especially rich in hard-to-locate agency reports. The library now boasts a combined collection of more than 300,000 items and is arguably the largest collection of Alaska resources reports found anywhere.

## ARLIS'S FMS COLLECTION STORY

ARLIS's early success resulted in its founding agencies looking upon the library favorably, after the initial period of grumbling about losing the "library down the hall" to an off-site shared facility. The original co-located library was busy, well used, and was strategically situated for great parking and quick access. Its combined collection was impressive following the co-location and merger. ARLIS was proving itself to be extremely successful in both satisfying the expectations of the agencies that funded it and being sought after by the private sector. Efficiencies resulting from the partnerships allowed each agency to enjoy an exponentially greater number of resources at its staff desktops, such as databases and journals, than they ever had before as a single-agency library operation. As a result of this initial success, individual agency staff members were coming up with schemes to empty out "office libraries" that had accumulated in offices, hallways, and storage rooms and thereby increasing ARLIS's collection. Hence the fortuitous situation presented itself not long after ARLIS's formation to be offered the furs, skulls, and bird mounts by Alaska Department of Fish and Game, Division of Wildlife Conservation (ADF&G).

It only takes one person to come up with a great idea. For the FMS collection, that one person was the ADF&G wildlife technician tasked with circulating the huge collection of furs, skulls, and bird mounts to the few local teachers who somehow got the information via word of mouth that ADF&G had these items available for loan. This staff person would need to make a trip to the storeroom where the items were jumbled together. The circulation occurred in a black plastic garbage bag, with the borrower's name and contact information scribbled on a sticky note, and off the item went.

This haphazard loaning arrangement involved phone calls, meet-ups, and all the foibles that go along with finding someone in a big confusing building who is simultaneously a busy technician on the move, more likely to be drawn away to answer a problem bear or moose incident than to be hanging around the building for teachers dropping in unexpectedly. It was certainly not a perfect process, and that immense collection was largely idle.

The excellent idea for ARLIS to become the central circulation home for the collection came to fruition in May 1998, only seven months after ARLIS's formation. The many good reasons for this idea included: (1) ARLIS, as a library with an integrated library system (ILS), retains borrower contact information electronically; (2) prior circulations resulting in fines or blocked cards would indicate if the potential patron may have a problem with returning materials; (3) ARLIS's ILS would track any overdue material; (4) ARLIS was staffed at its reference desk from 8:00 a.m. to 5:00 p.m., Monday through Friday, to circulate materials as a normal business practice.

Buy-in and approval by the division's top brass resulted in an informal agreement (see Appendix F) and a modest appropriation to purchase the initial plastic boxes and totes for circulation. That was the end of circulations in black plastic trash bags! The agency also purchased the tags that identify each item as being provided by ADF&G.

## Augmenting the Collection

Why does a state resource agency end up with so many of these items? A primary source is roadkill that falls under the agency's jurisdiction. Depending on the impact, skulls may be salvageable. Sometimes, when citizens exercise their right to "Defense of Life or Property" (defined as an unprovoked animal attack), the skulls or furs may be salvaged by the agency. Alaska is a state of numerous hunters, many of whom already have a house full of mounts and bear rugs. Avid huntsmen will often donate their overabundance of furs that they do not want to keep in their personal collation to ADF&G. Widows who want to take the opportunity of their new single lifestyle to redecorate are also a big source of donated mounts. Alaska state troopers who oversee wildlife actively confiscate illegal specimens and turn them over to ADF&G for an annual sale or donation to ARLIS. Lastly, ADF&G has a "sealing" requirement that brings hunters into the office to report their kills and present in person the hide or skull, as regulatory mandated, for bear, sheep, lynx, wolf, and wolverine, and in some cases, bull moose. This interface with wildlife officials can sometimes result in donations of unwanted parts.

Publicity about the collection also has been an opportunity to grow the collection. An article in *Alaska Fish and Wildlife News* alerted its 6,000 subscribers that a raven mount was ARLIS's most frequently requested item (Rozen, 2015). Ravens are an iconic bird in Alaska and a big part of the urban and rural Alaskan outdoors. Their loud and expressive caw can be heard on downtown streets as well as on wilderness hikes. These intelligent birds have a rich social life and their antics are a delight to witness. Artists in particular and even English majors writing papers on Edgar Allan Poe have come to the library asking for a raven mount. As a result of the article, a frozen raven in a veterinarian's freezer was located, and a state permit to allow the taxidermist to create a mount was made available. In other states, bird treatment centers may also be a source of additional bird mounts. The high cost of taxidermy for raw specimens continues to be a consideration.

## Storing the Items

When designing the current library on the University of Alaska Anchorage (UAA) campus in 2004, ARLIS staff learned from its prior location what did not work and planned accordingly. Taking the enormity of the collection into account, adequate heavy-duty shelving was an important consideration in terms of quantity, adjustability to accommodate size variations, and an expansive shelf width to maximize available storage. The storage room for the FMS collection needed to be close to the reference desk so that long-term abandonment of the desk did not occur for every transaction. Protection of the items was key, so it was put in a staff-only area that would keep the curious out during UAA library's continuing open hours after ARLIS's more limited staffed hours. A mnemonic alphanumeric shelving location helps staff find items quickly as patrons patiently wait for their retrieval back at the reference desk.

## The Collection Gets Media Attention

Through a happy coincidence and without much effort on ARLIS's part, a string of publicity events fell into ARLIS's lap in 2015 that once again highlighted the unusual nature of its FMS collection. It is not often that a library is front-page news, featured in a national radio program, has a video expressly shot for CNN, and gets requests by local (but faraway) television broadcasters looking for opportunities to feature some homegrown Alaska reality TV, but all these events occurred within the same month. Most intriguing to the media was that anyone with a library card could check out a "dead animal just like a book." It all began with the checkout of a baleen (a fascinating and highly decorative elongated whale bone) by a day care center housed at the University of Alaska Anchorage that just happened to include the toddler of a local newspaperman in the mix. His enthusiasm for the collection followed by a prominent front-page, above-the-fold story got picked up by the Associated Press, and things spiraled out from there. Hence, the invitation for this book chapter as well!

## Education Curriculum Kits

ARLIS's success in becoming a central source of education curriculum kits has not attained the same heights achieved by the collection of furs, skulls, and bird mounts. It is not due to a lack of cooperation on the part of the agencies; in fact, cooperation has been widespread. Rather, it seems to result from diverse agencies believing these kits to be a tangential part of their mission. Although ARLIS itself has about 40 kits, many duplicative and unique kits exist through a multiplicity of efforts by federal and state agency education staffs and are searchable through an assortment of websites, each of which tell only a part of the access story for potential patrons.

The driving force of these related efforts seems to be the desire on the part of professional agency educators to interface with classroom educators directly, resulting in a glut of information that may be rather bewildering to potential users. Multiple websites posting varying lists to consult translates into different policies for users, especially regarding nonlocal use. Experiential access to kits with the same title but unequal content, depending on updates to newer technologies, is also a complicating factor. Instead of one cohesive effort, education kit endeavors in Alaska have been duplicative, fragmented, and unsystematic.

The sheer number of locations, changed names and phone numbers of contacts, agency relocations creating new addresses to track down, and versions of the guides are frankly confounding, and actually limit the effectiveness of these programs. In Anchorage alone, five sources are listed, potentially having educators running around town to chase down busy agency employees. The cacophony of options is more head spinning than helpful.

An important trend has been the separate efforts by various agencies to update the technology in their education curriculum kits. VHS players are almost extinct in schools, so a video must be provided in DVD format to be useful for today's teachers. This often involves an expense, regardless of whether the DVD is copied or purchased. Trade materials may not be copied due to copyright restrictions, but titles are not always offered for sale in the newer format. ARLIS found itself having to purchase "related" titles when replacing video cassettes with DVDs. Slides are another problematic format, as slide projectors are no longer readily available at schools, requiring scanning effort.

Individual libraries wishing to be resources for these materials are encouraged to check the U.S. Fish and Wildlife Service website for the many offices that offer such "conservation" kits to teachers. State fish and game agencies as well as state departments of education have proven to be alternative sources. The U.S. Department of Education made regional efforts to centralize the access of these useful classroom tools through 2005, but these regional "Eisenhower Consortia" now have an archived website. Whether libraries have a role in their retrieval is an open question, but this service does have a potential library audience.

## ADVICE IN HOW TO CIRCULATE THESE "THINGS"

Note: the use of brand names in the following sections is merely intended to assist with description and recognition and is not intended as brand endorsement.

### Enclosure Requirements

After ADF&G's initial purchase of boxes, ARLIS has relied on its own funding to purchase additional boxes to circulate these items and for taxidermy costs related to the existing and growing FMS collection. Boxes and other enclosures are critical to the mission of circulating this collection. It did not take long for ARLIS staff to realize that, although it was fine for kids in classrooms to handle furs to their heart's content, skulls and bird mounts were a different story. These items are delicate and easily damaged. Public services staff readily came to the conclusion that these items were meant only to be seen, not handled, and that they needed to stay inside their locked see-through boxes.

To avoid any more garbage bag checkouts, many plastic boxes were needed to accommodate the FMS items. The majority of furs could circulate in store-bought, Rubbermaid-type containers. The need for custom-made containers became apparent due to the unusual size, shape, or weight of some of these skulls and mounts. Although Anchorage is the biggest city in Alaska, only a very few businesses make custom acrylic boxes. These take careful planning on the staff's part to come up with standard sizes that accommodate a great variety of specimens. Another consideration is the expense involved in fashioning and fabricating these boxes, as a typical custom box averages $450 to $600 (Alaska pricing in 2015).

## Store-Bought Container Requirements

Store-bought Rubbermaid-type containers are used for the furs and smaller skulls. These come in a variety of sizes to accommodate the vastly different fur and skull sizes. They are durable and are easy to open and close with hinge-type lids preferable for small items and removable tops accommodating the stowing of larger items.

## Custom Box Requirements and Considerations

Through trial and error, and three rounds of custom orders, ARLIS staff has determined container specifications that adequately address the wear and tear of circulating these often-delicate items. Custom boxes are constructed from $3/16$-inch clear acrylic on a half-inch Sanalite base (Figure 15.2 depicts a few custom boxes). ARLIS affixes bar codes and circulates the custom box as well as the item inside the box. The 25-item checkout limit includes the boxes.

### Bird Mounts

As described, ARLIS invested in custom clear acrylic boxes in a variety of sizes to accommodate most of the birds that circulate. Some of the boxes are large enough to accommodate two birds at once, which also makes it easier for patrons to transport. Birds are fastened to the box (see the later section labeled "Velcro").

### Larger or Unwieldy Skulls

The larger skulls, those with protruding horns (such as musk ox or Sitka black-tailed deer) or that are naturally tippy due to uneven weight distribution (like the walrus skull) will often require a custom-made box, which, as described previously, incurs a sizeable expense. The larger skulls tend to be

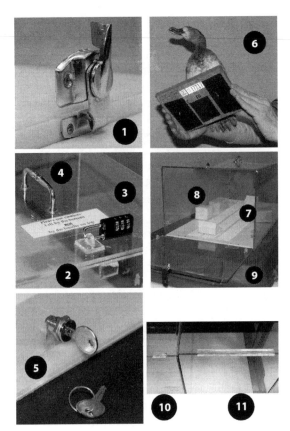

heavier and the Rubbermaid-type boxes do not adequately encase them. Horns and antlers eventually poke holes in the Rubbermaid-type boxes.

## Handles

ARLIS managers soon realized that these boxes and their contents were more vulnerable whenever patrons picked up the custom boxes by the handle on top. Items are better off being picked up when supporting the bottom of the box. Just having a handle on top is an open invitation to mishandle the box, so the handle option was eliminated on the second round of custom boxes.

## Doors

**FIGURE 15.2**  ARLIS Custom Circulation Cases and Details Regarding Their Construction and Usage, as Described in the Previous Section.

The placement of doors on these boxes was another lesson learned after some trial and error. Garage door–style openings with the hinge on top allow the circulation staff to rest the door on top of the box, rather than using a spare elbow to prop a side door open while handling a bird with a possible bobbing head or outspread wing, and were discovered to be the easiest to load (see Figure 15.2, view 11). Doors that have the hinge on the bottom (see Figure 15.2, view 9) tend to get more wear and tear on the hinge area through stepping or leaning on it. Boxes that were specially designed to be long and flat to hold a fish mount were better off with a door at each end, as none of the workers at ARLIS had arms long enough to push a long fish into a box from the tail end while simultaneously strategically placing the snout end. Getting the fish hung up on Velcro when it is partially in the box can be a frustrating experience.

## Hinges

After trial and error, ARLIS staff found that long acrylic hinges (see Figure 15.2, view 11) are more durable and pivot better than short acrylic hinges. Also, any acrylic hinges are preferable to brass hinges that screw in. Because the boxes are subject to constant use, the brass hinges began shedding their brass screws through wear and tear after only a few years. The brass clamps (see Figure 15.2, view 1) were also not a good solution, as it can be hard to match up the tops and bottoms, especially if the original top strays from the original bottom, due to inexact box specifications. Matching the brass clamps is a "hit-and-miss" experience and results in patrons witnessing much fumbling.

### *Locking Mechanisms*

The next logical step after the realization that bird mounts needed to be locked up during circulation was coming up with a locking system for the custom containers. The original boxes had acrylic hasps in which a mini-padlock was placed (see Figure 15.2, view 3). Heavy circulation broke these acrylic hasps after few uses (see Figure 15.2, view 2). Brass hasps were preferable, but the mini-padlocks became problematic. It is truly amazing how a mere three-number password on a padlock challenged everyone's memories. To prevent embarrassment in front of patrons, the preferable system was a lock and master key (see Figure 15.2, view 5) that works on all boxes and lots of spare keys that are conveniently placed.

## Other Circulation Essentials

In addition to having the right custom boxes, other elements related to processing and transport have made ARLIS's circulation of these furs, skulls, and mounts much easier.

### *Carts*

The logistics of transporting the items is a critical factor in patron satisfaction with the circulation transaction. Adequately sized carts allow patrons to check out many items at a time and transport the items to their car. ARLIS is favorably situated so that patrons can go to the backdoor loading dock to load their cars with checked-out items or to easily drop off FMS collection items upon return. Patrons can call the front desk to have a staff member meet them at the back door for returns. This makes quick work for patrons to return, and lends a no-hassle feeling to the transaction. Long flat carts are great for heavy objects, as they do not have to be lifted very high. A tiered cart with no shelf lip is another handy cart to employ for smaller boxes.

### *Velcro*

There is nothing like two-inch-wide, industrial-strength, self-adhesive Velcro (yes, there is such a product!) to keep a delicate bird mount from slipping around in the box. ARLIS staff puts the flat wiry side of the Velcro as a base in the bottom of the box, and the bird mount itself has the fuzzy side (see Figure 15.2, views 6 and 7).

## *Padding, Cushioning, and Propping*

Although furs can be simply tossed into a Rubbermaid-type container with no harm done, skulls, bird mounts, and fish mounts require a high degree of care to prevent transportation damage or overzealous handling by patrons. ARLIS has employed the use of Styrofoam, Bubble Wrap, hand-fashioned cardboard supports, found objects, and literally yards and yards of industrial-strength Velcro to prop, stabilize, or protect items (see Figure 15.2, view 8).

## *Item Identification Tags*

For ADF&G, owner of the items, to receive due credit with library patrons, who by definition are all residents and thereby constituents of this state agency, ADF&G originally supplied identification tags. ARLIS added the name of the species typed on the underside of the bar-code card. This feature was added so that teachers may have students guess the species before revealing the name on the tag. The plastic slipcase keeps the whole tag and identifying material clean and protected.

## **The Potential Perils**

Only two major incidents have occurred to date that resulted in materials being returned in an unsatisfactory state or needing repair. The polar bear fur was circulated to a summer camp that hires young people overseeing even younger people. The wrong people were left alone with sharp scissors, resulting in a diagonal cut through the polar bear fur that produced two unequal halves. Prior to this, it had been a prime specimen. In addition, a tundra hare, a very soft fur, was torn apart due to overzealous handling. It became evident that the polar bear and tundra hare were among the most difficult items to replace. Polar bears are protected by U.S. Fish and Wildlife Service (see the Marine Mammal section later for a discussion regarding the special restrictions on these furs). Furthermore, it is rare to encounter an available specimen. ARLIS was lucky to replace the torn polar bear in 2009, through a "Transfer of Property" form from U.S. Fish and Wildlife Service. This was a pelt in its entirety, but nowhere near as soft and white as the prior specimen.

ARLIS has a "tundra hare alert" circulating through Alaska Department of Fish and Game, but the sad situation is that these are much in demand, yet hard to find due to the annual predator cycles and the tundra hares' vulnerability. Also, trappers tend to keep these furs due their fine coats and usefulness. They are notoriously difficult to trap.

The skulls themselves are subject to some handling by patrons, but borrowers tend to be very careful with these, especially due to signing the Statement of

Responsibility (see Appendix H). Many are repeat borrowers who have a stake in maintaining the quality of the collection. Teeth do fall out, needing to be reglued, and skulls yellow with age. But for the most part, the items retain their integrity over many circulations because of patrons' due diligence. Aside from expected container wear and tear, this constitutes a very low rate of problem circulations during this program's 18-year history to date.

### Mothballs and Bugs

One incident that falls under "perils" literally became a staff health hazard. One of the last specimens that had been transferred in 1998 from ADF&G to ARLIS was infected by an unspecified bug that had been pervading the ADF&G office. This bug quickly infected the hundreds of specimens in the ARLIS collection, causing a mild case of hair and flesh loss, which for a short time increased the "ick" factor. After exploring a number of options, including leaving them outside in an unheated Conex rented trailer for the entire Alaskan winter to freeze out the critters, the ultimate solution by the hired exterminator was a heavy dose of naphthalene and lots of mothballs (more naphthalene) in every enclosure. Due to staff getting headaches from the smell, ARLIS had an environmental firm perform an airborne Naphthalene analysis. Although the existing OSHA standard of 10 parts per million (ppm) was underexceeded (results:<0.02 ppm), staff health complaints continued. The purchase of two air purifiers and the implementation of a plastic curtain to enclose the room holding the items, plus the passage of time, eventually conquered the smell.

### Federal Problems with Marine Mammals

An additional challenge is the legal limitation on the transport of marine mammal parts, which are subject to the Marine Mammal Protection Act (MMPA) of 1972 (16 U.S. Code §1361 et seq.). ARLIS's circulation of the marine mammal furs and skulls came under question during 2014 by federal authorities at U.S. Fish and Wildlife Service. At issue was whether users of ARLIS were inadvertently breaking the law by transporting marine mammal parts in violation of the MMPA.

Although attorneys for both the federal and state governments readily agreed that ARLIS's program did not violate the law and that the loan program could legally continue, the management team updated the Statement of Responsibility to include Use Agreement 3 (see Appendix H): "I agree to abide by the Marine Mammals Protection Act which prohibits taking marine mammal items over state lines." Although it is likely that such events have never occurred, patrons are duly warned, and ARLIS is protected.

## PUBLIC SERVICE ASPECTS OF THE FMS COLLECTION

This section outlines some of the major impacts that the FMS collection has had on ARLIS's policies, staffing, and outreach efforts.

## Current Practices and Policies

### Closed Stacks

It has become necessary to limit user access to ARLIS's realia collection. Patrons often express a wish to see the collection as a whole to bask in all their choices. Although ARLIS staff is proud of the collection and it is rather fun to show it off, this became problematic because the collection is stored in tight quarters within the "employees-only" area. Browsing became disruptive and interfered with staff work. In 2014, the ARLIS management team made the decision to make the FMS collection a closed-stacks collection, and instead created finding aids for patrons to browse. A sign to this effect is posted; additionally, a photo book of all available mounts, a brochure listing all items in the FMS collection, and a brochure of the available educational science kits can be perused at the circulation desk. Once the patrons have decided which items they would like, staff will retrieve them for checkout. The storage room is no longer used as a "patron selection room."

### Local Checkouts Only—Return Only to ARLIS

FMS collection items must be checked out in person at ARLIS, and returned in person at ARLIS. As part of a very large consortium, patrons can return most items to any member library. Not so with the FMS collection. Because of the fragile and valuable nature of the FMS items and the time necessary to ensure that a kit is returned in its complete state, it is required that these items be returned directly to ARLIS during open hours and that the transaction be in person. This limits the possibility of damage or loss in transit and any liability on the part of other libraries. It also allows ARLIS to determine any damage at the time of return. With both patron and librarian present for the transaction, it prevents disagreement surrounding returned condition and date of return, and most importantly prevents the loss of items with claims of return. Although ARLIS has had requests to mail realia to patrons in rural areas, the items contained in ARLIS's educational kits and in the FMS collection are quite fragile, making the risk of damage in transit too great to fulfill this request. For this reason, ARLIS does not make them available through interlibrary loan or via the holds system.

### Checkouts during Limited Hours

ARLIS is open 8:00 a.m. to 5:00 p.m. Monday through Friday. Patrons are asked to begin the checkout/return process no later than 4:45 p.m. to allow for the time-consuming process of browsing the finding aids, deciding which items to check out, retrieval from the storage shelves, and securing into boxes if necessary—all of which must happen prior to the circulation transaction. The items are then carted to the circulation desk for checkout. Once the items are checked out, often staff (with library cart) assistance is needed to get the items out the door to the patron's vehicle.

Checking items in requires that the items be inspected for damage and completeness. Thus, the time required for realia transactions can be great. End of the day is the most common circulation time for this collection. Sometimes the circulation desk is busy transacting with more than one patron, so the 4:45 p.m. time line is helpful in avoiding overtime and disruption of closing procedures.

This time frame can be troublesome for teachers, who are among the most frequent users of the FMS collection and the educational science kits, as their workdays are full and long. Often a family member will come to check out for a teacher, and sometimes they will check out well in advance of when their lessons will be presented so that they are assured of having the material on hand, because ARLIS does not reserve items. This often results in items being renewed past their original due date, which, up to this point, has not been a problem.

## Statement of Responsibility

ARLIS requires a Statement of Responsibility (see Appendix H) to be signed and dated by the patron when checking out any items from the FMS collection. This form addresses three areas: statement of personal and financial responsibility for loss or damage of the item, box, tag, or bar code; use guidelines; and repair/replacement costs.

It is also signed and dated by the ARLIS librarian. Notably lacking was a section requiring current contact information, which led ARLIS public services staff to rely on potentially outdated patron records. During the time that this chapter was written, the form was amended to require documentation of current contact information to assist with collection efforts.

## Agency Reserves Only

ARLIS is a composite of several government agency libraries, funded by those agencies. This structure informs ARLIS's unique mission in that founding and member agencies are given priority with regard to library resources. For this reason, ARLIS will accept reserve requests from its agency-affiliated patrons. For all other patrons, ARLIS does not reserve kits or items in the FMS collection. Instead, they are circulated on an as-available basis.

## Staffing Needs

The FMS realia collection is a fairly staff-intensive aspect of ARLIS. The logistics of circulating a realia item from closed stacks require a staff member to pull the desired item or items from the storage shelves. ARLIS's collection often involves packing an item in a locked acrylic box for safe transport, easy viewing, and damage control while checked out. For these reasons, the realia collection is available for checkout only during ARLIS's open hours, when the reference/circulation desk is staffed with one reference librarian. The circulation technician works in the afternoons in support of the reference desk and any circulation needs. Much of the circulation technician's time is devoted to the maintenance and handling of ARLIS's realia collection.

Many of the FMS items and kits are quite large and heavy, so they are usually moved by cart from the storage shelves to the circulation desk for checkout, then wheeled to the loading dock in back of the library for loading into the patron's vehicle. This requires that support staff be available during open hours to ensure that the desk is covered during realia transactions, requiring this to be a consideration in scheduling staff hours.

Maintenance issues regarding this collection range from fixing broken or tampered locks and hinges on the acrylic boxes to arranging for repair of a fur or mount. Pieces can break off from skulls; kits must be checked to ensure all contents are contained within upon return; and sometimes staff time is required to track down overdue items and send reminders that an item needs to be returned, or that fines are accruing.

## Challenging Public Service Aspects for Consideration

Unexpected publicity in the spring and summer of 2015 raised the profile of ARLIS's realia collection, bringing a surge in circulation, as well as some unanticipated issues. Since the publicity, many patrons from other libraries are interested in checking out FMS items. This has, by necessity, changed ARLIS's circulation routine by imposing the need to research each library account that a patron may have among the consortial libraries to ensure that the patron is in good standing. Some patrons have multiple cards, some with excessive fines; some patrons have an expired card or no card at all, so those details must be attended to prior to checkout. During the transition time from little publicity to a lot of publicity, the checkout process gaps are being found. The upside is that they can be addressed. The downside has been learning about them the hard way. Some items have been checked out to bad-risk patrons, and if they are true to pattern, much time is required to track down, notify, monitor, and continue communicating with the patron until valuable item(s) are returned.

Recognizing that updated patron information is important to the return of items, ARLIS revised the Statement of Responsibility form to ensure that current contact information is included. Also under consideration is whether to require a patron's ID in addition to their card, as ARLIS is developing a policy regarding when and how a patron's delinquency will impact future ARLIS transactions. Interesting questions regarding responsibility arise in the cases of items being checked out for others. ARLIS is considering whether a need exists to require some sort of deposit as well.

ARLIS's newfound publicity also resulted in a boost in use by the K–12 teaching community, but the items had been well used prior to being front-page news, as teachers spread the word to other teachers. With ARLIS being situated at a university that offers teaching degrees, it is well placed for knowledgeable instructors to share information about the collection to teacher trainees. In addition, ADF&G Division of Wildlife Conservation has a staff of educational experts who actively interface with teachers needing wildlife curriculum materials.

Forward thinkers in the field of wildlife education have produced guides that market hands-on teaching concepts. National curricula like *Project WILD K-12 Curriculum and Activity Guide* raise teacher awareness of the types of materials that serve wildlife teaching goals, such as those comprising the FMS collection

(Council for Environmental Education, 2009). Professional education literature is full of references to the benefits of hands-on learning (Crow, 1996; Klein et al., 2015; Tobin, 1997), and teachers seem well aware of its value.

The problem for ARLIS is getting the teachers into the library in a reasonable time frame so that ARLIS public services staff can accommodate their needs within a normal workday. Teachers are recognized as being prone to overwork (Schembari, 1994) and are extraordinarily busy during ARLIS open hours. Oftentimes, teachers will send in a proxy for the circulation transaction. This works well until someone with a compromised library record or no library card is dispatched to the library, resulting in repeat visits to obtain the items. To this end, teachers have expressed great appreciation for the easy return at the loading dock. The lack of weekend and evening transactions is acknowledged as a potential service limitation to teachers. However, the presence of the selection lists at the ARLIS website, the ADF&G Teacher Resources webpage, and the U.S. Fish and Wildlife Service-Alaska Region Educator webpage[2] helps to widen access, as these are available anytime and allow teachers to prepare their requests for same-day pickup.

## ADVICE IN HOW TO CATALOG THESE "THINGS"

According to Anglo-American Cataloguing Rules (AACR2), Rule 1.1C1, the word *realia* is an optional addition after the title in square brackets for three-dimensional objects. ARLIS makes use of the word [realia] in [square brackets] in the 245-title field, as the word is not on the piece itself. ARLIS uses the title term *fur* to describe what may synonymously be referred to as a "pelt," "hide," or "skin." If "otter" and "realia" are used as search terms, for example, one would find the river otter skull, river otter fur, sea otter skull, and the sea otter fur.

A note on the future use of [realia] as a General Material Designation (GMD): libraries that are undertaking the new Resource Description and Access (RDA) cataloging conventions should be aware that the GMD is being phased out. OCLC is planning to remove it from all records in WorldCat. The word *realia* cannot be found in in the RDA Toolkit, which makes mention instead to "objects." However, rather than searching the catalog, most people having repeated acquaintance with the collection will instead use the posted list (see Appendix G), which lists all the items. ARLIS keeps a steady supply of the paper list available at the reference desk as people like to check off the items they want. This makes it easy for the staff person to verify that all requested items are provided to the patron.

### Catalog Records

As ARLIS appears to be one of the few libraries with such holdings, ARLIS's cataloger is perhaps one of few nationwide with extensive experience in cataloging such "things" in particular. One caveat is that these records cannot be found in OCLC as they were input into the local system due to their solely local availability. They may instead be accessed by searching the ARLIS catalog at www.arlis.org.

AACR2 Chapter 10, "Three-Dimensional Artifacts and Realia," offers some guidance on "real, naturally occurring item[s]," but it provides no specifics on taxidermic materials. Library of Congress (LC) has no applicable rule interpretations for such items, nor has OCLC provided specific guidelines. In Example 10.3, Olson, Bothmann, and Schomberg (2008) offer a helpful example in how to catalog a naturally occurring item. In this case the item was a geode (rock).

## Advice on Specific Catalog Record Fields

The following section describes how ARLIS handles specific MARC fields when cataloging furs, skulls, and mounts.

### MARC Format: Titles

Most realia objects, unlike a book, do not come supplied with a title, so the cataloger devises one and makes a note indicating the source. At ARLIS we start with the name of the organism, followed by the item type (or body part), such as "Brown bear skull" or "Sea otter fur." If place of origin is important, the place may be included, such as "Algae from the Homer, Alaska area." For taxidermic items such as a mounted or stuffed animal, ARLIS uses only the name of the animal (for example, "Greater white-fronted goose"). ARLIS does not follow these formats: "Mounted organism" or "Organism mount," nor the inverted format: "Body part of organism."

In records cataloged under AACR2 1.1B7, the devised title is entered in square brackets. No brackets are used under RDA. A note for the source of title is required under both systems (AACR2 10.1B1 and 10.7B3; RDA 2.3.2.10 and 2.17.2.3), as in a 500 note indicating "title supplied by cataloger." However, for a collection that was given a title, or a single item that was distributed under a title, use that title supplied from the container or labeling. A natural object might have been purchased or obtained under a name, or may be named on a plaque. Give the source of that title in a note.

### General Material Designator (GMD)

AACR2 includes [realia] in [brackets] after the designated title in subfield-h after any subfields-a, n, and p. RDA does not include the GMD. For example:

| | | |
|---|---|---|
| AACR2: | 245 00 | [Black bear fur] ‡h [realia]. |
| RDA: | 245 00 | Black bear fur. |
| Both: | 500 | Title supplied by cataloger. |

### Content, Media, and Carrier Types

RDA uses these fields in place of the GMD. OCLC allows the addition of these fields in AACR2 hybrid records that contain the GMD.

336    three-dimensional form ‡b tdf ‡2 rdacontent
337    unmediated ‡b n ‡2 rdamedia
338    object ‡b nr ‡2 rdacarrier

### MARC Fixed Fields

When using OCLC Connexion, typically the fixed-field table is encountered in the manner shown in Table 15.1.

### Field 007

There is no specific 007 field (physical description fixed field) for realia and three-dimensional objects. A 007 field had been defined in MARC21 for unspecified category of material (007/00 'z'), but OCLC did not implement it until several years later in August 2011. It is an optional field. Until guidance is published, the most logical coding of this field for realia is subfield-a "z" and subfield-b "u" (or "m" if there are multiple forms in a collection), as in:

007    z ‡b u

### Publication Information

For naturally occurring objects that are not commercially packaged or distributed there is no AACR2 Publication Area (AACR2 10.4.C2). RDA simply makes no mention of recording such statements in the pertinent rules 2.7 to 2.10. Thus, this field may be entirely omitted. The date is not to be assumed.

### Subject Headings

ARLIS uses Library of Congress subject headings. There is no rule regarding realia in LC's Subject Heading Manual. For subject access, ARLIS has decided to use LC subject headings using the tag 655 for genre/form instead of the more common tag 650 for topical terms, as the objects being cataloged are not about the animal but instead are physical manifestations of the item named. ARLIS generally assigns one heading for the organism and one for the type of object.

### TABLE 15.1   OCLC Connexion

| Type | r | ELvl | I | Srce | d | Audn | | Ctrl | Lang | zxx |
|---|---|---|---|---|---|---|---|---|---|---|
| BLvl | m | Form | | GPub | | Time | nnn | MRec | Ctry | xx |
| Desc | a | TMat | r | Tech | n | DtSt | n | Dates | uuuu.uuuu | |

*Note*: Blank fields are intentionally blank.

## TABLE 15.2  Explanatory Table of MARC Fixed Fields

| Field Name | OCLC Mnemonic | Field Definition | Code for Realia |
|---|---|---|---|
| Type of Record | Type | Type of MARC Record | r |
| Encoding Level | ELvl | Degree of completeness of the MARC record | I—full-level input by OCLC participant (other codes are also possible) |
| Cataloging Source | Srce | Original catalog source of the record | d—other (most libraries use this code; some cataloging agencies may use other codes) |
| Target Audience | Audn | Intellectual level | |
| Type of Control | Ctrl | Archival control status | |
| Language Code | Lang | Language of the item | zxx |
| Bibliographic Level | BLvl | Bibliographic level of the record | m—monograph item c—a collection |
| Form of Item | Form | Form of the material | |
| Government Publication | GPub | Publication of a government agency | |
| Running Time | Time | Running time of motion pictures and video recordings | nnn |
| Modified Record | MRec | Modification of bibliographic information | |
| Country of Publication | Ctry | State or country of publication | xx |
| Descriptive Cataloging Form | Desc | Form of descriptive cataloging according to ISBD | a—AACR2 c—RDA without ISBD punctuation i—RDA using ISBD |
| Type of Visual Material | TMat | Type of Visual Material | r |
| Technique | Tech | Technique to creation motion | n |
| Type of Date | DtSt | Type of publication date | n |
| Dates | Dates | Date 1 and Date 2 | uuuu,uuuu |

*Note:* Blank codes are intentionally blank.

**Sample LCSH organisms:**    **Sample LCSH objects:**

| | |
|---|---|
| Black bear | Antlers |
| Dall sheep | Fur |
| Lynx | Head |
| Pike | Jaws |
| Sablefish | Vertebrae |

However, because ARLIS specializes in research on animals, we prefer to use a form subdivision to help identify such three-dimensional objects. ARLIS uses the form subdivision "‡v Specimens." Because LC's official definition of this subdivision does not conform to ARLIS usage, we use second indicator "4" to mark the field as a local heading so it will not be "corrected" by another agency or by a vendor in a database cleanup.

| | |
|---|---|
| 655 _4 | Polar bear ‡v Specimens. |
| 655 _4 | Fur ‡v Specimens. |
| 655 _4 | Chinook salmon ‡v Specimens. |
| 655 _4 | Jaws ‡v Specimens. |

An example of a fully cataloged bear mount, following current AACR2 standard catalog rules follows:

OCLC record:  54057850

| | | | | | | | |
|---|---|---|---|---|---|---|---|
| Type: | r | ELvl: | l | Srce: | d | Audn: | Ctrl: | Lang: zxx |
| BLvl: | m | Form: | | GPub: | | Time: nnn | MRec: | Ctry: xx |
| Desc: | a | TMat: | r | Tech: | n | DtSt: | n | Dates: uuuu,uuuu |

| | |
|---|---|
| 007 | z ‡b u |
| 043 | n-us-ak |
| 245  00 | [Black bear] ‡h [realia]. |
| 300 | 1 black bear mount : ‡b black phase ; ‡c 134 x 66 x 114 cm., on base 72 x 48 x 78 cm., overall 155 x 70 x 100 cm. |
| 500 | Title supplied by cataloger. |
| 500 | Standing 3/4 high, mouth open with teeth showing, ears back (full body mount in defensive threat pose). |
| 500 | "Male black bear taken in western Prince William Sound in 1993. Donated in memory of James P. Green"–Plaque. |
| 500 | Styrofoam mount. |
| 500 | Mounted on wooden base with accompanying faux lichen and other foliage. |
| 500 | Details about bear supplied by Rick Sinnott, ADF&G Anchorage area biologist (February 2004). |
| 655 _4 | Black bear ‡v Specimens. |

RDA Differences:

| | |
|---|---|
| Desc: | i |
| 245 | no GMD (subfield "h") and brackets |
| 336 | three-dimensional form ‡b tdf ‡2 rdacontent |
| 337 | unmediated ‡b n ‡2 rdamedia |
| 338 | object ‡b nr ‡2 rdacarrier |

**FIGURE 15.3**   A Complete Catalog Record for a Full-Sized Black Bear Mount under AACR2 Rules, as Specified by Olson et al. 2008, with RDA Standards Noted (Note: Thanks to Julie Moore and her team of cataloging interns in 2004 for their creative work. Updates provided by Ed Kazzimir).

However, ARLIS generally uses only brief records created via its ILS for the specimens, so the records do not appear in OCLC. A typical record follows:

| Rec_Type | r | Bib_Lvl | m | TypeCtrl | | Enc_Lvl | k |
|---|---|---|---|---|---|---|---|
| Desc | a | Entrd | 980820 | Dat_Tp | n | Date1 | uuuu |
| Date2 | uuuu | Ctry | xx | Illus | | Audience | |
| Repr | | Cont | | GovtPub | | ConfPub | 0 |
| Festschr | 0 | Indx | 0 | Fiction | 0 | Biog | |
| Lang | zxx | Mod_Rec | | Source | d | | |

| Tag | Ind. | Contents |
|---|---|---|
| 099 | | FMS F-O88 |
| 245 | 00 | [Sea otter fur]\|h[realia]. |
| 300 | | 1 fur. |
| 655 | 4 | Sea otter\|vSpecimens. |
| 655 | 4 | Fur\|vSpecimens. |

**FIGURE 15.4**   A Brief Record for a Sea Otter Fur, as Depicted from a SirsiDynix WorkFlows Display.

## MISSION-RELATED CONSIDERATIONS

As ARLIS has evolved into a major Alaskan library, and broadened its appeal through this popular collection, it is firmly connected to its agency roots through its service orientation and its pride in promoting and helping to fulfill founding agency missions. This strong connection keeps ARLIS relevant to individual agency staff members in getting their work done and to agencies as a whole in being a vital part of their operations. ARLIS remains strongly aligned with its agencies' missions.

ARLIS's primary service orientation and funding source is the federal, state, and university agencies that originally came together to form ARLIS. In those terms, ARLIS considers itself a "special" library. Yet, from the public's perspective, ARLIS is also a "public" library in the sense that anyone from the general public or private sector may walk in during open hours with reference questions, research projects, or casual interest in its collection and services. Checkout privileges are easy to obtain and services are identical, no matter the affiliation of the nonfounding agency walk-in, call-in, or e-mail user.

The "public" aspect of ARLIS services originated with a 1972 secretarial order that mandated the Department of Interior in Alaska to establish and operate a library that served the public. This need was identified due to "heavy demands on the department" to provide Alaska resources information. This management authority was transferred to the Bureau of Land Management (BLM) via an organizational change memorandum authorized by the director of BLM in 1986.

This authority as carried forward by the BLM is the main driver for ARLIS's commitment to providing public services, and the BLM funding level assures this service continues. As stated in the organizational change plan, "[a]ll traditional library services are provided by the library including reference, telephone reference, interlibrary loan, circulation and online bibliographic searching."

Through the FMS collection, ARLIS's deep commitment to serve the public has grown stronger. This service orientation is manifested by staffing a reference desk during all open hours (45 hours per week), maintaining telephone and e-mail reference services, licensing its scientific journals and databases to be available to on-site visitors, sharing a library catalog with public libraries throughout the state, participating in a patron-initiated holds program, creating brochures and LibGuides that direct users to its more hidden collections, and serving all on-site users and providing them with free parking.

The FMS collection, by far, is the largest draw for the public to ARLIS. Cub Scout troops use the furs to symbolize moving up from Wolf to Bear ranks. Established and aspiring artists draw inspiration from the shape and shadowing of skulls. According to the Alaska Department of Fish and Game (2005), teachers often use animal skulls as a "tool for teaching about the diversity of Alaska's wildlife and the special role each animal plays in its natural environment" (p. 7). Camp counselors envisioning fun activities, event planners needing decoration, and parents helping kids with in-class presentations are attracted to ARLIS specifically and sometimes exclusively to this collection.

Some have surprised staff with new and innovative uses for this collection. Staff did not initially envision that the spotted owl would be used for Harry Potter events. The most notorious use was by the movie, *The Frozen Ground,* which was filmed in Anchorage and re-created serial killer Robert Hansen's basement lair using ARLIS materials, for which the library was never listed in the credits, despite the pivotal role the "trophy room" played in the movie. However, the film producers paid for repairing the walrus skull they borrowed, so ARLIS benefited from foregoing its prohibition of circulating these items to nonresidents. Their movie credit to "The wonderful people of the City of Anchorage and State of Alaska" likely included the people who work at ARLIS. Those curious to see the trophy room can fast-forward to minute 23, but be prepared for gory violence.

## Conformity with ARLIS's Collection Development Policy

ARLIS's collection scope is addressed in the following collection statement. The concept that most closely addresses the FMS collection is ARLIS's service to the constituency of its founding agencies:

> The ARLIS collection will focus on the research and information needs of its founding agencies, primarily in the areas of natural resources and cultural resources management in Alaska. Subject area emphases are wildlife and fisheries biology and habitat, arctic issues, traditional knowledge, resource development, mineral industries, land use planning, earth science, environmental studies, pollution studies, oil spills, and conservation. The ARLIS collection will likewise serve as an information resource for the constituency of its founding agencies, the public, university students, the business community, and individuals and groups involved in natural resources conservation and development. ARLIS will acquire materials

appropriate to the use of these groups in the designated subject areas. ARLIS will participate in cooperative collection development with public and university libraries to minimize duplication and to perpetuate a largely unique collection in Anchorage.

The circulating FMS collection was initially amassed by Alaska Department of Fish and Game to serve its active constituency of wildlife educators and enthusiasts of all types. ARLIS is upholding that service, expanding it, and broadening its reach to the public at large.

### Other Mission-Related Considerations

Libraries considering the adoption of a wildlife realia collection have a number of factors to consider, including the ease of the circulation transaction in light of the library's physical layout, adequate and accessible storage, and the labor and expense of circulating the items, which involves an investment in boxes, allocating circulation staff, etc. Core mission is certainly a fundamental consideration. In ARLIS's case, being founded by natural resource agencies allowed access to the materials, and a special order to serve as a public library allowed ARLIS to offer these materials widely, hence the agency-related need to have these items publicly available was inherent in its library operation. A mission consideration for ARLIS would have been to circulate to teachers only in conformance with the ADF&G model, but ARLIS chose to instead extend their access to any user "on the road system" having the capability to return the items, and therefore broadened the library's appeal to the general public.

Although a more traditional special library serving agency clientele may have access to FMS-like items, they may have neither the mandate to serve the public nor adequate staff to do so. Conversely, a traditional public library may have clientele that would like access to these types of materials, such as teachers and Scout leaders, but the jurisdiction to acquire these materials from state or local agencies may be lacking. Although the advice to librarians to seek out these materials through contact with the proper agencies may be freely given, there is little evidence that other libraries have done so. A single university library[3] was identified in the research leading to this chapter as offering science kits that include specimens like the items within the FMS collection, but it serves only its own college population and area teachers. The source for these materials is not indicated. The central theme of this chapter is that realia collections are the exception rather than the norm, and it is hoped that other libraries will find ARLIS's experiences with these items helpful in examining whether the expansion to such a program will conform to an individual library's existing mission or become a worthwhile expansion of mission.

## CLOSING OBSERVATIONS ABOUT HANDS-ON TEACHING TOOLS IN THE CLASSROOM

According to Tobin (1997), teaching using the hands-on method "gives students an active role in their own learning. . . . [S]tudents . . . need to explore,

justify, predict, synthesize, conjecture, solve, infer, model and otherwise participate in the learning process. One effective way of encouraging the active involvement of students is to incorporate hands-on activities into classroom teaching"
(p. 371).

Current teaching literature advocates the use of skulls to "provide an additional learning resource through the tactile modality; connect practical, real-
world knowledge to more abstract concepts; and improve memory through
physical actions" (Klein et al., 2015). Curriculum-based texts acclaim this
approach for teaching science in elementary and secondary grade levels. Tobin
(1997) notes that "co-participation among the teacher and students requires
all participants to communicate with one another using a shared language
that evolves over time, [that] use of the language is a critical part of the learning process . . . as students engage the tasks that constitute the curriculum"
(p. 400). The FMS collection allows for this type of learning experience.

However, the use of wildlife realia in the classroom presents unique challenges. The Alaska Department of Fish and Game (2005) give the following
cautions to teachers: "Skulls should be handled carefully. Students should be
sitting down when handling skulls, using both hands to pass them, preferably
over carpeted floor. . . . When teaching about Alaska mammals, it is important
to note that there are some cultural mores where it is inappropriate to talk about
a particular species. For example, the Athabascan culture traditionally discour-
ages women from speaking about bears" (p. 71).

These furs, skulls, and bird/fish mounts, as well as educational kits, are
used to inspire students. A recent article in the *Anchorage Daily News* discusses
one high school teacher's use of this collection. The teacher annually checks
out a variety of items for a three-day lab that "allows students to get up close
to the things that they'll be studying each year. . . . It gets them excited about
being in biology class. It starts the year off on a good foot" (Caldwell, 2015).
When hearing these stories from teachers over the reference desk, the excitement in the teachers' voices carries over the shared experiences from the classroom into the library and gives staff an inkling of the encounter with science
that occurred in the classroom through the use of this collection.

## NOTES

1. Another notable example is the StreamNet Library in Oregon.
2. See ARLIS: www.arlis.org/docs/vol2/a/Furs_mounts_skulls.pdf; ADF&G: www
.adfg.alaska.gov/index.cfm?adfg=educators.teachingkits; USFWS: www.fws.gov
/alaska/external/educators.htm.
3. Illinois State University, Milner Library, Teaching Materials Center. Educational Kits: illinoisstate.libguides.com/c.php?g=30483&p=191309.

## REFERENCES

Alaska Department of Fish and Game, Division of Wildlife Conservation. (2005).
*Skulls of Alaskan mammals: A teacher's guide.* Juneau, AK: ADF&G.
Caldwell, S. (2015, Oct. 6). Check out this stuff. *Anchorage Daily News,* pp. A1, A6.

Council for Environmental Education. (2009). *Project WILD: K-12 curriculum & activity guide.* Gaithersburg, MD: Project WILD.

Crow, T. (Ed.) (1996). Active learning with hands-on resources (special issue). *ENC Focus, 2*(2).

Klein, J. L., Gray, P., Zhbanova, K. S., & Rule, A. C. (2015). Upper elementary students creatively learn scientific features of animal skulls by making movable books. *Journal for Learning through the Arts, 11*(1).

Olson, N. B., Bothmann, R. L., & Schomberg, J. L. (2008). *Cataloging of audiovisual materials and other special materials: A manual based on AACR2 and MARC 21* (5th ed.). Westport, Connecticut: Libraries Unlimited.

Rozen, C. (2015, Nov.). ARLIS: Furs, skulls, mounts, kits and so much more. *Alaska Fish and Wildlife News.* Retrieved from www.adfg.alaska.gov/index.cfm?adfg =wildlifenews.view_article&articles_id=748.

Schembari, P. (1994). Teacher workload in elementary and secondary schools. *Education Quarterly Review, 1*(3):11–16.

Tobin, K. (1997). The teaching and learning of elementary science. In G. D. Phye (Ed.), *Handbook of academic learning: Construction of knowledge.* San Diego: Academic Press.

# Part V

Best Practices

# 16

# Best Practices: Building Your Own Library of Things

*Lindley Shedd and Mark Robison*

We close this volume with suggestions for starting and maintaining things collections in your own libraries, or possibly improving an existing collection. This chapter is structured as a directed, useful list of topics, modeled after the life cycle of other library materials, including planning, securing funding, acquisition, cataloging, processing, housing, circulation, policy development, in-house training, maintenance, advertising, outreach, and ongoing assessment of the collection. Each topic is summarized and cites specific advice offered by this book's contributors.

## PLANNING

### Tying Your Collection to a Mission

Things collections can be, well, a lot of things. So how do you determine what yours should be? Will it be a limitless collection in a public library, like Sacramento Public Library's Library of Things (see Chapter 7), or will it be a focused collection, like Virginia Commonwealth University's (VCU) scopes collection (Chapter 14)? The answer to this question starts with the mission of your library. The importance of mission and its role in the creation and continued support of these things collections is vital. Brian Burns (author of Chapter 8) talks about diversifying holdings (that is, creating limitless collections) at small colleges to make a real impact on student life. Mitchell Shuldman's (Chapter 11) description of the multimedia instruction program at UMass Lowell is a story

227

of mission. As your mind starts racing with the possibilities, stop, sit down, and evaluate the mission of your organization, the needs of your community, and the impact that your things collection could have locally. A great starting point would be to look for local partners. Partnership possibilities mentioned in this volume include local businesses, garden clubs, STEM clubs, and student organizations, just to name a few. Local partners will have their own insights on what resources are needed to meet community needs, sparing you the burden of having to start entirely from scratch.

## Community Needs Assessment

A community needs assessment is a great starting point for identifying opportunities and the possible local impact of a things collection. Knowing which things resources your community actually needs can keep your library from wasting precious time and assets on building a collection that seems trendy or appealing, but that will not provide any long-term benefit. This needs assessment can take many forms. If you already know of a need in your community, your needs assessment might be a formalization of informal, existing information. If you are not sure what the needs are, you might take a very open approach to possible collections. Holding open meetings and extending meeting invitations to all imaginable stakeholders, such as Athens County Public Libraries (Ohio) (Chapter 3) and the Berkeley Tool Library (Chapter 2) did, is one idea. When Sacramento started its Library of Things (Chapter 7), it offered a series of public, online surveys, in which users could suggest and then vote on the items destined for the limitless things collection. Their efforts resulted in thousands of votes from their community. Conducting community meetings or surveys is a good opportunity to make sure all stakeholders within the library, including administrators and board members, are on the same page.

The process for your community needs assessment will differ based on the size and spread of your user community, your library's mission, and the funding opportunities available. In addition to helping you avoid misguided efforts, conducting a community needs assessment is a way to generate excitement and anticipation for your collection long before the collection is launched.

## Pushing Innovation

Although identifying a community need is one method of introducing a things collection, sometimes libraries need to be the ones to innovate and to push their communities. Sometimes, a community's responses are limited by traditional notions about what libraries are, as characterized by the thought: "I didn't know my library could/would do that." Chapter 12, the story of the reinvention of the University of Nevada, Reno's DeLaMare Library, is one example combining both responsiveness and innovation: librarians responded to a need, saw their efforts be less successful than was hoped for, pushed to change and expand with renewed effort, reengaged their community, and ultimately created a successful program. The University of North Texas (UNT) Libraries' game collection

(Chapter 13) is another example of the library introducing a new things collection and carving out a user community. If your library is going to introduce a new collection, be strategic about your selection, identify strong possible collaborators, and work with those collaborators as you consider the depth and breadth of your collection.

# FUNDING

Many of the programs discussed in this volume were established using one-time funds in the form of local, state or federal grants, gifts, or monies from a foundation, a larger project on campus, or a provost's office. No matter the origin of these one-time funds, the challenge remains the same: how to continue to circulate the things collection when those start-up funds run out or the relationship with the external contributors changes. The Library of Things (Chapter 7) began as part of a larger program, Library Unexpected, which was funded by an Institute of Museum and Library Services (IMLS) grant. Now they turn to the Friends of the Library group, but those funds are already stretched thin. Ultimately, the library is working to integrate funding for the Library of Things into the system-wide collections budget. Likewise, the Berkeley Tool Library (Chapter 2) started with a HUD grant, but long-term funding was shifted to the city's general fund when the HUD funding became inconsistent.

Think beyond short-term funding from the very beginning. When writing your proposal for such a collection, address how you can use both one-time funds and your plan for long-term sustainability. These one-time funds can be used to demonstrate the collection's feasibility and its potential long-term impact, but be thinking about long-term concerns from the outset. For example, one option is a staggered funding proposal, with money for the pilot coming from one-time funds, showing success through that pilot, transitioning to a mixed fiscal model of one-time funds and bridge funds, and eventually moving the funding to a permanent budget line.

Some things collections find it is necessary to charge fees to supplement the budgets they receive from their libraries or organizations. After years of offering its services free of charge to users, the Tool Library at Rebuilding Together Central Ohio began charging modest annual membership fees in 2016.[1] Borrower fees should be considered in the context of your community, political atmosphere, and need, but should not be discounted outright.

# ACQUISITION AND PURCHASING

## Collection Development

As with other library materials, the selection of things collections requires careful consideration in light of mission, need, popularity, availability, purpose, maintenance concerns, cost, and other factors. Although the materials needed for a specialized collection, such as tools and toys, seem more straightforward, it might be easy to assume that more comprehensive things collections lack collection development policies, purchasing at random whatever feels right. However, both of the limitless things collections in this volume address the question of collection policies. Alvarado, Azevedo, and Calhoun (see Chapter 7) describe how the goal of building the Sacramento Library of Things into the library system's collections budget requires that the collection also have explicit language about what it collects. This policy language will benefit the collection moving forward, streamlining questions about what to purchase and which directions to grow. In making collections decisions, Burns (Chapter 8) recommends prioritizing need and purpose before cost, and then finding the desired item in a cost range that is affordable. Both of these collections are seemingly random in many ways, but fundamentally, the ruling collection development principle is to respond to a community need within a set of very broad parameters set by the library.

The issue of donations is another facet of collection development appearing in a number of chapters (see, Chapters 4, 5, 7, 13, 15). UNT's (Chapter 13) collection development policy is very open to donations, while seed libraries have to consider local seed laws before accepting donations from members (see Chapter 5).

# Durability

Overwhelmingly, the topic of durability of things is a common collection development topic among our contributors. A summary across all of these ideas, object types, and types of collections comes down to this: either buy high quality, or buy a lot of whatever it is that you have decided to purchase cheaply. For example, Burns (Chapter 8) makes the argument for purposefully buying inexpensive tripods for undergraduate use, to lessen replacement costs and keep the inventory fresh. Durability considerations will differ across things collections. For Book-a-Bike (Chapter 3), a desire for durability meant consulting with a local bicycle shop on bike models and consciously making the choice to buy cruisers over mountain bikes or road bikes, purposefully limiting the types of use, while the University of Delaware's Student Multimedia Design Center (Chapter 10) found the durability of battery compartment doors and slides to be an unforeseen problem.

Along with durability, many authors mention keeping spare parts and pieces to allow for quick turnaround of objects that might just need a replacement piece to get back into circulation. For example, GoPros are directly mentioned by four of the authors in this volume (see Chapters 7, 8, 10, and 14), with both Burns (Chapter 8) and Johnson (Chapter 14) addressing the need for extra parts, like the small thumbscrews that secure the cameras to different mounts. By having these spare parts on hand, item downtime is minimized.

Durability considerations and parts needs must be an element of your collections plan. We recommend researching existing things collections that already have the kind of objects you want to circulate to learn about the relevant durability issues. This topic, more so than many others in this chapter, is mostly trial and error that can only be worked out with time.

# CATALOGING AND DESCRIPTION

Cataloging is essential to any item's discoverability by patrons, but the formats of things collections present unique challenges. Some libraries are able to adapt the existing Anglo-American Cataloguing Rules (AACR2) and Resource Description and Access (RDA) rules to describe their things. Librarians at Alaska Resources Library and Information Services (ARLIS) (see Chapter 15) provide many helpful suggestions for describing realia, such as generating consistent titles based on the type of organism. In adding subject headings, ARLIS suggests using the 655 Genre/Form field, rather than the 650 Topic Terms field, as the subject headings apply to an item's physical description (for example, antlers, fur) rather than its subject content.

In generating call numbers, many libraries struggle with how to group similar items together. Harvey and Krueger (Chapter 9) describe how the Curriculum Materials Center (CMC) at the University of Nebraska at Kearney classifies things by format type, followed by accession number. However, the reliance on accession number can lead to similar items not being collocated, if they were purchased at different times. Alternatively, the CMC at Bowling Green State University uses Dewey call numbers, adding a Cutter number according to the publisher's name, making collocation more likely. The gaming collection at UNT (Chapter 13) uses the same accession number for all iterations of the same game, regardless of platform, to avoid confusion and expedite retrieval.

The key is to develop a system for describing your things collection that balances user discoverability with ease of service. If users will be exploring a things collection mostly through physical browsing, similar items should be together. This aim might best be achieved using locally generated systems and categories, and creating minimal catalog records for use by library staff only but suppressed from public display. (This approach should only be taken if functionalities such as patron-generated holds and recalls are not applicable.) But if a collection is closed stacks or discovered primarily through the catalog, catalog records should be as complete as possible and the organizational system can be designed for library personnel's convenience. Consider that images might be an important part of electronic discoverability, especially for young children or other patrons without English reading literacy. Kirschner (Chapter 6) tells of creating an electronic toy database, complete with images.

# PROCESSING

Their three-dimensional format, multiple pieces, mixed textures, and technology challenges make things collections complicated to process. Many items will need to be repackaged in a box or bin, to provide protection and to simplify storage and use. Rozen, Woods, and Kazzimir (see Chapter 15) describe how ARLIS's furs and more durable skulls are stored in bins, while the fragile items are securely placed in transparent boxes, to allow viewing but no touching. Johnson (Chapter 14) warns that, although it might seem convenient, storing equipment in its original box can create more hassle for patrons due to assembly concerns.

Processing is also an opportunity to protect an item from future damages. When processing games, UNT (Chapter 13) reinforces box corners, places game pieces in bags, put cards in plastic sleeves, and adds a band to keep the box closed during transport.

As with any other library item, things should be properly labeled and identified. Labeling is especially important with things that might not be readily recognizable as library items. Although labeling is straightforward for boxed and cased items, items such as puppets and toys can be labeled using tags. Because cleaning is a necessary part of circulating some items, consider how tags will be affected by water or other cleaning processes. Kirschner (Chapter 6) explains how the Cuyahoga County Public Library secures tags to its toys using reusable nylon cable ties, which can be easily cut off when the toy is washed and then reattached.

One challenge of processing things collections lies in the fact that many of them have multiple components, such as board game pieces or parts of a kit. Some libraries choose to bar-code each piece individually. UNT (Chapter 13) bar-codes the individual components that accompany a video game console, such as HDMI cables and power cords. However, the records for the accompanying pieces are suppressed, to ease patrons' confusion in using the catalog. Other libraries, such as Delaware's Student Multimedia Design Center (Chapter 10), include a list of all items in a kit, many of which might be too small to bar-code individually. This sheet helps keep patrons accountable for returning all pieces. Rather than bar-code all the components of a tabletop game, UNT simply weighs the game boxes upon check-in, to ensure no pieces are missing. In processing your things collection, consider whether it is worthwhile to spend the time and resources bar-coding and labeling each individual piece in a kit, or whether bar-coding the main items and including a parts checklist would suffice.

Many technology objects in things collections are designed for personal, single-owner use, creating additional processing challenges. Reno's DeLaMare Library (Chapter 12) lends Google Glass and Apple Watches. The library created dummy accounts as a work-around so that users are not required to use their personal accounts. However, the library cannot prevent someone from using a personal account, creating the potential for the library to be unintentionally involved in a breach of personal privacy. DeLaMare's solution to this challenge is to require a full reset and reconfiguration back to the dummy account following check-in. If your things collection will include electronics or computer technology, consider whether establishing dummy accounts will be a necessary part of your processing workflow.

## STORAGE AND SHELVING

As you look over the topics presented in this chapter, we expect that many come as no surprise. However, the topic of storage, shelving, and containers might make you stop and wonder. This topic is included and identified as a top-level concern because the storage and repackaging of things collections objects takes effort, planning, and money. Some of the top concerns identified by our authors include maximizing and optimizing available storage space (Chapters 2,

5, 13); unification of containers for easier storage, item durability, and ease of discoverability and retrieval (Chapter 2, 5, 6, 9, 10, 13); security of storage, such as using locking cabinets (Chapter 14); and balance between the best fit from a space perspective versus maintaining the integrity of the object, such as the unforeseen curling of art prints that were stored vertically (Chapter 9). The storage and shelving needs of a things collection cannot be an afterthought. It is necessary to consider space needs and limitations from the beginning, as part of initial conversations with internal and external stakeholders, with regard to the planning, budgeting, and processing for these types of collections.

# CIRCULATION

## Limits and Loan Periods

Most things collections have relatively short circulation periods to allow more users to access a relatively small pool of resources. For example, Sacramento's Library of Things (Chapter 7) limits checkout to a single item at a time. In the case of the media centers represented in this volume, the University of Delaware's Student Multimedia Design Center (Chapter 10) and Reno's DeLaMare Library (Chapter 12) allow three-day checkouts, which is the same circulation time of many media centers around the country. However, it is possible for loan periods to be too restrictive. DeLaMare learned that having some of their items limited to a single day or to in-house use only made it impossible for users to utilize the equipment properly, so they shifted to the three-day checkout rule mentioned.

## Multiple Locations

A few of this volume's authors are in systems with multiple locations or branches and address the issues inherent to making things collections work in such an environment. For the Toy Library at Cuyahoga County Public Library (Chapter 6), the approach to serving multiple locations was to start with offering the toys at one branch, establish a solid program, and eventually expand to other branches by allowing toys to be requested and delivered to all 27 locations within their system. It took many years, administrative changes, and the implementation of a system of delivery trucks to transition from serving a single location to multiple. Sacramento (Chapter 7) notes that keeping the collection in one branch creates a "destination library" that brings people in from other areas. However, they also plan to consider expanding to other locations. Whether circulating out of one branch, having items located in multiple branches, or allowing patrons to request delivery between branches, there is no doubt that adding multiple locations with varying personnel increases complication. Starting out at one location allows a library to test the collection and prove that it will work before expanding.

Cataloging will also impact the coordination of item delivery between locations. Users at other branches will be exploring and requesting delivery of the collection's holdings using the online catalog. Starting a things collection with incomplete cataloging, though perhaps acceptable for a single-location project, can limit the ability to expand to multiple locations in the future.

# POLICIES AND PROCEDURES

## Paperwork and Requirements for Borrowing

Things collections contain objects with a lot of working parts, consisting of many pieces. Things collections see heavy, active use, are often very costly, and commonly have higher fees associated with late returns, repairs, and replacement. In many cases, the basic documentation policies of a library may not be sufficiently detailed for things collections. Early in the existence of a things collection, particularly as the library itself is learning about the nuances of these things, additional documentation may be needed. However, there should be an effort to achieve balance. The Book-a-Bike program (Chapter 3), Delaware's Student Multimedia Design Center (Chapter 10), and the UNT Library (Chapter 13) all discuss how they loosened their paperwork and requirements over time, to reduce turnaround time and create more streamlined processes. Sacramento Public Library (Chapter 7) mentions allowing policy simplification based on staff feedback.

From a long-term, positive service model, it creates a positive experience to reduce or relax a rule and a negative experience to add one. Keep this thought in mind when determining which additional requirements or borrowing processes are necessary. Some things collections will undoubtedly necessitate new policies and red tape because of liability and safety concerns. However, extra paperwork and restrictions impact customer service and turnaround time, and so should not be implemented solely out of fear. Find a happy medium of gathering enough information to hold borrowers accountable and to learn about your users' needs, while not making the process so burdensome as to detract from service and damage public perception.

## Legal Concerns

Be sure you understand federal, state, and local laws and ordinances that might impact your things collection. Legal issues related to things collections differ widely. In some cases, a simple "hold harmless" agreement will meet your needs, but development of some collections will need a greater understanding of the law. For example, some of the legal concerns touched on in this volume include: an Ohio state law requiring cyclists to use front and rear lights within a half hour of sunrise and sunset leading to the purchase of bike reflectors (Chapter 3); the legal concerns around federal and state seed laws, such as the illegality of saving or sharing patented seeds, laws regulating how and where seeds can be exchanged, and the ongoing changes in state seed laws and how judges are interpreting their implications for libraries (Chapter 5); a lack of multiplayer licensing for born-digital games limiting purchase options (Chapter 13); the Federal Aviation Administration action concerning unmanned aerial vehicles leading to the removal of drones from DeLaMare's collection (Chapter 12); and ARLIS's knowledge of and work within the Marine Mammal Protection Act of 1972 (Chapter 15).

## STAFF TRAINING

Because of how things collections are used, training library staff in how to support these items requires extra effort. Personnel must be able to successfully check an item in and out, account for all of its parts, be able to confirm that it is in working order, know the cleaning process if relevant, and, in many cases, be able to demonstrate to users how it works. Establishing clearly defined minimum expectations is key to successful staff training. For example, McCoy (Chapter 10) covers library personnel using new gear before it is put into circulation and mentions being able to record, play back, and delete footage on a camcorder as a minimum expectation related to that device. Johnson (Chapter 14) notes that not everyone will become an expert, but a basic level of understanding for those interacting with the objects of things collections is a reasonable expectation. He, too, addresses the need for personal familiarity with the things by actually using the devices. Staff training should not be seen as a one-time event. Rather, as a things collection continues to grow and change, library personnel should have regular opportunities to use equipment, learn about its features, and ask questions. Having staff members who are helpful in showing patrons how to use things collections and who can articulate the collection's value can be its own form of marketing.

## MAINTENANCE

Things collections provide objects that support accomplishing a task. They are, by definition, used for an active purpose. This use necessitates a maintenance plan for most things collections, which requires both time and money. Many chapters of this volume, ranging from Berkley Tool Library (Chapter 2) to ARLIS (Chapter 15), address the topic of maintaining their things collections. Common subjects include cleaning (Chapters 3, 6, 10, 12, and 13), maintaining spare replacement parts (Chapters 8, 10, 12, 13, and 14), considering potential maintenance costs as part of the purchasing decision (Chapter 2), difficulty in replacing fragile or older material or systems (Chapters 13 and 15), and fixed maintenance schedules (Chapters 2 and 10; also see Appendix A). Maintenance processes range from the simple, such as spraying wearable items with products such as Lysol or RID (Chapters 6 and 12), to completely rebuilding demolition hammers (Chapter 2). The takeaway is that maintenance is a necessary and time-intensive aspect of most things collections and must be included in your planning, space, staff training, and budgeting processes and considerations.

# ADVERTISING

By their definition, things collections have a "wow" factor and will be appealing to patrons. First, however, patrons have to know the collection exists. Involving community members in the initial planning stages will generate buzz around the collection. Keep the momentum going by updating patrons on your progress toward unveiling the project, such as through social media or signage within the building.

When your collection is ready to go live, consider making its launch a major event, as Athens County Public Libraries did when it threw a party to roll out the Book-a-Bike program (Chapter 3). To market the Library of Things, Sacramento Public Library organized its #librarybrag campaign (Chapter 7), taking out magazine ads and purchasing vehicle wraps for its book delivery trucks. Consider leveraging the local and even national press to gain some free publicity for your collection. Many of the libraries in this chapter have garnered a great deal of media attention, such as the LibraryFarm's coverage in the *New York Times* and various magazines (Chapter 4) and National Public Radio's coverage of ARLIS's furs, mounts, and skulls (Chapter 15).

Remember that word of mouth is invaluable in advertising your collection to niche audiences. For best results, identify and pitch to your target market from the start. For example, after an initially lukewarm reception to calculators for loan, Reno's DeLaMare Library (Chapter 12) successfully got through to its target audience (the university's computer science and engineering department), built a relationship, expanded its collection, and went directly to the department's senior capstone class with information about its collection of drones. Whether specific communities of users, like gamers and game designers for UNT's collection (Chapter 13), or a community based on need, like Berkeley's Tool Library (Chapter 2), remember: people talk. Use this fact to help advertise your things collection.

# OUTREACH

## Building Community Early

We mention early in this chapter that planning and building a successful things collection might include a community needs assessment. In the context of building a community of users and supporters, how you go about the needs assessment is your first opportunity to build community. The Berkeley Tool Library (Chapter 2) held community meetings during the planning stage, while the creators behind the Book-a-Bike program (Chapter 3) sent community meeting invitations to groups, such as bike shops, schools, the health department, nonprofits, and others, looking for their advice and input. Other chapters also mention collaboration with nonprofits and community agencies (Chapters 4 and 5).

After or as part of the needs assessment, one of the next steps is to select the first items for your collection, which is another opportunity to build community.

The DeLaMare Library (Chapter 12) counted on community input when deciding what initially to add to their collection, while the UNT Libraries (Chapter 13) talks about the balance between the newest technology and what your users actually need, which is best determined through active feedback loops and user input when creating or expanding collections. One suggestion is to set some parameters around what you know you can and cannot do related to cost, types of objects that will be in the collection, and maintenance. Having an established collection development plan will give those involved in the decision-making process some understanding of the project's intent and limitations, while still allowing the needs and ideas of the community to be incorporated. Of course, your plan should be flexible enough to recognize a great community suggestion when you hear it.

### Workshops and Instruction

Although including the community in the early planning and launch of your things collection is a useful way to create interest and draw attention, the larger challenge in outreach and community building is sustaining that community, bringing in new members, and creating a long-term impact. Most of our authors address the challenge of being asked *how to use* the things in their collections. Among the academic libraries (Chapters 8 to 14), the most successful outreach efforts involved direct integration in the classes (Chapters 10, 11, and 13) and holding events (Chapter 12). For the academic libraries, building community was achieved by way of building relationships with faculty, different divisions of campus, and some long-term, repeat student users. But given that students are eventually supposed to graduate and leave, they build community by sharing their knowledge of the collection with a friend, who comes in, loves the program, and shares some more.

On the public library side (Chapters 1 to 7), not only are the library personnel themselves teaching workshops and giving users advice, members of those user communities are also providing instruction. Inclusion of those in the community willing to share their knowledge with others is an invaluable outreach opportunity, particularly if you develop a limitless things collection. Sacramento (Chapter 7) incorporates outreach for the Library of Things into its library programming; during its volunteer-led sewing classes, the availability of sewing machines is promoted, and when local musicians play in the building, the library seizes the opportunity to advertise the collection's musical instruments.

## ASSESSMENT

As with other materials, a things collection should be assessed periodically for quality. Harvey and Krueger (Chapter 9) discuss the need to evaluate the currency of curriculum materials and to replace outdated materials. Things collections bring the added challenge of format obsolescence. Older audiovisual materials that are still useful might need to be replaced with newer formats, and multimedia equipment and accessories will inevitably become obsolete.

Long-term budgeting should consider replacement costs along with those for maintenance.

Also consider how you will demonstrate the value of a things collection to your stakeholders. For some collections, traditional quantitative metrics such as circulation statistics and workshop attendance numbers can measure the impact. Other things collections produce easily observed deliverables, such as the student video projects facilitated by Media Services at UMass Lowell (Chapter 11). Such projects reveal the qualitative impact of a things collections and make for a nicer story than raw data. If your things collection will be used to generate finished products, consider how you might gain access to those products for assessment purposes. Although you should be mindful of patrons' privacy, many might voluntarily share pictures of the garden they grew using your seed library or of the event they organized where your equipment was utilized. If you use such finished products in qualitatively demonstrating your collection's value, be sure to obtain all necessary permissions.

Qualitative impact could also be captured through focus groups and surveys, which might reveal both the things your collection is doing well and the opportunities to improve it. Radniecki and Colegrove (Chapter 12) caution that the community feedback loop is a double-edged sword; the library should be prepared to engage in authentic dialog with the public and then follow through accordingly.

## CONCLUSION

As we argue in the introduction of this work, things collections are neither "nontraditional" nor "unique." This collected chapter of suggestions for building things collections in your own libraries touches on many topics that librarians have long been addressing. Focused things collections, and the emerging limitless things collections, present an opportunity for librarians to leverage and adapt our profession's long-established strengths and knowledge to provide new services and satisfy previously unmet needs in our communities. We hope this volume helps you to meet those needs.

## NOTE

1. See www.rtcentralohio.org/tool-library.

# APPENDIX A: GENERAL MAINTENANCE OF HAND AND ELECTRIC TOOLS

## From the Berkeley Tool Lending Library

### Maintenance

- Electric Weed Eaters (Stihl FSE-60): Every time we rewind spool, clean out debris, and add a couple drops of 3-IN-ONE oil at bearing; check buttons for wear and replace when they are severely worn down. Also, as soon as we buy these weed eaters, we pin the front nut to the shaft with a 3d penny: drill through the soft nut and shaft, slide a nail in, clip it off, and peen both ends flat to the faces. This will keep the nut from slipping if a patron overheats it. Also, we only use 14-gauge cords with these to prevent overheating.
- Straighten out the bin of digging bars, and arrange wheelbarrows, lawn-mowers, carts, and stepladders.
- Straighten out bins of picks and shovels.
- Put up hooks and rearrange tools on the peg boards (a constant evolution). Untangle cords; check for broken-off ground pin.
- Shelve books.
- Enter new tools into the database.
- Engrave and mark new tools.
- Change handles on shovels, eye hoes, and picks.

### Frequent Sharpening

- Hand hedge clippers: Use 7-inch disc sander or hand stone.
- Loppers: Use mill bastard file.
- Pruning shears: Use mill bastard file.
- Chisels: Use bench stone for "quickie" and bench grinder for hollow ground.
- Hand planes and draw knives: Sharpen like chisels.
- Floor scrapers, paint scrapers, and burn-off scrapers: Use 7-inch disc sander.
- Axes, mauls, and wedges: Use 7-inch disc sander to sharpen, and 4½-inch mini-grinder to remove mushroomed metal and burrs.
- Brush-cutter machete and hand sickle: Use 7-inch disc sander on machete and hand stone on sickle (too sharp a curve for disc).

### Less Frequent Sharpening

- Flat spade bits: Use bench grinder with regular (blue) stone wheel.
- Rotary hammer bits: Use bench grinder, green stone for carbide.

- Ship auger bits: Use disc sander or triangular file, depending on the shape.
- Hoes and garden tools: Use disc sander.
- Pole pruners: Use mill bastard file.

## Infrequent Sharpening

- Electric hedge trimmers: Sharpen every one to two years: open gearbox and dismantle blades on Little Wonder trimmers. Sharpen each blade in vise with disc sander or mini-grinder: needs 4 passes to sharpen both edges of both sides. Then place on flat surface (clean bench) and clean up burrs and grind flat with oil and hand stone. Check wear on both gears and replace grease. When reassembling, tighten blade screws all the way, then back off three-quarter turn (270 degrees) and tighten nuts. For Stihl trimmers, just separate blades and sharpen without dismantling.
- Push lawnmowers: Back lap every spring using hand crank and grinding compound from lawnmower sharpening kit. Add grease before replacing wheel.

## Inspect and Change Blades

- Jig saws: Change often.
- Utility knives, wallpaper razors: Change or add blades as necessary.
- SKILSAWs: Change as necessary, every couple weeks or so.
- Chop saws: Change as necessary, send out blades for sharpening.
- Table saws: Change as necessary, send out blades for sharpening.
- Pole saws: Change seasonally, once to twice a year, send out blade for sharpening.

## Small Tool Repairs

- Inspect and repair extension cords: Check for ground plug and replace if missing; repair cut cords.
- Cords on tools: Replace cord if ground is missing for grounded tool, particularly SKILSAWs and 4-inch belt sanders. Rewire cord inside tool if it has been nicked, and copper is showing, until it is too short to be safe. When possible, use brand replacement. If not, use similar gauge cord. Most switches have screws that tighten on terminal ends, which you need to crimp onto line. But some have a clamp, and you only need to insert some bare wire and screw it down, while others (for example, Milwaukee Sawzall) need to have solder dripped onto the wire, and then pushed into spring clamp on switch. If this is difficult and there is room in the case, one can use a crimp-on connector (tube-type) as long as you crimp it well for a good connection. When replacing SKILSAW cords,

be careful not to overtighten the handle screws, as it is easy to strip the plastic.

- Switch repair: If tool is not functioning and cord is okay, test switch with continuity tester and replace the switch.
- Replace broken or missing handles: Sometimes it is possible to replace a nut or bolt in a handle, as it usually gets tightened at the same point and the thread gets stripped. Note, Porter-Cable, DeWalt, Milwaukee, and so on, would be SAE, while Makita and Bosch would be metric.
- Change brushes: When brushes are short, they can spark, leaving a carbon residue on brush holder and armature. Clean out brush holder when you replace brush, using small triangular file, and use white pumice stick to clean armature.
- Bend tines on garden forks.
- Repair jammed staple guns: This is surprisingly finicky, but necessary, as patrons drop staple guns (Arrow T50) and then the staple guide needs to be fiddled with.
- Replace springs on pole pruners: This is absurdly awkward, and I have seen coworkers stab themselves with a screwdriver or worse. I use a vise and grip edge of spring with vise grips. For pole pruners I use the Marvin head, and put it on an 8-foot piece of painted closet rod, and then rope it with quarter-inch polypro. We separate the pruners and pole saws.
- Replace chucks on drills: This is clever. Chucks are threaded on to the end of the drill, but there is usually a left-hand screw holding it in place. Open the chuck all the way and you can see the screw at the bottom, then turn it clockwise to loosen and remove it. Then put a bar into the chuck keyhole and whack it quite hard with a small sledgehammer. This is to use the inertia of the motor to overcome the friction that holds the chuck screwed on.
- Milwaukee right-angle drills come with that "bar" as a chuck removal tool.

## Medium Tool Repairs

- Rebuild chop saws: Grease base and replace metal glides; replace bearings. There are three or four bearings on the Makita 10-inch chop saws—one or two in the gearbox and one on each end of the armature. Often only one needs to be replaced, and it can nearly double the life of the tool.
- Replace gears in hedge trimmers (Little Wonder). File and straighten cluster gear holder if it has been damaged (by the force that broke a tooth on the gear); clean out grease carefully to remove any metal bits from broken gear teeth.
- Rebuild table saws, replace bearings. For the old Makita tabletop model, it is pretty straightforward. There are two bearings on ends of armature. Remove brushes first and turn armature (by hand). Then use bearing remover and replace bearings. Reset with bearing press—essential to

keep straight and not damage new bearings. Sometimes one needs to take the whole table saw apart. The handles are tricky, and in the old models you had to knock out a roller pin (tension pin) to get the handle off.

- Repair power snakes (General Mini-Rooter): Straighten or change cables; replace motor when burned out (awkward to wire, and hard to order correctly—there is a guide in the Grainger catalog on how to order a motor, using the existing nameplate to copy the hp, voltage, phase, body type, etc.), rewire foot pedal and switch; replace bearing and felt pad at rear of cable can.

- Service demolition hammers with service pack: This is lengthy, but well worthwhile, as you can triple the life of the Bosch demolition hammer from about 150 to 200 uses to 500 to 650 checkouts. And it is a straight-forward procedure. Lay out all parts on paper toweling as you disas-semble; clean carefully and regrease only with grease from service pack. Then replace all rubber rings with the new ones and reassemble. Here are a couple of cautions. One of the rings that is composed of a metal spring inside of rubber needs to face in one direction only—opening is away from the end of the tool, so watch it as you take it apart (hard to see on diagram). Also, some screws are tight, and you will want a cheater pipe on your Allen wrench. Lastly, the two needle bearings under the drive gear slowly get worn, and the needles can fall out. It is easy to order those new bearings from Bosch. I usually do the electrical end first (replace cord and strain relief if necessary, clean out brush hold-ers and clean up the armature) and then turn this tool over and clamp in the vise for the greasy stuff.

- Service spline hammers with service pack: This is more difficult than the demolition hammer, because this tool is both hammering and rotat-ing, and thus has more complicated gears. I used to sketch as I disas-sembled new things. Then I learned to take pictures on my phone! Here are two tips for the Bosch spline hammer. The inner assembly is fric-tion fit inside the outer steel tube, so you can slam the end down on a wooden surface to hitch it forward a bit, and/or go in from the top of the gear case and tap it carefully forward. Secondly, the gear train is a little complicated, so you need to keep them in order and facing the right way, with the several steel friction rings in the right places. And lastly, the insides of the nose and the very front slug (that drives the spline bit) are not drawn in the diagram, so you really need to watch this. That slug is held in by a split ring that is way down inside the tube, but it is accessed by several holes in the side. That way you can push the retainer ring inward from its groove while prying it up with some sort of long hook.

## Database Maintenance

- Clean up lists of items periodically.
- Delete broken tools from the database.
- Delete items that are labeled missing for more than one year.

## Ordering Parts and Tools

- Maintain lists of needed parts and tools.
- Check placed holds to determine need for buying extra items.
- Explore patron requests for new tools.
- Compare prices and availability from different venders; look for parts numbers and pricing online or from manufacturer.
- Be familiar with ordering process and ordering cheat sheet.
- Discuss proposed orders with coworkers.

# APPENDIX B: BOOK-A-BIKE LENDING AGREEMENT

last name: [                    ]

Athens County Public Libraries
**BOOK-A-BIKE LENDING AGREEMENT**

card # [                    ]

1. All factual data concerning the person borrowing the bicycle, the bicycle itself and the duration of the loan are described below. Athens County Public Libraries (ACPL) hereby loans the bicycle and equipment to the borrower upon the terms described below and upon the agreement by the borrower that if the bicycle or trailer or any accessories borrowed (such as helmets and locks) are not returned to ACPL on or before the end of the term, then the borrower shall pay ACPL the replacement cost of any bicycle or trailer not returned and $20 for any accessory not returned. The borrower agrees to lock the bicycle when not in use. The borrower agrees to follow the rules of the road and wear a helmet whenever riding the bicycle. When crossing railroad tracks or other obstacles that might "flip" the bicycle, the borrower agrees to cross such obstacles at a perpendicular angle.

2. By signing this lending agreement, the borrower agrees that bicycling is a dangerous activity and carries with it certain hazards and risks of which the borrower is aware. The borrower, on behalf of him/herself, his/her heirs, executors, administrators, personal representatives and assigns, hereby releases ACPL from any and all liability for any and all claims and causes of action which the borrower may sustain, or any loss of any sort, arising out of or relating to usage of the bicycle, whether caused by the negligence of ACPL or any other person. In additon, the borrower covenants and agrees not to sue ACPL and agrees to forever hold them harmless from any liability, claims, demands, actions or causes of action whatsoever arising from the usage of the bicycle, whether such liability, claims, demands, or actions are the result of negligence of the release or any other person. This release of liability, convenant not to sue, and hold harmless agreement shall be binding upon the borrower, the borrower's heirs, executors, administrators, personal representatives, and assigns, and share inure to the benefit of ACPL and its assigns.

3. The borrower agrees to indemnify ACPL and to assume and be responsible for all harm, injury, or damage caused by the borrower to ACPL, ACPL property or equipment, or other persons or other personal property used in conjunction with usage of the bicycle or other equipment.

4. Facts and information are as follows:

Name of borrower (please print): _____

Date of birth if borrower is under 18 years—
"Parental Consent" must be signed and attached: _____

Address: _____  City/State: _____

Phone number: _____  ☐ cell
☐ home

Email address: _____

Signature: _____

LIBRARY USE ONLY

Library card number: _____

Bike number: _____

Helmet number: _____

Lock number: _____

SAFETY CHECK COMPLETED: yes ☐

Date: _____

Staff/volunteer: _____

☐ signature on file noted in Koha

updated 6/20/13

244

# APPENDIX C: BOOK-A-BIKE PARENTAL OR LEGAL GUARDIAN CONSENT

last name: [                    ]

card # [                    ]

### Athens County Public Libraries
## BOOK-A-BIKE PARENTAL OR LEGAL GUARDIAN CONSENT

In consideration of my guardian's borrowing of a bicycle or riding in or on bicycle equipment from Athens County Public Libraries, the undersigned agrees as follows:

1. I am the parent or legal guardian of _____ .
I understand that my child/guardian's participation in this activity may include risks and hazards. I am aware of the risks and hazards inherent in my guardian's participation, and recognizing those risks and hazards, I hereby give my consent and approval to my child/guardian's participation.

2. On behalf of my child/guardian and myself, I hereby release ACPL and it employees, volunteers, and agents from any and all liability for any and all claims and causes of action that I or my child/guardian may hereafter have on account of any and all injuries and/or damage that I or my child/guardian may sustain, or any loss of any other sort, arising out of the negligence of ACPL or any other person. In addition, on behalf of my child/guardian and myself, I convenant and agree not to sue ACPL and agree to forever hold them harmless from any liability, claims, demands, actions, or causes of action whatsoever arising from my child/guardian's or my participation in Book-a-Bike, whether such liability, claims, demands, or actions are the result of the negligence of ACPL or any other person. This release of liability, convenant not to sue, and hold-harmless agreement shall be binding upon me, my child/guardian, my heirs, and/or my child's heirs, executors, administrators, personal representatives, and assigns, and shall inure to the benefit of ACPL and their assigns.

3. I hereby agree to indemnify ACPL and to assume and be responsible for all harm, injury, or damage caused by me or my child/guardian to ACPL, ACPL property or equipment, other person, or personal property used in conjunction with this activity.

Parent or Legal Guardian's Printed Name:_____

Signature: _____ Date: _____

☐ My child/guardian has permission to ride bicycles with a caregiver other than myself.

☐ signature on file noted in Koha

☐ Koha information up-to-date

updated 6/20/13

245

# APPENDIX D: BOOK-A-BIKE SAFETY INSPECTION CHECKLIST

Last name: _____ Date: _____

Bike number: _____ Helmet number: _____ Lock number: _____

## Book-a-Bike Safety Inspection Checklist

HANDLEBARS    Left   Right     NOTES—

              NO    NO

loose*     ☐    ☐     _____

grips missing, loose,
    or torn     ☐    ☐     _____

bell loose or damaged   ☐     _____

BRAKES     Front   Rear

           YES    YES

levers move easily*   ☐    ☐     _____

calipers spaced evenly* ☐   ☐     _____

pads intact     ☐    ☐     _____

bike stops*     ☐    ☐     _____

REFLECTORS   Front   Rear

           NO    NO

damaged/loose   ☐    ☐     _____

missing     ☐    ☐     _____

TIRES & WHEELS   Front   Rear

           NO    NO

needs inflated   ☐    ☐     _____

excessive tread wear ☐   ☐     _____

loose/broken spokes* ☐   ☐     _____

SADDLE & FLAG

             YES

correct height   ☐     _____

   (demonstrate)     _____

seat cover intact   ☐

flag intact     ☐     _____

FORKS & FRAME

             NO

bent or cracked*   ☐     _____

CHAIN & GEARS

             NO

visible damage/rust   ☐     * indicates the bike is unsafe and should not

chain too loose   ☐       be circulated

shifting mechanisms ☐

   dirty or damaged      PASS/FAIL

                               YES NO

                 appears sound   ☐ ☐

HELMET & LOCK    YES

correct fit     ☐        Inspector _____

operates smoothly ☐     Time checked out: _____ Staff: _____

                 Time returned: _____ Staff: _____

# Seed Return Form

Please clean seed of all plant material.

Name:

Date:

Seed Library Location:

Contact Information (optional):

**1) Common Name**

Example: Tomato

**2) Variety Name**

Example: Nebraska Wedding

**3) Latin Name**

Example: Solanum lycopersicum

**4) Did you grow any other varieties of (insert common name)? If yes, please list.** Using above example: Did you grow any other varieties of tomatoes?

**5) If you answered yes to the previous question, did you hand-pollinate or isolate?** Example: If you are returning squash and grew more than one variety, hand pollination is necessary.

**6) Isolation distance**

**7) Seed Source**

Example: Common Soil Seed Library

**8) Choose One:** *Mark only one square.*
- ☐ Annual
- ☐ Biennial*
- ☐ Perennial*

**9) *If biennial or perennial choose one**

*Mark only one square.*
- ☐ Seed to seed (left in ground)
- ☐ Root to seed
  (root stored and replanted)

**Rate yourself as a seed saver**

*Mark only one square.*
- ☐ Beginner
- ☐ I have a clue.
- ☐ Done it for the last __ years!

**10)  Crop Location**

Example: Benson Community Garden

**11)  Linear or square feet of crop and/or population size**

**12)  Insect pests/pest damage/pest control applications**

**13)  Diseases/disease damage/disease control applications**

**14)  Cultivation Methods**

**15) Approximate % of crop discarded**

example: rejected because of disease/pest

**16)  Characteristics selected for:**

**17)  Other comments:**

247

# APPENDIX F: DRAFT AGREEMENT FOR HOUSING, MAINTENANCE, AND CIRCULATION OF COLLECTION OF SKULLS, FURS, AND BIRD MOUNTS

Draft Agreement between Alaska Department of Fish
and Game (ADF&G) and Alaska Resources Library and
Information Services (ARLIS) for Housing, Maintenance
and Circulation of the ADF&G Collection of Skulls,
Furs, and Bird Mounts

Date of Agreement: _____

Background: The Alaska Department of Fish and Game
(ADF&G) has amassed a circulating collection of skulls, furs,
and bird mounts that is heavily used by teachers and environmental educators in the community. These materials are listed in Appendix G.
ADF&G no longer has on-site storage to accommodate the display and circulation of
these materials in an area readily accessible by staff. Alaska Resources Library and
Information Services (ARLIS) was approached by ADF&G staff seeking a solution to the
problem of access of these materials. Providing access to this collection is appropriate
to the mission of ARLIS and is especially congruous with the existing environmental
education collection, consisting of videos, books, and classroom presentation kits, that
was transferred from U.S. Fish and Wildlife Service to ARLIS. The housing of the skull,
fur, and bird mount collection at ARLIS is beneficial to ADF&G in promoting access to
these materials that are in demand but that ADF&G can no longer adequately administer. The collection will remain the property of ADF&G. ARLIS will house the collection
and provide a central distribution point to which ADF&G may refer potential users. The
parties also agree to the following listed terms.

ADF&G agrees to:

1. Provide boxes appropriate for the storage of the furs and replace these as needed.
   These boxes will be labeled with the common and scientific names of the animal
   from which the fur was taken.
2. Provide labels for the bird mounts and skull mounts listing the common and scientific names of the animals represented.
3. Provide tags attached to the bird and skull mounts and to the furs identifying the
   items as ADF&G property and stating the need to return them to ARLIS. The tags
   should be an adequate size to allow affixing a bar code label.
4. Repair the collection as necessary and replace items that become worn from handling.
5. Assign monetary value to items to assist ARLIS with recovery from patrons who are
   delinquent with returns.

ARLIS agrees to:

1. Store the collection in the ARLIS storeroom and provide appropriate display materials alerting patrons to its availability.
2. Register borrowers who wish to check out items from the collection.
3. Comply with ADF&G protocol regarding the patron groups allowed borrowing privileges to the collection.
4. Keep accurate circulation statistics regarding the use of the collection.
5. Regularly send out notices to patrons who allow items from the collection to become
   overdue and ultimately bill for replacement value.
6. Alert ADF&G staff when materials require repair or replacement.

The undersigned agree to the conditions set forth above.

_____  _____
for Alaska Department of Fish and Game           date

_____  _____
for Alaska Resources Library and Information Services    date

# Furs, Mounts, and Skulls

### *Provided in cooperation with*

## Alaska Department of Fish and Game

## September 2015

Alaska Resources Library & Information Services
Suite 111 Library Building
3211 Providence Drive
Anchorage, AK 99508
(907) 27-ARLIS (272-7547) reference@arlis.org
www.arlis.org
Hours: Monday–Friday, 8 a.m.–5 p.m.

# ARLIS Furs, Mounts, and Skulls

The furs, skulls, and mounts listed as follows are made available at ARLIS by the Alaska Department of Fish and Game, Division of Wildlife Conservation, U.S. Fish and Wildlife Service, and private donors. Most items may be checked out from ARLIS for a two-week period and may be renewed once for an additional two weeks.

These items are available on a first-come/first-served basis. Please check the catalog for availability by doing a key word search using the name of the animal or bird exactly as it appears in the list. If the search produces too many hits, add key word *realia*.

ARLIS is open Monday through Friday, 8:00 a.m. to 5:00 p.m., but furs, mounts, and skulls may only be checked out until 4:45 p.m. Items must be returned to ARLIS during open hours. Unlike books, these items cannot be returned to other Anchorage libraries. For assistance, please contact the ARLIS reference desk at 272-7547 or reference@arlis.org.

**Furs** Search the catalog by key word using the name of the animal or bird exactly as it appears in the list. If the search produces too many hits, add key word *realia. Please handle furs with care.*

| Fur Name | Shelf Location | Number of Items/Notes |
| --- | --- | --- |
| Alaskan hare fur | FMS F-H32 | 1 |
| Beaver fur | FMS F-B4 | 2 sheared; 4 full coat |
| Black bear fur | FMS F-B32 | 4 |
| Black bear cub fur | FMS F-B32j | 3 |
| Brown bear fur | FMS F-B33 | 5 |
| Brown bear cub fur | FMS F-B33j | 1 partial with radio transmitter |
| Caribou fur | FMS F-C3 | 1 |
| Coyote fur | FMS F-C6 | 1 |
| Cross fox fur | FMS F-F63 | 1 |
| Deer fur | FMS F-D4 | 1 |
| Harbor seal fur | FMS F-S45 | 3 |
| Lynx fur | FMS F-L9 | 2 |
| Marten fur | FMS F-M3 | 2 |
| Mink fur | FMS F-M5 | 1 |
| Mountain goat fur | FMS F-G66 | 1 |
| Musk ox fur | FMS F-M8 | 1 head detached |
| Muskrat fur | FMS F-M9 | 1 |

*(continued)*

| Fur Name | Shelf Location | Number of Items/Notes |
|---|---|---|
| Polar bear fur | FMS F-B37 | 2 |
| Red fox fur | FMS F-F67 | 5 |
| River otter fur | FMS F-O87 | 7 |
| Sample furs | FMS F-F8 | black bear, brown bear, mountain goat, lynx, sea otter, and sheep fur samples |
| Sea otter fur | FMS F-O88 | 9 |
| Snowshoe hare fur | FMS F-H37 | 1 winter coat |
| Steller sea lion pup fur | FMS F-S37j | 1 |
| Wolf fur | FMS F-W6l | 5 light coat |
| Wolf fur | FMS F-W6d | 3 dark coat |
| Wolverine fur | FMS F-W7 | 1 |

**Mounts: Birds** Search the catalog by key word using the name of the animal or bird exactly as it appears in the list. If the search produces too many hits, add key word *realia*.

*Mounts are checked out in clear boxes and are meant to be viewed through the box to prevent damage to these fragile items.*

| Bird Name | Shelf Location | Number of Items/Notes |
|---|---|---|
| Bird boxes for circulating bird mounts | Storage | Small, medium, large, and extra large sizes are available. |
| American wigeon mount | FMS-3 | 2 |
| Canada goose | FMS-13B | 2 unmounted bird specimen |
| Common goldeneye mount | FMS-4 | 1 |
| Common loon mount | FMS-6 | 1 |
| Common loon mount | FMS-52 | 3 in self-contained boxes |
| Gray partridge mount | FMS-12 | 1 |
| Great horned owl mount | FMS-8 | 3 |
| Greater Canada goose mount | FMS-1 | 3 |
| Greater scaup | FMS-13B | 1 unmounted bird specimen |
| Greater white-fronted goose mount | FMS-5 | 1 |
| Greater yellowlegs mount | FMS-7 | 1 |
| Green-winged teal mount | FMS-3 | 2 |
| Harlequin duck mount | FMS-4 | 2 |
| Lesser Canada goose mount | FMS-2 | 2 |
| Lesser scaup mount | FMS-4 | 1 |

*(continued)*

| Bird Name | Shelf Location | Number of Items/Notes |
|---|---|---|
| Mallard drake mount | FMS-3 | 2 |
| Mallard hen mount | FMS-3 | 1 |
| Mew gull mount | FMS-7 | 2 |
| Northern harrier | FMS-13A | 1 unmounted bird specimen |
| Northern hawk owl mount | FMS-11 | 1 |
| Pacific loon mount | FMS-5/6 | 3 |
| Puffin | FMS-13B | 2 unmounted bird specimen |
| Red-breasted merganser mount | FMS-4 | 1 |
| Red-throated loon mount | FMS-6 | 1 |
| Ring-necked pheasant | FMS-13B | 1 unmounted bird specimen |
| Ring-necked pheasant mount | FMS-15 | 1 in display case |
| Rough-legged hawk mount | FMS-11 | 1 |
| Sandhill crane mount | FMS-15 | 1 |
| Snowy owl mount | FMS-10 | 2 |
| Sooty shearwater mount | FMS-7 | 1 |
| Spruce grouse | FMS-13A | 1 unmounted bird specimen |
| Spruce grouse mount | FMS-12 | 2 |
| Willow ptarmigan mount | FMS-12 | 1 |

**Mounts: Fish** Search the catalog by key word using the name of the fish exactly as it appears in the list. If the search produces too many hits, add key word *realia.*

*Mounts are checked out in clear boxes and are meant to be viewed through the box to prevent damage to these fragile items.*

| Fish Name | Shelf Location | Size |
|---|---|---|
| Fish boxes for circulating fish mounts | Storage | large, medium, and small sizes are available |
| Bigmouth sculpin | FMS FISH-10 | medium |
| Bering wolfish | FMS FISH-8 | large |
| Black rockfish | FMS FISH-9 | medium |
| Chinook (king) salmon | FMS FISH-14 | large |
| Coho (silver) salmon | FMS FISH-15 | large |
| Dark rockfish | FMS FISH-4 | medium |
| Dusky rockfish | FMS FISH-1 | medium |
| Great sculpin | FMS FISH-11 | medium |
| Harlequin rockfish | FMS FISH-5 | small |

(*continued*)

| Fish Name | Shelf Location | Size |
|---|---|---|
| Northern rockfish | FMS FISH-2 | small |
| Pacific cod | FMS FISH-12 | large |
| Redstripe rockfish | FMS FISH-3 | small |
| Sablefish | FMS FISH-7 | medium |
| Sockeye (red) salmon | FMS FISH-13 | medium |
| Yellow Irish lord | FMS FISH-6 | small |

**Mounts: Mammals** Search the catalog by key word using the name of the animal or bird exactly as it appears in the list. If the search produces too many hits, add key word *realia.*

*These mounts are large and do not have clear boxes; they should be handled carefully and only during transport to prevent damage.*

| Mammal Name | Shelf Location | Number of Items/Notes |
|---|---|---|
| Black-tailed deer fawn mount | FMS M-D48 | 1 |
| Land otter mount | FMS M-O87 | 1 |

**Skulls** Search the catalog by key word using the name of the animal or bird exactly as it appears in the list. If the search produces too many hits, add key word *realia.*

*Skulls must be handled with the utmost care as most are extremely fragile and difficult to replace.*

| Skull Name | Shelf Location | Number of Items/Notes |
|---|---|---|
| Antelope skull and horns set | FMS S-A6 | 1 skull and 4 horns |
| Arctic ground squirrel skull | FMS S-S63 | 2 |
| Beaver skull | FMS S-B4 | 6 |
| Beluga whale skull & vertebrae disc | FMS S-W52 | 1 |
| Bird skull kit | FMS S-B5 | 1 display box with 16 skulls: bald eagle, common loon, sandhill crane, glaucous-winged gull, raven, great horned owl, snipe, woodcock, Lapland longspur, mew gull, [unknown], Steller's eider, white-winged scoter, pine grosbeak, double-crested cormorant, gray jay |

*(continued)*

| Skull Name | Shelf Location | Number of Items/Notes |
|---|---|---|
| Black bear skull | FMS S-B32 | 6 |
| Bobcat skull | FMS S-B8 | 3 |
| Brown bear skull | FMS S-B33 | 7 |
| Caribou skull | FMS S-C3 | 1 |
| Coyote skull | FMS S-C6 | 6 |
| Dall sheep horns | FMS S-S53h | 5 small horns |
| Dall sheep skull and horns set | FMS S-S53 | 2 |
| Dog skull | FMS S-D6 | 1 |
| Harbor seal skull | FMS S-S45 | 2 |
| Harbor seal pup skull | FMS S-S45j | 1 |
| Lynx skull | FMS S-L9 | 5 |
| Marten skull | FMS S-M3 | 5 |
| Mink skull | FMS S-M5 | 5 |
| Mountain goat skull | FMS S-G66 | 1 skull and 2 jawbones |
| Moose skull | FMS S-M6 | 1 |
| Musk ox skull | FMS S-M8 | 2 |
| Muskrat skull | FMS S-M9 | 4 |
| Northern fur seal skull | FMS S-S46 | 2 |
| Opossum skull | FMS S-O6 | 1 |
| Polar bear skull | FMS S-B37 | 6 |
| Porcupine skull | FMS S-P6 | 2 |
| Raccoon skull | FMS S-R3 | 1 |
| Red fox skull | FMS S-F67 | 7 |
| Red squirrel skull | FMS S-S67 | 2 |
| River otter skull | FMS S-O87 | 3 |
| Sandhill crane skull | FMS S-S2 | 1 |
| Sea otter skull | FMS S-O88 | 1 |
| Sitka black-tailed deer antlers | FMS S-D47a | 1 |
| Sitka black-tailed deer skull | FMS S-D47 | 4 |
| Small furbearers skull set | FMS S-F8 | 1 display box with 13 skulls: Arctic fox, northern ground squirrel, red squirrel, mink, tundra hare, snowshoe hare, little brown bat, muskrat, marten, shrew, vole, short-tailed weasel, least weasel |
| Snowshoe hare skull | FMS S-H37 | 3 |

(continued)

| Skull Name | Shelf Location | Number of Items/Notes |
|---|---|---|
| Steller sea lion skull | FMS S-S37 | 3 |
| Walrus skull | FMS S-W3 | 2 |
| Short-tailed weasel skull (ermine) | FMS S-W47 | 1 |
| Wild boar skull | FMS S-B7 | 1 |
| Wolf skull | FMS S-W6 | 5 |
| Wolverine skull | FMS S-W7 | 6 |

**Miscellaneous Specimens** Search the catalog by key word using the name of the animal or bird exactly as it appears in the list. If the search produces too many hits, add key word *realia*.

*Specimens must be handled with the utmost care as most
are extremely fragile and difficult to replace.*

| Name | Shelf Location | Number of Items/Notes |
|---|---|---|
| Bird feet set | FMS-8 | 12 feet in 1 container |
| Brown bear paws set | FMS F-B33p | 2 paws |
| Class Insecta | FMS Z-I5 | 1 display box of various insects |
| Moose, fractured bone | FMS S-M6f | 1 fractured bone in 2 pieces |
| Moose, miscellaneous bones | FMS S-M6m | 4 bones |
| Polar bear paws set | FMS F-B37p | 2 paws in display box |
| Walrus jaw bone | FMS S-W3j | 1 |
| Walrus jaw bone, juvenile | FMS S-W3jj | 1 |
| Walrus tusk | FMS S-W3t | 1 |
| Whale baleen | FMS Z-W5 | 1 baleen plate |

# APPENDIX H: FURS, MOUNTS, AND SKULLS COLLECTION/EDUCATIONAL SCIENCE KITS STATEMENT OF RESPONSIBILITY

Suite 111 Library Building, 3211 Providence Drive, Anchorage, AK 99508
(907) 27-ARLIS (272-7547) / (907) 786- 7652 fax
http://www.arlis.org

## Furs, Mounts, and Skulls Collection/Educational Science Kits
### Statement of Responsibility
* To check out items, you must have an active, eligible library card. ←

**Responsibility**

1. I understand that furs, mounts, skulls, and kits must be returned to ARLIS during open hours, 8-5, M-F, and that, unlike books, these items may not be returned to other Anchorage libraries.
2. I understand that the furs, mounts, and skulls are my responsibility while checked out in my name and agree to take all reasonable precautions to protect them. If others use them while they are checked out in my name and damage or loss occurs, I understand that I will be held liable for any loss or damage that may occur.
3. I agree that I will be responsible for the cost of repair or replacement of the furs, skulls, and mounts due to any loss, damage, or theft. I understand that repair or replacement costs will be current market price and may be in excess of $1,000 for rare specimens.
4. I understand that I am responsible for the tags and bar codes of each specimen. If these are removed or damaged, I consent to pay the cost of replacing these items.
5. I understand that it is my responsibility to make arrangements with Alaska Resources Library & Information Services (ARLIS) to pay any and all charges incurred as a result of improper use, damage, loss, or theft of furs, mounts, or skulls checked out to me. Failure to do so may result in the loss of library privileges at ARLIS and the Joint Catalog partner libraries.
6. I understand that if furs, mounts, or skulls are stolen while checked out to me, I must notify ARLIS library personnel at the ARLIS reference desk immediately and file a theft report with the Anchorage Police Department or University Campus Police if the theft occurs on the UAA campus.
7. Checkout is for two weeks. Items may be renewed once. Fines accrue at the rate of $1.00/day for each item.

**Use Agreements**

1. I understand that mounts are checked out in clear boxes and are meant to be viewed through the box to prevent damage. I agree that mounts shall remain in their locked boxes while in my custody.
2. I understand that skulls must be handled with the greatest care; most are extremely fragile and difficult to replace. I understand that furs may be touched with the condition that they must be handled with care. Children are to be supervised when handling furs and skulls. I agree to handle items in my custody accordingly, with the utmost care.
3. I agree to abide by the Marine Mammal Protection Act, which prohibits taking marine mammal items over state lines.
4. **I understand that labels, tags, and bar codes must not be removed or damaged, and that a $10 fine may be charged for each tag that is damaged or removed.** If labels need to be covered for testing purposes, I agree to use impermanent materials, such as sticky notes or painter's tape applied to the tag only. Under no circumstances will I apply tape to the furs, mounts, or skulls.

**Repair/Replacement Costs**
Repair or replacement due to loss or damage, including failure to return the item, will be charged at the current market price as determined by the ARLIS Management Team.

I have read this document and fully understand its terms and my obligations. Breach of these terms may affect future borrowing privileges. I understand that this document is contractual in nature and my signature below indicates my agreement with all terms.

Print name_____ Signature_____ Date_____

Current Home Phone Number _____ Current Cell Phone Number_____

Employer_____ Work Phone Number_____

E-mail address_____ Home address _____

ARLIS Librarian_____ Date_____ ***Signed copy for file/Give one copy to borrower***

# About the Editors and Contributors

MICHELLE COLEMAN ALVARADO is the cataloging supervisor at Sacramento Public Library. She has an MLIS from San Jose State University.

JUSTIN AZEVEDO is the youth materials selector for Sacramento Public Library. He previously served as the supervisor of the system's Arcade Branch, which houses the Library of Things.

ADAM BRONER was born in New York City and raised in the Midwest. He has worked at Berkeley's Tool Lending Library since 1991. He is also a professional carpenter, the music critic for the *Piedmont Post,* a contributor to the *Berkeley Times,* and the cofounder of Repeat Performances.

BRIAN BURNS is the media librarian in the Fuqua Technology Commons at Hampden-Sydney College's Bortz Library. Prior to joining Hampden-Sydney College in 2003, Brian spent 12 years in the media center at the University of Florida. He has a passion for providing high-quality service to all library users.

AMY CALHOUN is the communications and virtual services manager at Sacramento Public Library. Her conference presentations and webinars include *Library Journal*'s "Using Data to Better Serve Your Community" and GALE Geek's "Connecting Digital Products to Physical Programming."

PATRICK "TOD" COLEGROVE, PhD, MSLIS, is a physicist, serial intrapreneur, and professional librarian. A recognized leader of the maker movement in libraries, and pioneer of its potential impact on learning, discovery, and engagement, Colegrove is head of the DeLaMare Science and Engineering Library at the University of Nevada, Reno.

BETSY GOODMAN is an organic farmer, seed advocate, and community activist. She has worked with state legislators, nonprofit organizations, American Seed Trade Association, USDA, and community supporters to change legislation in Nebraska and beyond to allow for the free and open sharing of seeds in libraries and other public spaces.

JENNIFER HARVEY has worked in and managed curriculum centers at University of Nebraska at Kearney and Bowling Green State University. Her research in collections and differentiated instruction has culminated in related articles and presentations. She coauthored a chapter in *Just Plains Folks: Studies of the People of the Great Plains*.

JAMES HILL is actively involved in the bicycling community of Athens, Ohio. He is assistant director for Athens County Public Libraries.

ERIC D. M. JOHNSON is the head of the Innovative Media department for Virginia Commonwealth University Libraries. He has previously published in *Library Quarterly* and in *#Alt-Academy*. He has an MA in U.S. history from George Mason University and an MSLIS from Florida State University.

ED KAZZIMIR is the lead cataloger at Alaska Resources Library and Information Services (ARLIS) in Anchorage, Alaska, where his focus is the complex cataloging of technical and scientific material on natural and cultural resources of Alaska and northern regions. Previously, he has worked at university libraries and for OCLC.

SUE KIRSCHNER is youth literacy and outreach supervisor for Cuyahoga County Public Library. She is a board member of Reach Out and Read Greater Cleveland and the USA Toy Library Association. Sue has been published in *Children & Libraries*, wrote *Splash into Kindergarten* and *Whooo's Ready for School?*, and presents nationally on toys and literacy.

ROCHELLE HUNT KRUEGER is the curriculum librarian at the University of Nebraska at Kearney and serves as the liaison to the College of Education. She has also collaborated on a chapter in *Renewed Accountability for Access and Excellence*.

SHELLY MCCOY is head of the Multimedia Collections and Services department at the University of Delaware Library. She oversees the 30,000-square-foot Student Multimedia Design Center, the largest multimedia production-focused space in an academic library in the nation, and the film and video collection.

ERIN DEWITT MILLER is the head of the Media Library at the University of North Texas. Formerly, she was the electronic resources librarian, and before that worked as a high school librarian. Her research interests include streaming media, online video usability, and innovative services in academic libraries.

SUE PARKS is the associate dean for special libraries at the University of North Texas. Formerly, she was head of the Media Library and served as president of

Consortium of College and University Media Centers (CCUMC): Leadership in Media and Academic Technology. She is actively involved in the American Library Association (ALA), Association of College and Research Libraries (ACRL), and Library Leadership and Management Association (LLAMA).

TARA RADNIECKI, MLIS, MA, is the engineering librarian at the University of Nevada, Reno's DeLaMare Science and Engineering Library. She works with students, faculty, and staff to develop cutting-edge resource and service offerings and is interested in how academic libraries can impact innovation and entrepreneurship within their communities.

MARK ROBISON is assistant professor of library services at Valparaiso University. In addition to serving as liaison to several social science areas, he also oversees the information literacy program for first-year students. His research interests include transfer student success, libraries' engagement with social media, and things collections.

DIANE ROBSON is a librarian at the University of North Texas. She manages collection development and outreach related to games and gaming for the UNT Libraries. Robson is active on the ALA Games and Gaming Round Table and publishes on game collections and their use in academic libraries.

CELIA ROZEN is the Alaska Department of Fish and Game Librarian and serves the agency statewide. Celia was one of the dreamers who conceptualized Alaska Resources Library and Information Services (ARLIS). She also brokered the deal to get the realia collection to ARLIS. She has coauthored ADF&G reports, and coauthored prior articles on unique ARLIS collections.

LINDLEY SHEDD is a research and writing consultant for the New Media Consortium and a former librarian at the University of Alabama. Her writing, presentation, and workshop topics include educational technology, creating alternate reality games (ARGs) in libraries, incorporating multimedia assignments into curriculum, copyright and fair use, and creating staff training and evaluation.

MITCHELL SHULDMAN is a librarian emeritus with University of Massachusetts Lowell Library's Division of Media Services, where he worked for nearly 34 years. Recent publications focus on the integration of video production assignments into nonmedia disciplines, resulting in various relevant journal articles, as well as presentations at numerous conferences.

RENÉ TANNER is a science librarian at Arizona State University. She has contributed articles to *American Libraries* and *College and Research Libraries News,* as well as authored book chapters in *Focus on Educating for Sustainability: Toolkit for Academic Libraries* and *Computer Mediated Communication: Issues and Approaches in Education.*

HELEN WOODS is librarian for the *Exxon Valdez* Oil Spill Trustee Council, and is reference services coordinator for Alaska Resources Library and

Information Services (ARLIS) in Anchorage, Alaska. This is her first publication.

JILL YOUNGS is the manager of the Northern Onondaga Public Library at Cicero, located in Central New York State. Supporting green and sustainable programming, materials, and information for the community is a guiding vision.

# Index